100 Hikes in

SOUTHERN OREGON

William L. Sullivan

Navillus Press
Eugene

Wizard Island.

Published by the Navillus Press
1958 Onyx Street
Eugene, Oregon 97403

Printed in USA on Envirotext, 100% recycled paper

Cover: Devils Peak from Cliff Lake, Bigelow's sneezeweed.
Spine: Crater Lake. Back cover: Mt. Shasta from Gray Butte.
Frontispiece: Fog on York Butte.

SAFETY CONSIDERATIONS: Many of the trails in this book pass through Wilderness and remote country where hikers are exposed to unavoidable risks. On any hike, the weather may change suddenly. The fact that a hike is included in this book, or that it may be rated as easy, does not necessarily mean it will be safe or easy for you. Prepare yourself with proper equipment and outdoor skills, and you will be able to enjoy these hikes with confidence.

Every effort has been made to assure the accuracy of the information in this book. The author has hiked all 100 of the featured trails, and the trails' administrative agencies have reviewed the maps and text. Nonetheless, construction, logging, and storm damage may cause changes. Corrections and updates are welcome, and may be sent in care of the publisher.

Contents

ợ —Horses OK   ® —Bicycles OK

C —Crowded or restricted backpacking area

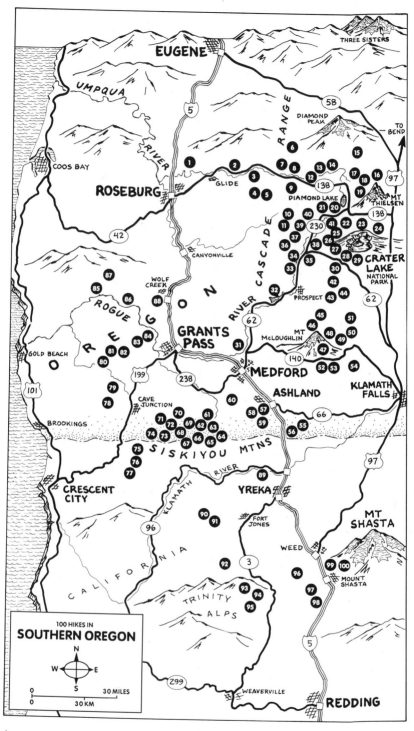

100 HIKES IN
SOUTHERN OREGON

0 ——— 30 MILES
0 ——— 30 KM

۵ –Horses OK   ۰ –Bicycles OK
C –Crowded or restricted backpacking area

NORTHERN CALIFORNIA . . . 194

🐎 --Horses OK   🚲 --Bicycles OK
C --Crowded or restricted backpacking area

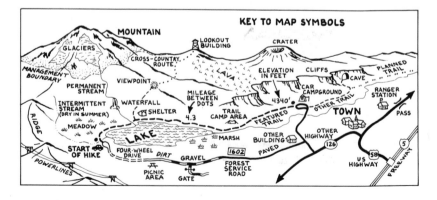

KEY TO MAP SYMBOLS

Introduction

Welcome to the spectacular trails of Southern Oregon and adjacent Northern California! This comprehensive guide proves there's more to this scenic region than just Crater Lake, the Rogue River, and Mt. Shasta. Come discover a hot springs in the hills behind Roseburg, a wildflower mecca near Ashland, and a historic cabin in the Trinity Alps. All of the trips are well suited for day hikers, but you'll also find 48 routes recommended for backpackers, 22 trails for mountain bikers, and 59 paths for equestrians. And don't hang up your hiking boots in winter. Special symbols identify 24 trails that are open all year.

The book features a variety of difficulty levels. If you're hiking with children, look for the symbols identifying 54 carefully chosen kids' hikes—trips that are easy enough for the whole family. Advanced hikers, on the other hand, can choose from 40 unabashedly difficult treks. And if you really want to get away from it all, a list at the back of the book describes 100 *more* hikes in Southern Oregon—little-known but intriguing treks for adventurous spirits.

HOW TO USE THIS BOOK

It's Easy to Choose a Trip

The featured hikes are divided into 7 regions, from the Upper Umpqua River to Northern California. To choose a trip, simply turn to the area that interests you and look for the following symbols in the upper right-hand corner of each hike's heading. Whether you're hiking with children, backpacking, or looking for a snow-free winter trail, you'll quickly find an outing to match your tastes.

 Children's favorites—walks popular with the 4- to 12-year-old crowd, but fun for hikers of all ages.

 All-year trails, hikable most or all of winter.

 Hikes suitable for backpackers as well as day hikers. No permits required. Crowds unlikely.

 Restricted or crowded backpacking areas. Avoid summer weekends. Advance permits for overnight stays are required in Crater Lake's backcountry and in the Trinity Alps Wilderness.

The Information Blocks

Each hike is rated by difficulty. **Easy** hikes are between 1 and 7 miles round-trip and gain less than 1000 feet in elevation. Never very steep nor particularly remote, they make good warm-up trips for experienced hikers or first-time trips for novices.

Trips rated as **Moderate** range from 4 to 10 miles round-trip. These routes may gain up to 2000 feet of elevation or may require some pathfinding skills.

Hikers must be in good condition and will need to take several rest stops.

Difficult trails demand top physical condition, with a strong heart and strong knees. These challenging hikes are 6 to 20 miles round-trip and may gain 3000 feet or more. Backpacking can break difficult hikes into manageable segments.

Distances are given in round-trip mileage, except for those trails where a car or bicycle shuttle is so convenient that the suggested hike is one-way only, and is listed as such.

Elevation gains tell much about the difficulty of a hike. Those who puff climbing a few flights of stairs may consider even 500 feet of elevation a strenuous climb, and should watch this listing carefully. Note that the figures are for each hike's *cumulative* elevation gain, adding all the uphill portions, even those on the return trip.

The **hiking season** of any trail varies with the weather. In a cold year, a trail described as "Open May through October" may not yet be clear of snow by May 1, and may be socked in by a blizzard before October 31. Similarly, a trail that is "Open all year" may close due to storms.

The **allowed use** of many featured trails specifically includes horse and bicycle riders. Note that 36 hikes do not have a "use" listing. These are open to *hikers only*. For a quick overview of paths recommended for equestrians or mountain bikers, refer to the table of contents. Incidentally, dogs are allowed on all trails except at Crater Lake National Park, Oregon Caves National Monu-. ment, Castle Crags State Park, the Mount Shasta Wilderness, and Table Rock.

All hikers should carry a topographic **map**, with contour lines to show elevation. Maps listed as "USFS" are available from U.S. Forest Service offices. Those tagged "USGS" are published by the U.S. Geological Survey and can be found at many outdoor stores. Or you can write to the USGS, PO Box 25286, Denver, CO 80225 to have maps sent postpaid. In addition, it's handy to have a visitor map of the Umpqua National Forest (for Hikes #1-21), the Rogue River National Forest (for Hikes #32-70), or the Siskiyou National Forest (for Hikes #72-86). These maps can be picked up at a ranger station for a couple dollars.

WILDERNESS RESTRICTIONS

Forty-two of the featured hikes enter designated Wilderness Areas—beautiful, isolated places protected by special restrictions. Conveniently, day hikers can still use all the trails described in this book without having to pick up permits at ranger stations. Advance permits are required only for overnight use in the Trinity Alps Wilderness (and Crater Lake National Park's backcountry), or for people planning to build campfires in the Marble Mountain, Siskiyou, and Russian Wilderness Areas.

Other important restrictions to expect in Wilderness Areas:

- Groups must be no larger than 12.
- Campfires are discouraged, and are banned within 100 feet of any water source or maintained trail.
- Bicycles and other wheeled vehicles (except wheelchairs) are banned.
- Horses and pack stock cannot be tethered within 200 feet of any water source or shelter.
- Motorized equipment, hang gliders, and fireworks are banned.
- Live trees and shrubs must not be cut or damaged.

Lilypad Lake in the Red Buttes Wilderness (Hike #65)

In addition, some rules apply to all federal lands:

- Collecting arrowheads or other cultural artifacts is a federal crime.
- Permits are required to dig up plants.

SAFETY ON THE TRAIL

Wild Animals

Part of the fun of hiking is watching for wildlife. Lovers of wildness rue the demise of our most impressive species. Wolves and grizzly bears are extinct in both Oregon and California. The little black bears that remain are so profoundly shy you probably won't see one in years of hiking. To keep them shy, it's important for backpackers to hang food at least 10 feet high and 5 feet from a tree trunk at night. Only where cooler chest goodies are easily accessible have black bears become campground nuisances, particularly at Crater Lake, in Castle Crags State Park, and at river-rafting campsites on the Rogue River.

Rattlesnakes, too, have become relatively rare. The State Health Division reports that only one Oregonian died from a rattlesnake in the most recent decade. Statistically, this makes rattlesnakes less of a threat than horses, bees, dogs, or even cows. Nonetheless, if you hear a rattle or recognize the snake's diamondback pattern, it's your cue to give this reclusive animal some space.

Ticks have received some publicity as carriers of Lyme disease, which begins with flu-like symptoms and an often circular rash. While this is a problem in the

Eastern states, only a couple of cases have been reported in Oregon. Nonetheless, brush off your clothes and check your ankles after walking through dry grass or brush.

Mosquitoes can be a nuisance on hikes in the Cascades, particularly in the Sky Lakes and Mt. Thielsen Wilderness Areas. To avoid them, remember that these insects hatch about 10 days after the snow melts from the trails and that they remain in force about a month. Thus, if a given trail in the Cascades is listed as "Open mid-June," expect mosquitoes there most of July.

Drinking Water

Day hikers should bring all the water they will need—roughly a quart per person. A microscopic paramecium, *Giardia,* has forever changed the old custom of dipping a drink from every brook. The symptoms of "beaver fever," debilitating nausea and diarrhea, commence a week or 2 after ingesting *Giardia.*

If you love fresh water and are willing to gamble, consider that the paramecium is spread only by mammals, enters the water by defecation, and moves only downstream. As a result, gushing springs and runoff immediately below snowfields are less dangerous. If you're backpacking, bring an approved water filter or purification tablet, or boil your water 5 minutes.

Proper Equipment

Even on the tamest hike a surprise storm or a wrong turn can suddenly make the gear you carry very important. Always bring a pack with the 10 essentials:

1. Warm, water-repellent coat (or parka and extra shirt)
2. Drinking water
3. Extra food
4. Knife
5. Matches in waterproof container
6. Fire starter (butane lighter or candle)
7. First aid kit
8. Flashlight
9. Map (topographic, if possible)
10. Compass

Before leaving on a hike, tell someone where you are going so they can alert the county sheriff to begin a search if you do not return on time. If you're lost, stay put and keep warm. The number one killer in the woods is *hypothermia*—being cold and wet too long.

COURTESY ON THE TRAIL

As our trails become more heavily used, rules of trail etiquette become stricter. Please:

- Pick no flowers.
- Leave no litter. Eggshells and orange peels can last for decades.
- Do not bring pets into wilderness areas. Dogs can frighten wildlife and disturb other hikers.
- Step off the trail on the downhill side to let horses pass. Speak to them quietly to help keep them from spooking.
- Do not shortcut switchbacks.

For backpackers, low-impact camping was once merely a courtesy, but is on the verge of becoming a requirement, both to protect the landscape and to preserve a sense of solitude for others. The most important rules:

- Camp out of sight of lakes and trails.
- Build no campfire. Cook on a backpacking stove.
- Wash 100 feet from any lake or stream.
- Camp on duff, rock, or sand—never on meadow vegetation.
- Pack out garbage—don't burn or bury it.

FOR MORE INFORMATION

All major Forest Service offices in the area collect reports of trail conditions in TRIS, a computerized trail information system available to the public. By typing a trail's name or number into a computer terminal at a Forest Service office, you can theoretically access updated information on snow levels, trail maintenance, and new construction. Unfortunately, the information is often sketchy or out of date. Nonetheless, it's a promising beginning, with the laudable goal of eventually cataloguing every trail on public land in the state.

If you'd like to check on a trail, and if TRIS is inconvenient for you, call directly to the trail's administrative agency. These agencies are listed below, along with the hikes in this book for which they manage trails.

Hike	Managing Agency
61-70	Applegate Ranger District — (541) 899-1812
57	Ashland Parks Commission — (541) 488-5340
52, 53, 58, 59	Ashland Ranger District — (541) 482-3333
31, 55, 56, 60, 86-88	Bureau of Land Mgmt, Medford — (541) 770-2200
1, 2, 4	Bureau of Land Mgmt, Roseburg — (541) 440-4930
43, 45, 46	Butte Falls Ranger District — (541) 865-2700
98	Castle Crags State Park — (916) 235-2684
16	Chemult Ranger District — (541) 365-7001
22-30	Crater Lake National Park — (541) 594-2211
8, 12-21, 40	Diamond Lake Ranger District — (541) 498-2551
80-83	Galice Ranger District — (541) 471-6500
85	Gold Beach Ranger District — (541) 247-3600
76, 77	Happy Camp Ranger District — (916) 493-2243
72-75, 78, 79	Illinois Valley Ranger District — (541) 592-2166
84, 88	Josephine County Parks Dept — (541) 474-5285
44, 47-51, 54	Klamath Ranger District — (541) 885-3400
96, 97, 99, 100	Mount Shasta Ranger District — (916) 926-4511
2-7, 9	North Umpqua Ranger District — (541) 496-3532
89	Oak Knoll Ranger District — (916) 465-2241
71	Oregon Caves Natl Monument — (541) 592-2100
33-35, 37-39, 41, 42	Prospect Ranger District — (541) 560-3400
90-95	Scott River Ranger District — (916) 468-5351
31	The Nature Conservancy — (541) 488-4485
10, 11, 36	Tiller Ranger District — (541) 825-3201
32	US Army Corps of Engineers — (541) 878-2255

Upper Umpqua River

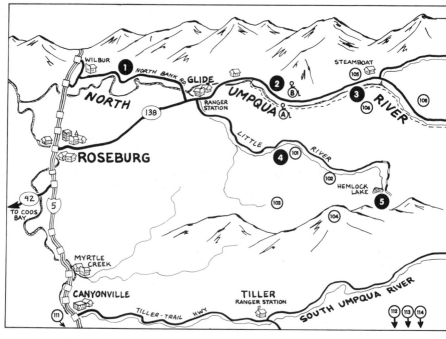

Above: Lemolo Falls (Hike #14).

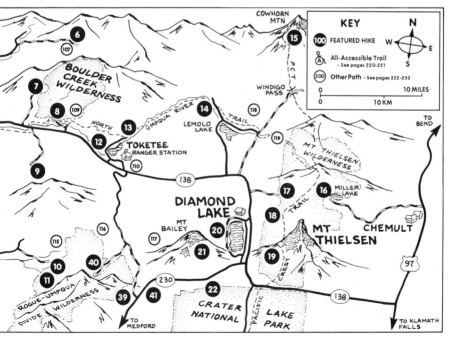

1 North Bank Deer Preserve

Easy (to South Knob)
3.4 miles round-trip
900 feet elevation gain
Open all year
Use: hikers, horses, bicycles
Maps: Winchester, Oak Cr. Valley (USGS)

Moderate (to Middle Knob)
6.7-mile loop
1220 feet elevation gain

Columbia white-tailed deer once roamed most of Western Oregon. But as pioneers began farming the deer's favored valley habitat and draining wetlands, the whitetails gradually lost ground to their larger, black-tailed cousins from the uplands. By 1970 fewer than 700 of the endangered breed survived, isolated in 2 small areas—near an island on the lower Columbia River and in the grassy hills around Roseburg. Today Columbia white-tailed deer are staging a comeback, thanks in part to the North Bank Habitat Management Area, a new 10-square-mile preserve overlooking the North Umpqua River near Roseburg.

The scenic preserve has become a haven for hikers and equestrians as well. Open all year and just 6 miles from Interstate 5, this quiet hideaway of rolling oak savannahs and forested valleys has been off-limits to unauthorized motor vehicles since 1994. Originally a vast cattle ranch, the preserve is laced with a network of ancient roads that have grown into pleasant, grassy tracks. Views from open ridgecrests sweep from the North Umpqua Rivers' dramatic Whistlers Bend to the Umpqua Community College campus at Winchester. And yes,

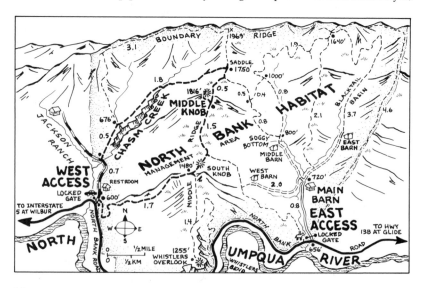

North Bank Habitat Management Area.   Opposite: White oak.

you really can expect to see the rare deer, with their gray eye rings and flashy white tails. Hawks, eagles, foxes, and blacktail deer are common too.

To drive here from Roseburg, take Interstate 5 north for 4 miles to Winchester exit 129, turn left toward Wilbur for 2 miles, and turn right on North Bank Road for 5.3 miles to a locked green gate on the left by a sign marking the North Bank Habitat area's west access. (If you're driving here from Eugene, take Wilbur exit 135, cross the freeway overpass, turn right for 4 miles to the middle of Wilbur, and turn left on North Bank Road for 5.3 miles to the west access gate.)

Walk past the green gate on a large gravel road 50 feet and promptly turn right onto a fainter track. This old roadbed parallels the highway a few hundred yards before climbing left up a broad grassy ridge of gnarled white oaks. In spring look for the fuzzy blue blooms of minty-smelling pennyroyal, the tall white plumes of camas, the small flowers of blue-eyed grass, and 2 kinds of cat's ears—one that's magenta and one with fuzzy white petals. In all seasons, poison oak is profuse along the trail, so it's a good idea to wear long pants. Long pants also reduce the risk of picking up chiggers—tiny insects that cause weeks of itching. Dogs are discouraged here not only because they collect chiggers, but also because they may chase the endangered deer's fawns.

After climbing 1.7 miles, keep left at a fork to reach a viewpoint in a grassy saddle beside South Knob—a possible turnaround point. For the longer loop, however, continue left along Middle Ridge's grassy crest 1.5 miles to a faint fork high on the side of Middle Knob. First explore the larger fork left 100 yards to a deadend at a panoramic viewpoint. Then take the smaller, right-hand fork around Middle Knob 0.5 mile to a saddle in a thicket of small incense cedars. Turn left and keep left for 1.8 miles, descending alongside the 20-foot gully of Chasm Creek (dry by summer) to the Jackson Ranch's large gravel road. Then turn left for 0.7 mile to your car.

Other Hiking Options

For a longer tour, follow faint, unmarked, grassy roadbeds along panoramic Boundary Ridge or to the old ranch's 4 metal-roofed barns, shown on the map. Equestrians most often start from the preserve's east access gate, located 7 miles farther east on North Bank Road, just after milepost 12.

2   Fall Creek Falls

Easy (to Fall Creek Falls)
1.8 miles round-trip
400 feet elevation gain
Open all year
Use: hikers, horses, bicycles
Maps: Old Fairview, Mace Mtn. (USGS)

Moderate (to all 3 waterfalls)
7.2 miles in all
800 feet elevation gain

The shady trail to Fall Creek Falls' plunging double waterfall follows a cascading creek and squeezes through a crack in a house-sized boulder. Because the path is short, it's fun to warm up with 2 easy hikes to other waterfalls nearby: Fern Falls and Susan Creek Falls.

If you plan to hike to all 3 waterfalls, start with the smallest, Fern Falls. To find its trailhead from Interstate 5 in Roseburg, take exit 124 and follow "Diamond Lake" signs east on Highway 138 for 22 miles. A mile past the Idleyld Park store, turn right at a "Swiftwater Park" sign, cross the river bridge, and park at the Tioga Trailhead on the left.

The North Umpqua Trail that begins here follows the river 79 miles up to its headwaters in the High Cascades. Although you can tackle longer portions of this well-built route (see Hike #3), here we'll focus on the first 1.6 miles.

From the Tioga Trailhead, the path sets off through a mossy old-growth forest of hemlock, cedar, bigleaf maple, Douglas fir 4 feet in diameter, and an occasional sugarpine—the source of foot-long pine cones along the trail. Big white 3-petaled trilliums bloom in March, while dainty pink calypso orchids bloom in May. The rush of the river masks highway noise from the far shore.

After 0.2 mile, a viewpoint on the left overlooks Deadline Falls, an 8-foot drop in the North Umpqua where salmon and steelhead trout leap. Beware of lush 3-leaved poison oak all around the viewpoint. The second side trail on the left leads to the bedrock shore—a prime sunbathing spot and the only good riverbank access of the hike. At the 0.4-mile mark, ignore side trails on the right leading to Swiftwater County Park's picnic shelter. Continue 1.2 miles, with glimpses down to the big green river, before reaching a satisfying turnaround point: the 70-foot bridge across Fern Falls, a mossy fan-shaped cascade where a small side creek pours into the North Umpqua River.

To try the Susan Creek Falls hike, return to your car, drive back to Highway 138, and head 6.3 miles east to the Susan Creek Picnic Area. It's on the right, beyond milepost 28, but the trail itself starts on the *left* side of the highway. This packed gravel path climbs very gradually through old-growth woods, ducks under a powerline, and crosses a footbridge at the base of Susan Creek Falls, a 70-foot punchbowl plume emerging from a slot. A rougher path continues 0.3 mile, switchbacking up a dry, rocky slope (with blue iris and reddish poison oak) to the Indian Mounds, a cyclone-fenced ridgetop of rockpiles and pits. Used as vision quest sites in Native American coming-of-age rituals centuries ago, the

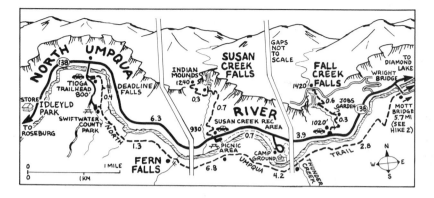

rockpiles have grown over with moss and gnarled madrone trees, concealing most of their original panorama.

To visit Fall Creek Falls—the grand finale if you're hiking all 3 short trails—drive another 3.9 miles east of Susan Creek on Highway 138 and park at the trailhead sign on the left, near milepost 32. After hiking 0.3 mile, ignore a fork for the Jobs Garden Trail on the right; this leads 200 yards to a small columnar basalt outcrop and rockpile. The main trail visits the misty plunge pool at the base of Fall Creek Falls' lower, 50-foot cascade, and then switchbacks up to a gravel road crossing the top of a smaller upper falls.

Fall Creek Falls.   Opposite: Oxalis (sourgrass).

North Umpqua River

Moderate (with shuttle)
5.5 miles one way
200 feet elevation gain
Open all year
Use: hikers, horses, bicycles
Maps: Mace Mtn., Steamboat (USGS)

In all, the North Umpqua Trail follows this whitewater river 79 miles to its headwaters in the High Cascades. If that seems too long a hike, try the 5.5-mile segment featured here—from Wright Creek to the settlement of Steamboat. This portion shows off the river at its best, with access to hidden beaches, rock riverbanks, and viewpoints. Along the way you'll pass the wooded campsite where Western writer Zane Grey fished. Because his earlier articles had crowded the Rogue River with anglers, Grey never named the North Umpqua in print.

To start the hike, take exit 124 of Interstate 5 in Roseburg and follow "Diamond Lake" signs east on Highway 138 for 33.5 miles. Beyond Fall Creek Falls 1.4 miles, turn right on Wright Creek Road across a bridge. Don't park at the hiker-symbol sign just beyond the bridge, but rather drive 0.2 mile farther to the signed Wright Creek Trailhead on the left. Park here and walk up the road another 100 yards to the actual start of the trail.

An old-growth forest lines the path, with droopy-limbed red cedars, vine maples, and 6-foot-thick Douglas firs. A shag carpet of moss covers the forest floor. Frequent side paths scramble left to the riverbank. Expect some traffic noise from the highway across the river.

After a mile the path dips to a glassy, green-pooled stretch of river where ducks paddle and osprey soar. A small sandy beach nestled among rock banks and wildflowers makes a good turnaround spot for hikers with small children.

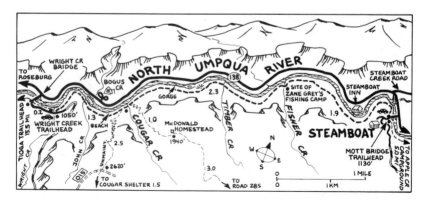

The North Umpqua River.   Opposite: Poison oak.

Poison oak is all but absent up to here, but beyond this point hikers should watch for its telltale triple leaflets along the trail.

After passing the small beach, the path visits 2 river gorges—rocky narrows where whitewater rafters flail and squeal. At the 3.6-mile mark the path bridges Fisher Creek, where a sign marks Zane Grey's former fishing camp. If you haven't arranged a car shuttle, this might be a good turnaround point. Otherwise continue 1.9 miles, skirting a few houses at the Forest Service settlement of Steamboat, to the Mott Trailhead parking area. To shuttle a car here, drive east on Highway 138 from Wright Creek Road for 5.1 miles and turn right across Mott Bridge to the trailhead on the right.

Other Hiking Options
Like to see more of the North Umpqua Trail? Downstream, the path starts 15.7 miles west of Wright Creek at Swiftwater Park (see Hike #2). Upstream from Steamboat, the path mostly traverses forested slopes well above the river for 12.3 miles before briefly joining Highway 138 to cross the river on Marsters Bridge. From there the trail skirts the Boulder Creek Wilderness (see Hike #8), leaves the river for 10 miles to Toketee Lake Campground, passes Umpqua Hot Springs (Hike #13) and Lemolo Falls (Hike #14), detours around the Lemolo Lake reservoir, and then climbs through the Mt. Thielsen Wilderness to the Pacific Crest Trail near Maidu Lake (Hike #16).

4 Little River Waterfalls

Easy (to Wolf Creek Falls)
2.6 miles round-trip
230 feet elevation gain
Open all year
Map: Umpqua National Forest (USFS)

Moderate (to all 4 waterfalls)
6 miles in all
Open April through December
870 feet elevation gain

A charming, little-known tributary of the North Umpqua, the Little River tumbles out of a long canyon full of hidden waterfalls. If you only have time to discover one, head for Wolf Creek Falls. The 1.3-mile creekside trail there is ideal for hikers with children. Waterfall connoisseurs will want to round out the day by driving upriver to visit 3 more cascades at the ends of short trails.

From Interstate 5, take Roseburg exit 124 and follow "Diamond Lake" signs east on Highway 138. At milepost 16, just before the town of Glide, turn right on Little River Road for 10.4 paved miles. Then park at a "Wolf Creek Falls Trail" sign on the right.

The trail starts by crossing the Little River on an arched, 150-foot bridge. In summer, the broad river's bedrock and warm, shallow pools invite wading. Beware of poison oak on the banks. Beyond the bridge go straight on the trail into a cool, shady forest of bigleaf maple and old-growth Douglas fir. In spring, trilliums bloom white in these woods. In summer look for tiny starflower and inside-out flower. In fall, expect a display of scarlet vine maple leaves. After 1.3 miles, the path skirts a 20-foot lower falls and ends at the base of a dramatic, 70-foot cascade. Listen here for the *zeet! zeet!* of robin-sized water ouzels flying along the creek.

To find the 3 other waterfalls, drive up Little River Road 5.4 miles past the

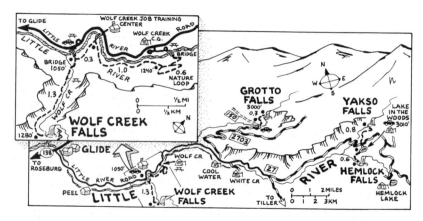

Wolf Creek Trailhead. Opposite Cool Water Campground turn left on gravel Road 2703 and keep left for 6.3 miles, following "Grotto Falls" signs to a trailhead just after a bridge. This 0.3-mile path climbs steeply across a 1970s clearcut and ends behind Grotto Falls' 45-foot curtain of water.

Now drive back to the junction by Cool Water Campground and continue up Little River Road (known here as Road 27). After 3 miles on pavement and an additional 6.3 miles on gravel, turn right into the Lake in the Woods Campground entrance. Park by a log cabin that survives from the days when rangers patrolled these woods on horseback. Walk past the cabin 120 yards on the lakeshore campground road. Then turn right at a "Hemlock Falls" sign and follow a switchbacking path 0.6 mile down a densely forested canyon to a 40-foot corkscrew-shaped cataract spilling from a moss-cushioned cliff.

To find the final waterfall, walk back past your car to Road 27. Immediately opposite the Lake in the Woods Campground entrance, take a relatively level 0.8-mile path through the woods to a pebbly beach at the misty base of 50-foot Yakso Falls. This cascade fans out like silver hair—and in fact *Yakso* means "hair" in Chinook jargon, the old trade language of Northwest Indians.

Other Hiking Options

A 3-mile trail climbs from the far end of the Lake in the Woods Campground loop road to Hemlock Lake (Hike #5), passing several small falls along the way.

Wolf Creek Falls.   Opposite: Footbridge over Little River at Wolf Creek Trail.

Hemlock Meadows.   Opposite: Shooting stars.

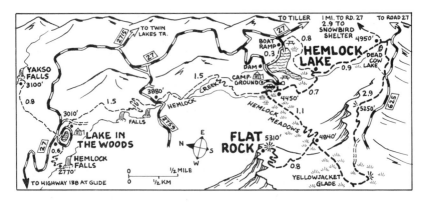

5   Hemlock Lake

Moderate (Yellowjacket Loop)
5.6-mile loop
910 feet elevation gain
Open June through November
Use: hikers, horses, bicycles
Map: Quartz Mountain (USGS)

Moderate (with Flat Rock detour)
7.2-mile loop
1380 feet elevation gain

The spectacular wildflower meadows on this loop trail have the subalpine feel of the High Cascades. But this patch of mountain scenery is less than an hour from Roseburg in an often-overlooked corner of the Old Cascades, the eroded remnants of a much older volcanic range. Thousands of trilliums and shooting stars line the misnamed Yellowjacket Loop in June. For a broader view, climb a side path to a lookout site atop Flat Rock.

To find the trail from Interstate 5, take Roseburg exit 124 and follow "Diamond Lake" signs east on Highway 138 to milepost 16, just before Glide. Then turn right on Little River Road (which becomes Road 27) for 18.8 paved miles and an additional 11.5 miles on gravel, following signs for Hemlock Lake. Finally cross the lake's earthen dam to a T-junction at the campground entrance.

The trail begins at a large mapboard straight ahead. After 100 feet, turn right at a trail junction to start the loop. Then keep left at all junctions for the rest of the hike. The path starts in a forest of Douglas fir and Shasta red fir, but soon crosses the first of many meadow openings. Yellow fawn lilies bloom here within days of the early June snowmelt, followed by white marsh marigolds, purple shooting stars, blue violets, and the huge green leaves of hellebore. Listen for the *ribbet* of frogs and the monotone call of the varied thrush, crying like a slow squeaky wheel in the treetops.

At the 1.1-mile mark, take time to detour right along the 0.8-mile Flat Rock Trail to a clifftop lookout site. The view stretches from Roseburg's valley to Crater Lake's rim. Diamond Peak rises to the left of Hemlock Lake, while Mt. Bailey is on the right, with Mt. Thielsen's spire peeking over its shoulder.

Back on the loop trail, you'll cross 2.5 miles of meadows, woods, and a recovering 1970s clearcut before reaching gravel Road 625 in a saddle. The trail is faint here, but just go up the little ridge straight ahead. In another half mile (still keeping left at junctions), you'll pass Dead Cow Lake, an innocent pond in the woods. Then descend 0.9 mile to Hemlock Lake and follow the shore path left to your car.

Other Hiking Options

A side trail from Dead Cow Lake continues 3.5 miles along the ridgetop east, passing Snowbird Shelter before ending at Road 2715. A proposed 4-mile extension would join the Twin Lakes Trail (Hike #9).

6   Bullpup Lake

Easy (around Bullpup Lake)
1.4-mile loop
250 feet elevation gain
Open June through November
Use: hikers, horses, bicycles
Maps: Chiltcoot Mountain, Reynolds
    Ridge (USGS)

Moderate (to outcrop viewpoint)
4.6 miles round-trip
1000 feet elevation gain

There are no crowds in the Calapooya Mountains. In fact, few Oregonians have even heard of this high, forested divide between the Willamette and North Umpqua rivers, just an hour's drive east of Roseburg. For a quick taste of this little-known range, try the delightful short trail to the shelter at rhododendron-ringed Bullpup Lake. For a better sample, hike past Bullpup Lake to a rock outcrop on a ridgecrest with views from Mt. Jefferson to Diamond Peak.

To find the trailhead from Roseburg, take Interstate 5 exit 124 and follow "Diamond Lake" signs east on Highway 138 for 38.4 miles—a bit beyond milepost 38. Then turn left on paved Steamboat Creek Road for 10.4 miles and fork to the right, following "Bullpup Lake" signs another 11.9 miles to the trailhead.

(If the "Bullpup Lake" pointers are missing, fork to the right off Steamboat Creek Road onto one-lane, paved Bend Creek-Washboard Road 3817 for 2.2 miles, fork to the right again on Road 3850 for 0.9 mile, fork left to stay on Road 3850 for 4.7 miles of gravel, keep left on Road 200 for 0.1 miles, and promptly fork left again onto Road 300 for 4 miles to a trail sign and parking area on the right.)

The trail climbs gradually through a forest of mountain hemlock trees draped with gray-green *Usnea* lichen, also called old man's beard. Look for three-leaved woodland wildflowers: small, shamrock-shaped oxalis, large vanilla leaf, and

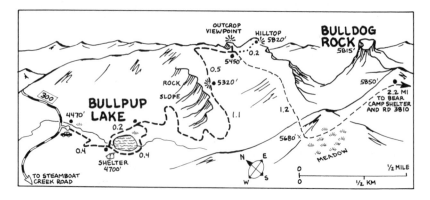

Bullpup Lake.   Opposite: Bullpup Lake shelter.

showy white trilliums. At a junction after 0.4 mile, go straight to the brushy shore of the shallow, forest-rimmed lake. The 3-sided, shake-covered shelter here was built in 1982, but leaks because of incorrectly lapped shakes.

To continue, hike past the shelter 0.4 mile around the lake to a T-junction with the Bulldog Rock Trail. The quick loop back to your car is to the left. For the ridgetop viewpoint, however, turn right and climb 1.1 miles to the top of a bare rock slope of gray andesite. This is the volcanic rock that built most of the 30-million-year-old, heavily eroded Calapooya Range. Only a few stonecrop, phlox, lomatiums, and pinemat manzanita plants have yet colonized this rock slope. Bullpup Lake is visible at the base of the slope, while flat-topped Bohemia Mountain—center of a 19th-century gold rush—dominates the horizon.

For a better view, continue half a mile farther up the trail. After the path switchbacks to the right and follows a wooded ridgecrest for 400 yards, look for a small rock outcrop on the left atop a 50-foot cliff. From this scenic lunch spot, broad Diamond Peak rises above green Bristow Prairie. To the left are the tips of the Three Sisters and the ghostly white pyramid of Mt. Jefferson.

Other Hiking Options

The Bulldog Rock Trail continues 3.4 miles along a wooded ridgecrest to Bear Camp Shelter at gravel Road 3810. (To shuttle a car there for a one-way hike, drive back to Road 3850 and follow "Boulder Creek Trail" signs left 5 miles.) Ironically, the trail bypasses Bulldog Rock itself. To see this rocky knob, hike to the outcrop viewpoint described above, continue 100 yards to where the path leaves the ridgecrest, and bushwhack 0.2 mile to the left, following the cliff-edged crest up to a wooded summit. To the right 100 feet is a viewpoint of Mt. Thielsen and Bulldog Rock. From this vantage point, adventurers with map and compass can lay out a path to the top of Bulldog Rock and the best viewpoint of all.

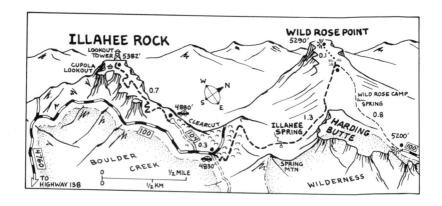

7

Illahee Rock

Easy (to Illahee Rock)
1.4 miles round trip
500 feet elevation gain
Open late May to late November
Use: hikers, horses, bicycles
Map: Illahee Rock (USGS)

Easy (to Wild Rose Point)
2.8 miles round trip
520 feet elevation gain

Two historic fire lookouts and a panoramic view across the Boulder Creek Wilderness await visitors to this cliff-edged peak. A natural rock garden of wildflowers lines the route to the top. And if the hike seems too short, add a jaunt to nearby Wild Rose Point—a lesser but wilder viewpoint that requires a little bushwhacking to reach.

To find the Illahee Rock trailhead from Interstate 5, take exit 124 in Roseburg and follow "Diamond Lake" signs east on Highway 138 for 47 miles. Just 0.3 mile beyond the Dry Creek Store, turn left on gravel Illahee Road 4760. Follow this one-lane road (ignoring a spur for the "Illahee Flat Trail") for 8 miles, go straight on Road 100 for 1.3 miles, and then turn left at a "Trail" pointer onto steep, rocky Road 104 for 0.2 mile to its end. If you have a low-clearance car you may want to walk this final stretch to the Illahee Rock trailhead.

Just 0.7 mile long, the trail up Illahee Rock is a joy, switchbacking from high forests with woodland flowers (rhododendrons, yellow violets, and more) to shaley rockslides with clumps of bright pink penstemons and fleshy-leaved stonecrop. Cliffs and crags flank the route. In June, whole slopes bloom with avalanche lilies—graceful white flowers with 6 white curving petals and spotted green leaves.

At the top are a 1925-vintage cupola-style lookout and its replacement, a

40-foot lookout tower from 1958. The newer lookout is staffed each summer during fire season. The older 12-by-12-foot building is one of only 8 remaining Oregon lookouts with a hipped cupola roof. After a painstaking restoration, the ground lookout may eventually be available to the public for overnight rental. Call the North Umpqua Ranger District (541-496-3532) for details.

Agile climbers can scale a rock outcrop near the old lookout for the area's best viewpoint. On the horizon, Mt. Thielsen's spire rises above the uncut forests of Boulder Creek's valley. To the right are broad Mt. Bailey, the tip of Mt. Scott, Crater Lake's rim, and the tip of Mt. McLoughlin. Far to the north, look for the tip of Mt. Jefferson above Wild Rose Point's rock bluff.

If you'd like a longer hike after returning from Illahee Rock, drive back 0.2 mile to Road 100, turn left for 200 yards, and park at a fork in the road. Between the forks is a small "Wild Rose Trail" sign. This path climbs 0.3 mile through a brushy clearcut and then contours a mile along a pleasantly wooded slope before reaching a small flat meadow atop a broad ridgecrest.

The main trail curves to the right into the woods (to deadend in 0.8 mile at a different Road 100), but to find Wild Rose Point, walk left through the meadow and then bushwhack 200 yards through the woods—*always keeping uphill* on the ridgetop. You'll reach a rocky bluff atop a 300-foot cliff with a view south to Illahee Rock. Many wildflowers spangle this bluff—red paintbrush, pink heather, yellow lomatiums, purple larkspur, and fuzzy white cats ears—but no wild roses.

Illahee Rock.   Opposite: View from the Illahee Rock lookout tower.

Boulder Creek

Moderate (to Pine Bench viewpoint)
5.5-mile loop
800 feet elevation gain
Open all year
Use: hikers, horses
Map: Boulder Creek Wilderness (USFS)

Moderate (to Boulder Creek)
8.9-mile loop
1100 feet elevation gain

One of Oregon's few official wilderness areas that's hikable in winter, the Boulder Creek valley features a plateau forested with stately ponderosa pines—a rarity west of the Cascades.

To drive here from Interstate 5, take Roseburg exit 124 and follow "Diamond Lake" signs east 54.7 miles on Highway 138. Between mileposts 54 and 55, turn left at a sign for Slide Creek, and *immediately turn left again* onto gravel Soda Springs Road for 1.4 miles to the Soda Springs trailhead parking area on the left. The trail itself begins on the right—and promptly ducks under a huge 12-foot steel pipe that's carrying most of the North Umpqua River to a power station. Because horses can't duck, equestrians have to ride another 200 yards down the road to find a detour path around the pipe.

Beyond the pipe, follow the trail 0.4 miles up to a junction and turn left. This path climbs steadily amid 4-foot-thick Douglas firs and incense cedars. Rhododendrons bloom here in June. Look for the massive trunks and foot-long cones of sugarpines, the world's largest variety of pine. At the 1.3-mile mark the trail finally levels out atop Pine Bench in a grassy forest of Douglas firs and ponderosa pines—easily identified by their 6-inch-long cones, foot-long needles, and orange bark. In June, expect white iris, fuzzy cats ears, starflower, and some mosquitoes. Also keep an eye out for poison oak.

Pine Bench's square-mile plateau is a remnant of a vast lava flow that once filled the North Umpqua's canyon from wall to wall at this elevation. Ponderosa pines are well adapted to such relatively dry spots for several reasons. First, they are among the few conifers with long taproots that enable them to extract water from deep ground layers. Second, they survive wildfire well because their needle clumps are located high in isolated clusters. The ponderosas' unusual bark helps them outlast fires, too, by flaking off in jigsaw-puzzle-piece shapes to dissipate the heat of flames.

Near the far end of Pine Bench, turn right at a T-shaped trail junction and continue 0.4 mile to an unsigned fork. Keep left for 100 yards and follow the sound of water to discover a delicious natural spring, pouring out of a cliff from 4 mossy spouts. Several campsites are just beyond. For the area's best viewpoint, scramble 50 yards out a rock promontory—using both hands and caution. The vista atop this 200-foot cliff shows how Boulder Creek's valley is recovering from a 1996 fire that swept through nearly half of this Wilderness, burning underbrush and leaving a healthier patchwork of old-growth forest.

Boulder Creek at the first trail crossing.   *Opposite: Cats ear.*

If you'd like to continue to Boulder Creek itself, walk back to the fork and take the main trail another 1.7 miles. The path crosses 20-foot-wide, pebbly creek on a fallen log. Flat campsites are scarce here, but lunch sites abound. In summer, it's fun to wade upstream 100 yards to a small waterfall and cold, swimmable pool. Backpackers can follow the Boulder Creek Trail another 6.8 miles beyond this first creek crossing. but the path climbs steeply away from the shore for 1.9 miles, then fords the creek 3 times before launching uphill on a switchbacking climb to Road 3810.

To return on a loop, hike back to Pine Bench and go straight at all trail junctions. You'll switchback down the Boulder Creek Trail across grassy slopes; watch out for poison oak. At the bottom of the hill the trail joins an ancient roadbed, which soon forks. For a short side trip, take the right-hand fork down 300 yards to a lovely footbridge across Boulder Creek. The pebbly beach here is not only a good place to cool off, it's also a place to see osprey, kingfishers, and ouzels. To complete the loop, however, take the ancient road's left fork 0.2 mile to the small Boulder Creek Trailhead, and continue 1.2 miles along the narrow dirt Soda Springs Road to your car. Although a car shuttle would eliminate this final 1.2-mile roadside walk, the road is rough enough and the river views are pleasant enough to make the walk a good option.

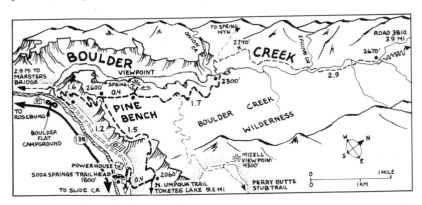

9   Twin Lakes

Easy (around both lakes)
3.2-mile loop
400 feet elevation gain
Open mid-June through November
Use: hikers, horses, bicycles
Map: Twin Lakes Mountain (USGS)

Moderate (to Twin Lakes Mountain)
5.4-mile loop
850 feet elevation gain

It's hard to imagine a better family backpacking destination than this pair of gorgeous turquoise lakes. The nearly level, 0.9-mile trail to the lakes ambles through old-growth woods and wildflower meadows. At the lakes themselves you'll find 2 large shelters and a hiker campground with picnic tables—but probably very few other people. If you'd like a bit more exercise, a well-graded 1.1-mile side path climbs to a breathtaking viewpoint atop a mountain cliff.

To start, take Interstate 5 exit 124 in Roseburg and follow "Diamond Lake" signs east on Highway 138 for 49 miles. Immediately after crossing the North Umpqua River on Marsters Bridge (and 0.7 mile before Eagle Rock Campground), turn right on Wilson Creek Road 4770. Follow this one-lane gravel road 9 miles to its end at the trailhead parking area.

The wide path sets off amid Douglas fir with an understory of vine maple, vanilla leaf, and Oregon grape. After 0.3 mile, pass a clifftop viewpoint of 3 distant, snowy Cascade peaks: Diamond Peak, Mt. Thielsen, and Mt. Bailey. At the 0.6-mile mark, turn right at a T-junction for 150 yards; then turn left through a wildflower meadow for 0.3 mile to a large plank-sided shelter by the lake. The meadow here brims with orange paintbrush, pink owl clover, mint, hellebore, and coneflower.

Turn right at the shelter to find 7 campsites, all with log picnic tables, lake views, and June-blooming rhododendrons. Continue around the large lake to

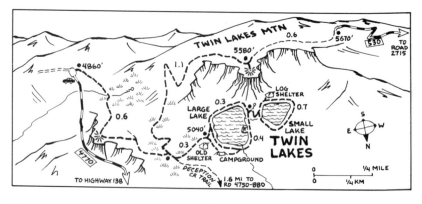

Large Twin Lake from Twin Lakes Mountain.   *Opposite: Shelter at Small Twin Lake.*

the far shore, where a short connecting trail leads to the smaller lake. Turn left around this lake 100 yards and look behind a house-sized boulder to find the 12-by-16-foot Twin Wolf Shelter, built of logs in 1995 by the Wolf Creek Job Corps and the Forest Service. Both shelters are open on a first-come-first-served basis.

For an optional climb after hiking around the Twin Lakes, head back toward the car but keep right at all junctions to find the trail up Twin Lakes Mountain. This path crests after a mile. Just a few hundred yards after the trail starts downhill, take a right-hand spur through rhododendron bushes to an amazing viewpoint atop a 300-foot cliff. The square-topped peak on the horizon above the small lake is Bohemia Mountain. Above the larger lake is the roadless Boulder Creek Wilderness (see Hike #8), with all Three Sisters peeking over that wild valley's rim.

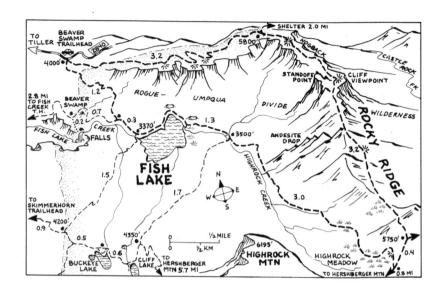

10   Fish Lake

Easy (to Fish Lake)
3 miles round-trip
630 feet elevation loss
Open May to mid-December
Use: hikers, horses
Map: Rogue-Umpqua Divide Wlds. (USFS)

Difficult (to Rocky Ridge)
12.6-mile loop
2800 feet elevation gain
Open July through October

    This Fish Lake (not to be confused with the larger, better-known reservoir near Mt. McLoughlin) won its name in 1889 when a group of explorers caught 70 trout in an hour using venison for bait. Fish still jump in this forest-rimmed, half-mile-long natural lake near the South Umpqua River's headwaters, but you'll find other wildlife too: ducks, eagles, and a cute family of river otters. If the stroll down to the lake seems too easy, you can continue on a moderate loop past 2 smaller lakes, or take a longer loop along Rocky Ridge past dramatic cliffs with views across the Rogue-Umpqua Divide Wilderness.

    To start, drive Interstate 5 south of Roseburg 25 miles (or north of Grants Pass 40 miles) to Canyonville exit 98. Following signs for Crater Lake, drive into Canyonville and turn east on 3rd Street—which becomes the Tiller-Trail Highway—for 23.3 miles to Tiller. On the far side of this hamlet, turn left on Road 46 toward South Umpqua Falls. After another 24.2 miles, veer to the right on one-lane, paved Road 2823.

Following "Fish Lake Trailhead" pointers, drive 2.4 miles on Road 2823, fork to the right on Road 2830 for 3.9 gravel miles, and then fork to the left on Road 2840 for 0.5 mile. Here you'll see the Fish Lake Trailhead—but don't park yet. Although this route to Fish Lake is pleasant enough (and well suited for equestrians), it's 2.3 miles longer than the trail from the Beaver Swamp Trailhead. To find the shorter path, drive onward on Road 2840 for another 4.6 miles to a trail sign on the right.

At this trailhead, take the right-hand path (the "Beaver Swamp Trail") down through a forest of Douglas fir, incense cedar, and ponderosa pine. In 1987 a 400-acre forest fire tidied up this area's woods, burning underbrush and downed logs, but leaving nearly all the large trees intact.

After 1.2 miles, turn left for 0.3 mile to the outlet of Fish Lake. To find the best shore access and lunch spot, hike 0.3 mile along the lakeshore trail to a peninsula. Because camping is banned within 200 feet of the shore, backpackers will want to continue 0.2 mile past the peninsula to an old-growth grove on the left with lots of permissible tent sites.

If you're not yet ready to turn back to your car, continue to a trail junction half a mile beyond Fish Lake. Here you have a choice of 2 loops.

For a moderate 8.6-mile loop hike, turn right and keep right for 4.4 miles. Climb through the woods to Cliff Lake and Buckeye Lake (see also Hike #11) and descend to the outlet of Fish Lake to join the trail to your car.

For the Rocky Ridge loop, a longer trip with the more dramatic views, turn left and keep left at all trail junctions. You'll climb steeply for 2.5 miles before skirting the left edge of Highrock Meadows, a subalpine slope full of wildflowers and huge-leaved hellebore. The sweet smell is mint. The musty smell is a white flower known as dirty socks. Beyond Highrock Meadows, still keeping left at junctions, you'll contour along Rocky Ridge, with clifftop views east to Fish Mountain and Castle Rock's lava plug. Then the path skirts Standoff Point's weird rock formations of flutes and spires, balances across a narrow hogback ridgecrest, and finally descends to your car.

Fish Lake.   Opposite: Pinnacles on Rocky Ridge

11 Buckeye and Cliff Lakes

Easy (to lakes)
3.4 miles round-trip
700 feet elevation gain
Open mid-May through November
Use: hikers, horses
Map: Rogue-Umpqua Divide Wlds. (USFS)

Moderate (to Grasshopper Mountain)
8.8-mile loop
1980 feet elevation gain
Open late June to early November

A monumental landslide crumbled half of Grasshopper Mountain about 1000 years ago, damming the Fish Lake Valley with 4 square miles of jumbled debris. Surprisingly, the scene of this ancient disaster has become one of the loveliest subalpine landscapes anywhere. An easy 1.4-mile trail, perfect for hikers with children, crosses the now thoroughly forested landslide to a pair of mountain lakes at the foot of a dramatic mile-long cliff—the origin of the slide. An extra 2-mile climb takes you through wildflower meadows to a viewpoint atop the cliff itself.

To find the trailhead, drive Interstate 5 south of Roseburg 25 miles (or north of Grants Pass 40 miles) to Canyonville exit 98. Following signs for Crater Lake, drive into Canyonville and turn east on 3rd Street—which becomes the Tiller-Trail Highway—for 23.3 miles to Tiller. On the far side of this hamlet, turn left on Road 46 toward South Umpqua Falls. After another 24.2 miles, veer to the right on one-lane, paved Road 2823 and begin following "Skimmerhorn Trail-head" pointers. After 2.4 miles these signs will direct you to fork to the right on Road 2830 for 3.9 gravel miles and then turn left on Road 600 for 1.8 miles to road's end.

The trail starts amid ponderosa pines, sugarpines, and June-blooming rhodo-dendrons. After 0.2 mile, turn left at a T-junction. In another half mile the path sets off across the hummocky surface of the ancient landslide, now overgrown

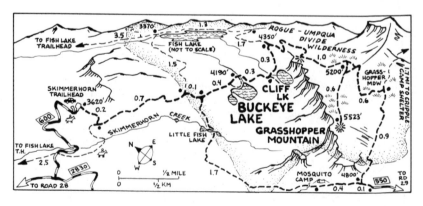

Buckeye Lake. Opposite: Cliff Lake from Grasshopper Mountain.

with Douglas fir, mountain hemlock, and Oregon grape. Enormous boulders remain from the slide's debris.

Keep straight at 2 junctions to reach Buckeye Lake. There, a small loop trail to the right tours a scenic peninsula where camping is banned. (Tents must be 200 feet from the shore.) Watch for the lake's playful resident river otter. Also try the echo off Grasshopper Mountain's cliffs.

The main trail continues, crossing Buckeye Lake's outlet below a beaver dam. In 0.3 mile a spur trail to the right leads to Cliff Lake—a smaller pool with a closer view of the landslide cliff. The stripes in the cliff are a cross section of the black basalt lava flows, greenish ash layers, and reddish soil layers that built this portion of the Old Cascades range 16 to 25 million years ago.

If you're not yet ready to turn back, continue on the main trail 0.3 mile, turn right for an uphill mile to a meadow, and fork right for 0.6 mile to the summit of Grasshopper Mountain. From the crumbling cliff edge of this former lookout, Buckeye and Cliff Lakes look like blue-green eggs in a huge forest-furred nest. To the east, note Highrock Mountain's cliffs and the tips of Rabbit Ears' rock spires.

It is quickest to return as you came, but if you keep right at all junctions on the way down you can return on a loop. Longer by 1.6 miles, this route visits Grasshopper Meadow, Mosquito Camp, and shallow Little Fish Lake.

12 Toketee and Watson Falls

Easy (to Toketee Falls)
0.8 miles round-trip
100 feet elevation loss
Open except in winter storms
Map: Toketee Falls (USGS)

Easy (to Watson Falls)
0.8-mile loop
300 feet elevation gain
Open mid-March through December
Map: Fish Creek Desert (USGS)

Left: Bridge over Watson Creek.

A pair of easy 0.4-mile trails lead to the North Umpqua's most spectacular waterfalls—90-foot Toketee Falls, whose name means "pretty" in the Northwest Indians' Chinook jargon, and 272-foot Watson Falls, tallest in Southern Oregon. Both tumble from the eroded edges of basalt lava flows that coursed down this valley from the High Cascades thousands of years ago.

To find the Toketee Falls Viewpoint trail, drive 58.6 miles east of Roseburg (or 20 miles west of Diamond Lake) on Highway 138. Between mileposts 58 and 59, turn north onto Toketee-Rigdon Road 34. Then keep left at all junctions for 0.4 mile to the well-marked gravel parking lot and a small picnic area.

The trail sets off through a forest of big Douglas fir, red cedar, and bigleaf maple, brightened in April and May with the showy blooms of white trilliums and pink rhododendrons. Elaborate stone and wood staircases help hikers clamber past a churning gorge and descend to the trail's end at a railed deck with a frontal view of the falls. The deck is built around 2 Douglas fir trees and a large yew—the legendary tree species that once provided flexible wood for Native Americans' bows and more recently yielded the cancer-fighting drug taxol.

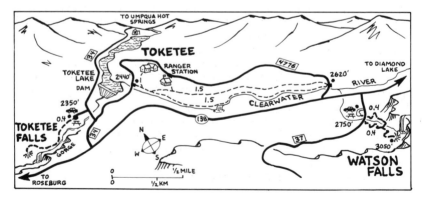

Below the viewpoint, Toketee Falls pours out of columnar basalt cliffs to smash into a wave-tossed pool. It's hard to imagine how huge this cascade must have been before the North Umpqua hydroelectric projects tapped the river. The enormous 8-foot-thick pipeline alongside this hike's trailhead is shunting most of the river around the falls, from Toketee Lake's reservoir to a power plant at Soda Springs.

To find Watson Falls, drive back to Highway 138 and turn left 2.3 miles. Between mileposts 60 and 61, turn south on Fish Creek Road 37 for 200 yards and park in a gravel lot at a picnic area on the right. The trail begins at the end of a gravel turnaround and promptly climbs to a crossing of paved Road 37—where parking is banned.

After crossing of the road, the path switchbacks up 0.3 mile to a 70-foot, zigzagging footbridge over bouldery Watson Creek. Just beyond is a T-shaped trail junction. To the left is a 100-yard path up to the misty base of Watson Falls' amazingly tall horsetail plume. To the right is the loop's return trail down to the Road 37 crossing and your car.

13   Umpqua Hot Springs

Easy
0.6 mile round-trip
100 feet elevation gain
Open except in winter storms
Use: hikers, horses, bicycles
Map: Potter Mountain (USGS)

Right: Umpqua Hot Springs shelter.

Unmarked but deservedly popular, this 0.3-mile path leads to a rustic shelter with a spa-sized 105-degree F hot springs pool overlooking the North Umpqua River. Less well known is an equally easy trail on the far shore that leads to a pair of astonishing *cold* springs—a roaring gusher and a mysterious waterfall with no apparent source or outlet.

Start by driving 58.6 miles east of Roseburg (or 20 miles west of Diamond Lake) on Highway 138. Between mileposts 58 and 59, turn north onto Toketee-Rigdon Road 34. After 0.2 mile keep left alongside Toketee Lake's dam. Continue 2 miles, fork right onto gravel Thorn Prairie Road 3401 for precisely another 2 miles, and look for a huge parking lot on the left.

The only sign here is a small notice on the outhouse: "Nude bathing is common at Umpqua Hot Springs. If this makes you uncomfortable, we recommend you not go into the area. Please remain conventionally clothed at the parking lot and on the trail."

The trail starts at the right-hand end of the parking area and immediately

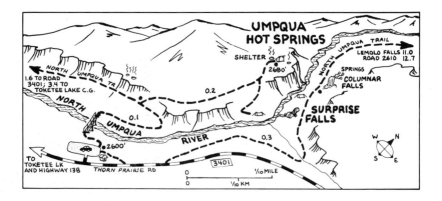

crosses the North Umpqua River on a 150-foot bridge. This is a portion of the 79-mile North Umpqua River Trail, but after following this path 100 yards into the second-growth Douglas fir woods on the far shore, take a steep side trail up to the right for 0.2 mile to the hot springs. Just before the shelter, ignore a small trail down to the right; it leads to riverside campsites.

All the springs in this area resulted when geologically recent High Cascade lava flows buried thousands of stream channels, leaving snowmelt to percolate underground to find an outlet. At Umpqua Hot Springs the water has seeped through an active fault, heating it to 100-115 degrees F. Such hot water dissolves and carries minerals well. Umpqua Hot Springs doesn't smell of sulfur, but it has carried enough alkali over the centuries to build a 100-foot dome-shaped rock knoll above the river's bank.

On summer weekends, expect to wait an hour for a turn in the hot springs. The pool in the shelter holds 4 or 5 people, while an open-air pool just outside holds 2 or 3. Smaller pools have been fashioned in the runoff creek. A less hot spring down on the riverbank below the shelter is covered by the river during high water.

After soaking a while and hiking back to the parking lot, why not take another short hike to see the cold springs? This trail starts beside the parking lot's outhouse, climbs to the road, follows it 100 feet, and then descends into the woods. Officially known as the Dread and Terror Segment of the North Umpqua Trail, this path is named for Dread and Terror Ridge, a nearby hill cursed by early fire fighters for its brushy thickets. Since then this lovely and remote 13-mile section of river trail has only terrorized maintenance crews. Ice and windstorms in early 1996 felled 1100 trees across the path, closing most of it for 2 summers.

Sample the trail with an easy 0.3-mile stroll to Surprise Falls, which roars out of the ground just below the trail, and Columnar Falls, where lacy springs spill down the angled columns of a mossy basalt cliff and immediately seep back into the ground, vanishing without a trace. This makes a good turnaround point, although backpackers can continue on the North Umpqua Trail either upriver to Lemolo Falls (see Hike #14) or downriver to the Boulder Creek Wilderness (see Hike #8).

14 Lemolo Falls

Easy (to Warm Spring Falls)
0.6 mile round-trip
80 feet elevation loss
Open May through November
Use: hikers, horses, bicycles
Map: Lemolo Lake (USGS)

Easy (to Lemolo Falls)
3.4 miles round-trip
400 feet elevation loss

Right: Trillium.

Huge waterfalls are the star attractions of these 2 short hikes below Lemolo Lake, but the North Umpqua River Trail is attractive in its own right, passing countless smaller chutes and cascades.

Drive Highway 58 east of Roseburg 70 miles (or west of Diamond Lake 6 miles) and turn north on paved Road 2610 at a sign for the Lemolo Lake Recreation Area. After 5 miles, cross Lemolo Lake's dam. Then keep left on Road 2610 for 0.6 mile.

The North Umpqua River Trail crosses the road here, and a bridge across a canal to the left leads to a parking area for the Lemolo Falls hike. But if you'd like to warm up first with a short walk to Warm Spring Falls, continue driving straight on Road 2610 for 2.4 miles, turn left on paved Road 680 (which soon turns to gravel), and follow it 1.6 miles to a partly hidden "Warm Spring Falls Trail" sign on the left.

This path ambles 0.3 mile through a Douglas fir forest full of rhododendrons (with pink blooms in June) and trilliums (with white May blooms). The path ends at an unrailed viewpoint of the massive 70-foot waterfall beside a 100-foot cliff of columnar basalt. This rock is part of a geologically recent lava flow that poured down the North Umpqua River canyon from the Cascades. The river and many side creeks now tumble over the lava flow's eroded lip.

For the second, longer hike to Lemolo Falls, drive back to the North Umpqua

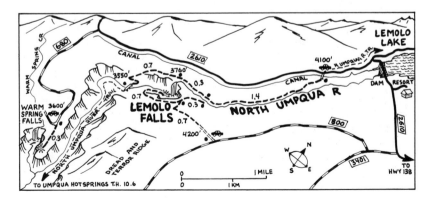

River trailhead at the canal bridge. Yellow Oregon grape, white vanilla leaf, and other forest flowers bloom along this riverbank path. Children can splash in pools below small chutes and cascades. At the 1.7-mile mark, a short left spur leads to the top of 100-foot Lemolo Falls—not a safe place for children. For a side view of the falls, continue a few hundred yards on the main trail. If you hike an additional 0.7 mile down the path you'll reach a long footbridge across the river—a pleasant spot for lunch before heading back.

Other Hiking Options

The best view of Lemolo Falls is actually on an older trail on the south side of the river. Although the 2 trails aren't quite connected, it's not hard to scramble from one to the other. From the top of Lemolo Falls, hike the North Umpqua River Trail about a quarter mile upstream, cross the river on a fallen log, and scramble up the far bank less than 300 feet to the old trail. Keep right on this well-built path for a mile to its end at a wave-wracked splash pool below Lemolo Fall's thundering plume.

If you'd rather drive to the old trail, take Road 2610 south of the Lemolo Lake dam 0.5 mile to a curve, turn west onto poorly marked Thorn Prairie Road 3401 for 0.5 mile, turn right on Road 800 for 1.6 miles, and park at a "Lemolo Falls Trail" sign on the right. The path follows an abandoned road 0.6 mile to its end. Keep right through an old picnic area 200 yards to a trail junction and turn left for 0.7 mile to the falls.

Warm Spring Falls.   Opposite: Cowhorn Mountain from the Pacific Crest Trail.

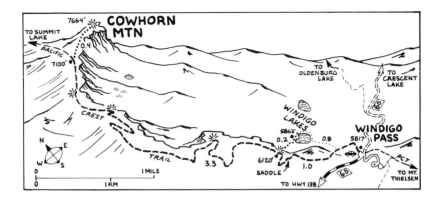

15   Cowhorn Mountain

Difficult
9.4 miles round-trip
1900 feet elevation gain
Open mid-July to late October
Use: hikers, horses
Maps: Cowhorn Mtn, Tolo Mtn (USGS)

Cowhorn Mountain has been one of the least recognized High Cascade peaks ever since its cowhorn-shaped spire toppled in a 1911 storm. But the summit view is still breathtaking, and few mountain climbs are this convenient. All but the last 0.4 mile of the route follows the well-graded Pacific Crest Trail. On the return trip, hikers can bushwhack a few hundred yards off the trail for a swim at the lovely, rarely visited Windigo Lakes.

To start, drive Highway 138 east of Roseburg 73.5 miles (or north of Diamond Lake 5 miles). Between mileposts 73 and 74, turn north onto Windigo Pass Road 60. Follow this wide, washboard gravel road 4.5 miles to a junction for Lemolo Lake. Curve right, continue on Road 60 another 7.6 miles to Windigo Pass, and park in a large pullout on the left with a trail registration box. Ignore a spur road to the right marked "Windigo Pass Trailhead;" it is for hikers headed south.

From the parking pullout, the Pacific Crest Trail climbs gradually northwards through a sparse forest of small mountain hemlock, lodgepole pine, and noble fir. After 0.8 mile the trail dips to a saddle and then switchbacks up 400 yards to the trail's only viewpoint of West Windigo Lake. Make a note of the spot if you'd like to swim on return trip.

The PCT passes increasingly dramatic cliff-edge viewpoints ahead to Cowhorn Mountain every mile or so as it climbs to alpine elevations with western Pasque flower, purple penstemon, and gnarled whitebark pines. At the

4.3-mile mark, look for a rock cairn where the PCT curves left to descend into the woods on Cowhorn Mountain's shoulder. Leave the PCT here and follow a faint trail up the ridgecrest, directly toward the summit. At timberline, the route steepens in cinder scree. Crest a false summit of bare black rock, cross a cinder hogback, and scale the actual summit crag on the left—a non-technical scramble requiring the use of hands.

The summit is the eroded remnant of a much larger stratovolcano. The shaley gray andesite is riddled with wall-like dikes, where black lava squeezed into fractures as it rose. But it's the view of Crescent Lake that steals the show at the summit. To the left are the Three Sisters, the sinuous shore of Summit Lake, snowy Diamond Peak, the U-shaped canyon of the Middle Fork Willamette River, and Sawtooth Mountain's bare gray slopes. To the south look for broad Mt. Bailey, Crater Lake's jagged rim, and Mt. Thielsen's spire.

If you decide to visit the Windigo Lakes on the return trip, don't leave the PCT until the lake viewpoint 1 mile from the trailhead. Then bushwhack steeply down 200 yards and continue straight 200 yards to the green lake, an 8-foot-deep pool with a sandy bottom and relatively warm water. Explorers can shortcut back to their cars from the lake's far, southern shore by hiking directly away from the view of Cowhorn Mountain, traversing along a slope 600 yards *without going downhill,* and turning left on the PCT.

16   Miller and Maidu Lakes

Easy (around Miller Lake)
5.1-mile loop
100 feet elevation gain
Open mid-June through October
Use: hikers, horses, bicycles
Map: Mt. Thielsen Wilderness (USFS)

Moderate (around Maidu Lake)
8.4 miles round-trip
750 feet elevation gain
Open early July through October
Use: hikers, horses

The glaciers that once spanned the crest of the Cascade Range in the Ice Age left behind a broad, forested mountain pass north of Mt. Thielsen. Today hikers can cross this pass on a trail from Miller Lake, on the range's eastern slope, to Maidu Lake, the source of the North Umpqua River. For a shorter hike from the same trailhead, try the 5.1-mile path around Miller Lake, a route popular with anglers. On either trip, be prepared for mosquitoes throughout July.

Access to the trailhead is via the town of Chemult, on Highway 97 halfway between Bend (65 miles to the north) and Klamath Falls (72 miles to the south). Half a mile north of Chemult, between mileposts 202 and 203, turn west onto a side road at a large brown sign for the Chemult Recreation Site. After half a mile of pavement, continue straight for 12 dusty gravel miles to road's end at Digit Point Campground. Keep left to park at the end of the lakeside picnic area loop.

Miller Lake from Digit Point.   *Opposite: Miller Lake from Pacific Crest Trail viewpoint.*

The trail starts at the left edge of the picnic area beach and follows Miller Lake's shore amid mountain hemlock woods with red huckleberry bushes. The path crosses 2 small inlet creeks, where lupines bloom and beavers fell trees. After 0.8 mile, just beyond a campsite, you'll reach a trail junction where you have to make a decision.

For the easy loop around Miller Lake, simply go straight. This trail follows the shore to the sunny side of the lake, where the forest shifts to pine, the underbrush includes huge, creamy Cascade lilies, and the views feature snowy Howlock Mountain. After 2.3 miles you'll meet the gravel entrance road. Follow it 100 yards to find the continuation of the trail, which then traces the shore for another 2 miles back to your car.

For the longer trip to Maidu Lake, however, turn left at the junction near the start of the hike. Bicycles aren't allowed on this route. The path bridges Evening

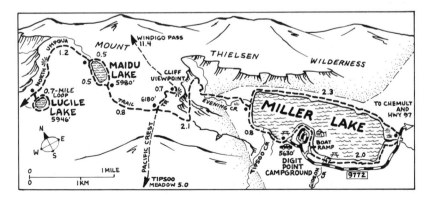

Creek twice in meadows of lupine and mountain bluebells (mertensia). Then it climbs steadily through lodgepole pine woods to a junction with the Pacific Crest Trail at the pass. (There are no views at the pass, but if you don't mind a small side trip, you can turn right on the PCT for 0.7 mile to a rock promontory with a fine overlook of Miller Lake's U-shaped glacial valley and Howlock Mountain.)

To go to Maidu Lake, cross the PCT at the pass and descend 0.8 mile to the shallow, forest-rimmed lake. If you're camping, choose a site at least 100 feet from the shore. To help disperse use near this fragile pool, the Forest Service removed an old shelter in 1990 from the open area where the trail meets the lake. Circle the lake on a 1-mile shoreline loop trail before returning the way you came.

Other Hiking Options

For a look west down the huge U-shaped valley left by Maidu Lake's vanished glacier, take the North Umqua River Trail 0.7 mile beyond the far end of the Maidu Lake loop to a clifftop viewpoint. On the horizon, look for Sawtooth Mountain, snowy Diamond Peak, and the spire of Cowhorn Mountain. Once you've come this far, you really should continue 0.5 mile and turn left for 100 yards to a 0.7-mile loop path around Lucile Lake, Maidu Lake's little sister.

17 Tipsoo Peak

Moderate
6.2 miles round-trip
1784 feet elevation gain
Open late July to mid-October
Use: hikers, horses
Map: Mt. Thielsen Wilderness (USFS)

One of the few 8000-foot Cascade peaks with a well-graded trail to its summit, Tipsoo Peak offers a panoramic view from the Three Sisters to Mt. Shasta, with nearby Mt. Thielsen looming above an alpine pumice plain.

To find the trailhead, drive Highway 138 east of Roseburg 75 miles (or north of Diamond Lake 4 miles. Near milepost 75, turn east onto gravel Cinnamon Butte Road 4793. After 1.7 miles, go straight on Wits End Road 100 for 3.2 miles to a wide spot with a small "Tipsoo Trail" sign on the right. The last half mile of the drive is a bit bumpy.

The trail climbs through a mountain hemlock forest with red huckleberry bushes. Grayish green old-man's-beard lichen grows profusely on tree trunks here, but only above the 8-foot depth of typical winter snow. At the 2.8-mile mark the trail climbs through a corner of Tipsoo Meadow, a vast alpine field of pumice that was blasted here when when Mt. Mazama collapsed to form Crater Lake. The intervening 7700 years have allowed wildflowers to spread—dwarf

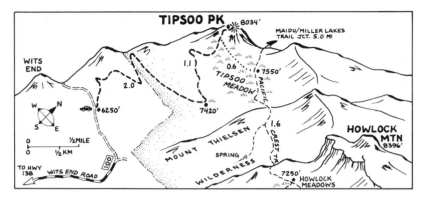

blue lupine, tiny purple penstemon, white partridge foot, and pink heather. At this elevation the sparse, wind-bent mountain hemlocks and whitebark pines grow no larger than Christmas trees.

Finally the trail turns right at a snowy pass and climbs a ridgecrest of craggy, black and red lava to the summit. The view to the south, across Tipsoo Meadow, includes Howlock Mountain and the Matterhorn-shaped Mt.Thielsen. Completing the panorama to the right are Diamond Lake, Mt. Bailey, Lemolo Lake, snowy Diamond Peak, Cowhorn Mountain, and the Three Sisters. The green lakes at the north base of Tipsoo Peak are Lucile and Maidu Lakes, while larger Miller Lake lies to the east.

If you'd like to explore Tipsoo Peak's high country, or if you're backpacking, it's easy to walk down 0.6 mile cross-country through Tipsoo Meadow to the Pacific Crest Trail—but note your route carefully for the return trip. Once on the PCT, you could either go 5.8 miles north to Maidu Lake (see Hike #16) or head south 1.6 miles to Howlock Meadows (see Hike #18).

View south from Tipsoo Peak.   Opposite: Lupine leaves.

Diamond and Crater Lakes

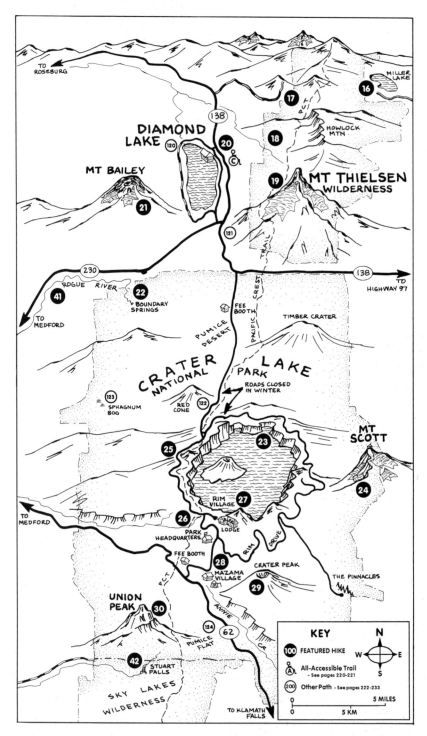

Opposite: Wizard Island from the Pacific Crest Trail (Hike #25).

18 Thielsen Creek

Difficult (to Thielsen Meadow)
11.4 miles round-trip
1650 feet elevation gain
Open end of July through October
Use: hikers and horses
Map: Mt. Thielsen Wilderness (USFS)

Difficult (to Howlock Meadows)
15.7-mile loop
2000 feet elevation gain

Mt. Thielsen looms like the Matterhorn above Thielsen Meadow, an alpine glen with a bubbling mountain stream. If you have extra energy after hiking to Thielsen Meadow you can return on a Pacific Crest Trail loop via Howlock Meadows, a broader field at another mountain's base. In either case, be prepared for mosquitoes from late July until mid-August and expect horse traffic on the first few dusty miles from the trailhead.

To find the trailhead from Medford, follow "Diamond Lake" signs east on Highway 62 for 57 miles and go straight on Highway 230 for another 23.6 miles. Then turn left at a "Diamond Lake Recreation Area" sign and follow Road 6592 for 4.2 miles to the Howlock Mountain Trailhead on the right, opposite a gas station. If you're coming from Roseburg, take Highway 138 east 78.6 miles. Between mileposts 78 and 79, turn right at a "Diamond Lake Recreation Area" sign for 0.3 mile, and park at the Howlock Mountain Trailhead on the left.

A commercial stable offers horse rentals and guided rides at this heavily used trailhead. Park at the message board at the far end of the parking loop and set off on the left-hand trail. In 0.2 mile follow the path through a tunnel under Highway 138. Then continue straight, ignoring horse loop trails to the left. The sparse lodgepole pine trees, pinemat manzanita bushes, and white lupines here

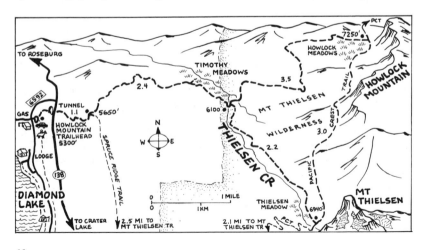

Thielsen Meadow.   Opposite: Snow-bent lodgepole pine.

are struggling to grow in 6 feet of dusty pumice and ash dumped here by the eruption of Crater Lake's Mt. Mazama 7700 years ago.

After 3.5 miles you'll be glad to reach Thielsen Creek, in a cool, grassy oasis at the head of Timothy Meadows. Cross on a log and walk 100 feet to a trail junction. Turn right on a path that parallels the creek upstream 2.2 miles to the Pacific Crest Trail. Just before the PCT, a short spur to the right leads to Thielsen Meadow, where the creek meanders through a heather glen overtowered by Mt. Thielsen's spire 2000 feet above. If you're backpacking, do not camp on the fragile meadow, but rather on forest duff well away from the creek.

If you're interested in the longer loop hike, turn left on the PCT. This route contours 3 miles through mountain hemlock woods to Howlock Meadows, a pumice barrens. At the far side of the field, where a sweeping view opens up of Howlock Mountain's cliffs and Mt. Thielsen's spire, turn left at a pointer for Diamond Lake and descend 3.5 miles to Thielsen Creek and the trail back to your car.

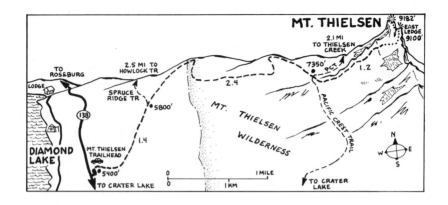

19   Mount Thielsen

Difficult (to Pacific Crest Trail)
7.6 miles round-trip
1950 feet elevation gain
Open end of July through October
Map: Mt. Thielsen Wilderness (USFS)

Very Difficult (to summit)
10 miles round-trip
3800 feet elevation gain

Towering above Diamond Lake, Mt. Thielsen's stony spire commands views from Mt. Shasta to the Three Sisters. A popular path climbs to the Pacific Crest Trail on Mt. Thielsen's flank. Hardy hikers can follow a scramble trail to a dizzying ledge at the base of the summit spire, and many dare to scale the final pitch as well.

Originally a broad, 11,000-foot volcano, Mt. Thielsen stopped erupting about 100,000 years ago when a lava plug blocked its throat. Since then, erosion by Ice Age glaciers has left this hard lava core exposed as the summit spire. The peak's nickname, "Lightning Rod of the Cascades," reflects both its shape and its weather. Lightning has left the summit boulders spattered with black *fulgurite*— glassy recrystalized rock. The name Thielsen (pronounced *TEEL-sun*) honors a Danish-American pioneer railroad engineer.

To drive here from Medford, take Highway 62 east and follow "Diamond Lake" signs a total of 81 miles. At that point *do not* take the "Diamond Lake Recreation Area" turnoff. Instead continue 300 yards to a "Roseburg" pointer and turn left onto Highway 138. In 1.4 miles you'll find the Mt. Thielsen Trailhead parking area on the right. If you're coming from Roseburg, take Highway 138 east for 81.6 miles. Ignore a "Diamond Lake Recreation Area" turnoff and continue 3 miles to the large trailhead sign on the left.

The trail climbs a dry, sparsely forested ridge, so bring plenty of water. As you gain elevation, lodgepole pine trees and manzanita bushes give way to mountain hemlock and red huckleberry. Notice how the trail cut exposes tan pumice gravel blasted here by the eruption of Crater Lake's Mt. Mazama 7700 years ago. Since then, only an inch or two of forest duff has managed to form atop the debris.

After 3.8 miles the path officially ends at the Pacific Crest Trail, but a climbers' trail continues straight up the ridgecrest. The best views are up this unofficial path, which climbs through the purple penstemon blooms and gnarled whitebark pines of timberline. To the north, the snowy peaks on the horizon are the Three Sisters and Diamond Peak. To the west, Mt. Bailey rises above Diamond Lake. To the south is Crater Lake's jagged rim.

Above timberline the braided, rocky path gives out amidst slippery scree and broken rock. Only sure-footed hikers should venture upward. The correct route veers slightly to the right, spiraling around to a dizzying ledge at the eastern base of the summit spire. This ledge, practically overhanging Thielsen Creek 2000 feet below, is an excellent place to declare victory and turn back. The final 80 feet are nearly vertical and require the adept use of hands and feet to chimney up cracks in the rock. Hikers attempting this do so at their own risk.

Mt. Thielsen.   Opposite: Mt. Thielsen's summit register.

20 Diamond Lake

Easy (North Shore)
3.4 miles round-trip
No elevation gain
Open mid-May through November
Use: hikers and bicycles
Map: Diamond Lake (USGS)

Easy (Silent Creek)
2.3-mile loop
100 feet elevation gain

Difficult (entire lakeshore)
11.5-mile loop
100 feet elevation gain

Crater Lake may be a dramatic draw for out-of-staters, but Oregonians visit neighboring Diamond Lake 5 times as often. This popular getaway is surrounded by mountain views, over 400 campsites, 5 boat ramps, a resort lodge, and a paved 11.5-mile loop trail. It's easiest to tour the lakeshore trail by bicycle, but a quiet section along the lake's north shore makes a lovely stroll, and the beautiful, unpaved spur trail through the wildflower meadows of glassy Silent Creek is open only to foot traffic.

The 3,015-acre lake has an average depth of only 20 feet, so it becomes swimmably warm in August. It's also stocked to provide 3 million catchable trout each year. Boats are limited to 10 miles per hour. Mosquitoes are a problem in June.

Diamond Lake's basin once cradled a broad Ice Age glacier that descended from the flanks of Mt. Thielsen, Mt. Bailey, and Crater Lake's volcano, Mt.

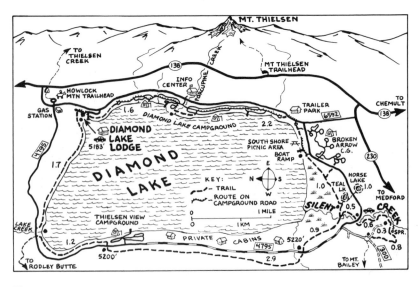

Mt. Thielsen from Diamond Lake.   *Opposite: Silent Creek.*

Mazama. A lake had replaced the glacier by the time Mt. Mazama's eruption sent a glowing avalanche of frothy pumice and hot gases racing at freight-train speed toward the North Umpqua River canyon. The lake did not vaporize under that hot blast, perhaps because smaller, earlier eruptions had left a thick blanket of pumice floating on the lake's surface as an insulating bridge.

The Diamond Lake Lodge makes a good starting point for a lakeshore tour. To find it, turn off either Highway 138 or Highway 230 at "Diamond Lake Recreation Area" signs and follow paved Road 6592 to a "Lodge" pointer. Turn here and drive past the boat ramp before parking on the left at the lodge. The compound includes not only a restaurant and store, but also a marina shop where you can rent boats and bicycles.

If you're hiking, simply walk to the sandy picnic beach in front of the lodge, follow the lakeshore to the right, and climb to the paved bike path. If you're pedaling, bike from the lodge parking lot directly away from the lake (past a "Dead End" sign) for 150 yards to the paved path on the left.

Ducks, shadowy trout, and zillions of dragonflies patrol the lapping shore. Raucous gray jays and scampering golden-mantled ground squirrels watch passersby. Look on the grassy banks for tiny blue forget-me-nots and large mountain bluebells (*mertensia*). At times the trail dips into a forest of Douglas fir, lodgepole pine, and long-needled ponderosa pine. Look here for white trilliums in May and star-flowered smilacina in June. Views ahead are to broad Mt. Bailey (Hike #21). Spire-tipped Mt. Thielsen (Hike #19) is behind you.

After 1.7 miles, the trail briefly joins a road to cross Lake Creek, the lake's outlet. This is a good turnaround spot for hikers with children. If you're continuing, you'll find the trail wedged between the shore and the road for the next 1.2 miles. Beyond this the paved path crosses the road, traverses a viewless forest slope for 2.9 miles to avoid private cabins, recrosses the road, strikes off across brushy marshlands for 1.9 miles to the South Shore boat ramp, and then mostly follows campground roads (where the route is identified by painted bike symbols on the pavement) for the final 3.8 miles back to the lodge.

Perhaps the most beautiful short hike at Diamond Lake follows Silent Creek to the largest spring feeding the lake. To find this unpaved trail from the Diamond Lake Lodge, drive 2.7 miles south on Road 6592, turn right at a "South Shore Picnic Area" pointer, follow Road 4795 for 1.5 miles, and park on the left immediately after the Silent Creek bridge.

This path heads upstream through an oasis in the dry lodgepole pine forests. In June, Silent Creek's mossy banks are ablaze with white marsh marigolds, purple shooting stars, and yellow violets. Alas, the mosquitoes here are thickest when the flowers are at their best. After the trail passes the spring it curves to the right through dry woods and meets a faint dirt road at the 1.4-mile mark. The official trail follows this track left 100 yards to a dusty trailhead on Road 300, but for a pleasant loop route back to your car, turn right instead. Follow the faint road 0.3 mile to its end, bushwhack straight ahead 20 feet through the woods, and turn left on the Silent Creek Trail for 0.6 mile to your car.

21   Mount Bailey

Difficult (from upper road)
5.4 miles round-trip
2330 feet elevation gain
Open end of July through October
Map: Diamond Lake (USGS)

Difficult (from lower road)
9.8 miles round-trip
3130 feet elevation gain
Left: Mt. Bailey from the south summit.

The 2 major mountains looming on opposite sides of Diamond Lake are both popular climbing goals for hikers. Mt. Thielsen is taller and has a more dizzying view, but the route to its top ends with a trailless scramble and a hair-raising rock climb (see Hike #19). Mt. Bailey is almost as challenging, but its steep trail leads all the way to the top. What's more, the final mile is full of surprises: a hidden crater, a rock garden of wildflowers, a double summit, and a rock wall with a window overlooking Diamond Lake.

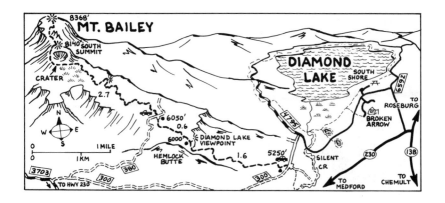

Most hikers start the climb at a lower trailhead on Road 300, which is easily accessible for passenger cars. If you're driving a high-clearance vehicle, however, it's possible to shorten the hike by 2.2 miles (and 800 feet of elevation) by starting at an upper trailhead on a deeply rutted dirt road full of large rocks.

To find the lower trailhead, drive Highway 230 or 138 to Diamond Lake, take the "Diamond Lake Recreation Area" turnoff, drive along Road 6592 to a "South Shore Picnic Area" pointer, and turn onto paved Road 4795 for 1.7 miles. Continue 400 yards past Silent Creek (and possibly a "Road Closed to Thru Traffic" sign) and turn left on dirt Road 300 for 0.4 mile to a dusty parking area in a stand of lodgepole pines.

The trail starts by a sign on the right and soon climbs from the lodgepole pine woods into a forest of Shasta red fir and manzanita. After 1.6 miles you'll get a first teasing glimpse of Diamond Lake through the trees; take a 200-foot side trip up a rock knoll to the right for a better viewpoint. Then continue on the main trail, which levels off for 0.6 mile to a dirt road.

If you have a rugged vehicle, you can drive to this upper trailhead by taking Highway 230 west from the Diamond Lake turnoff toward Medford 3 miles. Near milepost 21, turn right on gravel South Umpqua Road 3703 for 2 miles, turn right on rutted dirt Road 300 for 0.2 mile, and fork left on unmarked Road 380 for 1.5 miles.

From this upper trailhead the path launches steeply up through a dense mountain hemlock forest. The trees become smaller and the rocks larger as you climb. Finally the path reaches a ridgecrest with views across Diamond Lake to Mt. Thielsen, and across the Crater Lake rim to Mt. Scott. The forest thins to a few gnarled whitebark pines, but flowers brighten the black lava rockfields. Look for purple penstemon, white partridge foot, blue lupine, fuzzy pasque flower seedheads, and 3 colors of buckwheat blooms.

The trail skirts a snowfield in a 300-foot-wide crater and climbs to Mt. Bailey's south summit. While enjoying the view here, notice the glacier-carved valley to the east, where a massive 1980 winter avalanche mowed down forests halfway to Diamond Lake.

If you're not wearing boots with soles that grip well, consider turning back at the south summit. Ahead, the path dips across a cinder saddle, climbs along the left side of a 30-foot rock wall with a window-like peephole, edges briefly across the slippery top of a talus scree slope, and then climbs steeply to a ridgecrest and the true summit, a broad rockfield with alpine dandelions.

Rogue River at Boundary Springs.   Opposite: Monkeyflower.

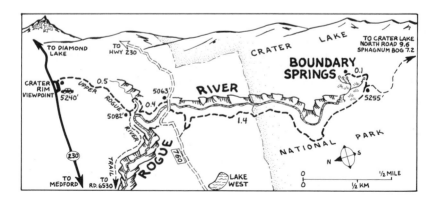

22   Boundary Springs

Easy
4.8 miles round-trip
480 feet elevation gain
Open June to mid-November
Map: Pumice Desert West (USGS)

Few rivers begin as dramatically as the Rogue. At Boundary Springs, in the dry forests of Crater Lake National Park, the river pours out of the ground 20 feet wide, rushes through a meadow of yellow monkeyflowers, and tumbles over a 15-foot waterfall. Pets are banned on park trails and camping is forbidden within a quarter mile of the springs.

The headwaters of the Rogue were buried by the eruption of Crater Lake's Mt. Mazama 7700 years ago, when a glowing avalanche of hot pumice roared 40 miles downstream in a few minutes. Below Boundary Springs the river has managed to wriggle loose by carving a 100-foot-deep canyon into the vast debris field. Above the springs, snowmelt from the Crater Lake high country still has to percolate underground. Other than this seepage, the springs are not an outlet for Crater Lake itself, as was once believed.

The hike to Boundary Springs starts at Crater Rim Viewpoint, a Highway 230 pullout located 5 miles west of the junction with Highway 138 at Diamond Lake. To drive here from Medford, take Highway 62 east 57 miles and continue straight on Highway 230 toward Diamond Lake for 18.6 miles to the viewpoint on the right, between mileposts 18 and 19.

Start out on the Upper Rogue River Trail through open woods of lodgepole pine, Shasta red fir, and mountain hemlock. After half a mile turn left on the Boundary Springs Trail and begin following the Rogue River. Along the river look for robin-sized water ouzels that dip in the river, lush blue lupine (best in July), and green islands of monkeyflowers.

At the 0.9-mile mark you'll meet a dirt road. Turn right on it 100 feet to find the continuation of the trail upstream. After another 1.4 miles the trail forks at the edge of a brushy meadow. Keep left 100 yards to a 3-foot-wide spring. The trail peters out here, but don't turn back. Contour onward around a low ridge toward the sound of water 200 yards to find Boundary Springs' massive vent.

Other Hiking Options

If you'd like to shorten this hike by 1.8 miles, start at dirt Road 760. To find this trailhead from the Crater Rim Viewpoint, drive east on Highway 230 for 2.2 miles and turn right past a "Lake West" sign for 3.4 miles. If you'd like to lengthen the hike, head downstream. From the junction of the Boundary Springs Trail and Upper Rogue River Trail it's 4.2 miles downriver to Rough Rider Falls (see Hike #41), and 47.4 miles to trail's end at Prospect.

Wizard Island

Easy (to Cleetwood Cove)
2.2 miles round-trip
654 feet elevation gain
Open late June to mid-October
Maps: Crater Lake East and West (USGS)

Moderate (to Wizard Island summit)
4.7 miles round-trip
1420 feet elevation gain
Open early July to early September

The switchbacking trail down to Cleetwood Cove's tour boat dock is the most popular path in Crater Lake National Park—and the only route to the lakeshore. To explore the inside of Crater Lake's collapsed volcano more fully, however, take the boat tour as far as Wizard Island and climb to that cinder cone's summit crater. Pets are not allowed on park trails.

To drive here from Crater Lake's Rim Village, take the Rim Drive clockwise 10.6 miles to the trailhead. If you're coming from the park's north entrance off Highway 138, turn left along the Rim Drive for 4.6 miles. If you plan to take the boat tour, be sure to stop by the ticket trailer in the large parking lot across the road from the trailhead.

Weather permitting, boat tours leave every 45 or 60 minutes between 10am and 4:30pm from early July to early September. The ticket trailer opens at 8:15am, and if you want to be visit Wizard Island on a busy summer weekend, it's not a bad idea to arrive by 9am. A private concession company sets the prices; expect to pay at least $12 for adults and $6.50 for kids under 12. To make sure hikers don't miss their boat, sales for each tour stop 40 minutes before it leaves. Passengers are not allowed to disembark on Wizard Island after 3pm and cannot stay overnight.

The trail down to the boat dock is wide enough that the concessioner's lawn tractor can shuttle boat supplies on it. The route passes lodgepole pines, Shasta

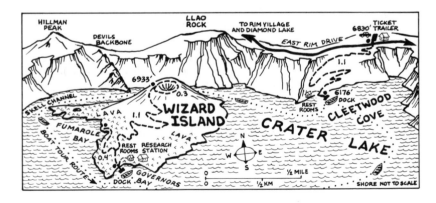

Cleetwood Cove.   Opposite: Wizard Island from the boat tour.

red firs, mountain hemlocks, manzanita bushes, and lots of glimpses down to the glowing blue lake. The amazing color results from the lake's purity (it has no inlet other than precipitation) and its 1932-foot depth (it is the deepest lake in the U.S.). In recorded history the lake has only frozen twice and its surface level has only fluctuated 16 feet.

Gutsy swimmers sometimes brave the 50-degree water at the dock's rocky shore. Fishing has been permitted without a license ever since rangers realized that introduced trout and kokanee salmon are hurting the lake's biological balance. Still, angling in this vast transparent pool is all but hopeless.

The roofless tour boats are packed school-bus-fashion with 60 passengers and an interpretive ranger. It's a 45-minute ride to Wizard Island. Those who get off here are given numbered passes. The pass numbers determine your priority for a ride back, because on busy days the only space available before 4:30pm is if someone else gets out.

Wizard Island is actually one of 2 cinder cones that erupted from the ruins of Mt. Mazama shortly after its cataclysmic collapse 7700 years ago. The other, Merriam Cone, was left under 486 feet of water after rain and melting snow gradually filled the lake. Wizard Island was named by Crater Lake's early promoter William Steel, who thought the cone resembled a sorcerer's hat. Although Steel helped win national park status, it's lucky many of his development schemes were ignored. He not only pushed for a rim road and a lodge, but also a highway tunnel through the rim, a lakeshore loop road, a highway bridge to Wizard Island, and an aerial tramway from the rim to the island's top.

The Wizard Island trail sets off through blocky black basalt lava colonized by golden-mantled ground squirrels, the red blooms of bleeding hearts, and gnarled Shasta red firs. Take the trail's right fork to switchback up the cinder cone. At the top, a path circles the 90-foot-deep crater's rim amid storm-blasted pines, red paintbrush, and constant panoramas. On the way back down, don't miss the rocky 0.4-mile side trail to the house-sized lava boulders and emerald lakeshore at Fumarole Bay.

The return boat trip passes the place where an unauthorized private helicopter crashed in 1995. It promptly sank with its passengers in 1500 feet of water and has never been recovered. The boat tour also circles Phantom Ship, a small craggy island that is actually a remnant of a 400,000-year-old volcanic plug—the oldest rock exposed on the lake. On the return trip, sharp-eyed passengers sometimes spot the Old Man of the Lake, a floating vertical log that's been roaming the lake for a century. Bring warm clothes for the sometimes chilly boat ride, and be sure to save energy for the 1.1-mile climb back to your car.

24 Mount Scott

Moderate
5 miles round-trip
1030 feet elevation gain
Open mid-July through October
Map: Crater Lake East (USGS)

Mt. Scott's lookout tower is the only place where hikers can fit the whole breathtaking sweep of Crater Lake into an average camera viewfinder. And although this is a major mountain—tenth tallest in Oregon's Cascades—the trail is so well-graded that even families with children sometimes tackle it.

Heavy winter snows make the Rim Drive near Mt. Scott the last road in Crater Lake National Park to open each summer. If you're driving here from Medford or Klamath Falls on Highway 62, turn north past the park entrance booth 4 miles and turn right on East Rim Drive for 11 miles to a parking pullout and trail sign on the right. If you're coming from Diamond Lake, turn left on East Rim Drive for 13 miles to the trailhead. Remember that pets are banned on park trails.

The trail begins as an ancient road track amid 5-needle whitebark pines and sparse meadows. Expect to cross a few snow patches until August. Also expect the company of Clark's nutcrackers, the gray-and-black cawing birds that tempt visitors to defy the park's ban on feeding wildlife. In fact, these "camp robbers" don't need handouts. Their sharp, strong beaks are adapted to break open whitebark pine cones for seeds, which they eat or cache for later. In return, the rugged whitebark pines, which only grow above 7000 feet, rely on the nutcrackers to spread their seeds from peak to peak.

The trail's second mile switchbacks up a slope of pumice pebbles, strewn like ochre hailstones from Mt. Mazama's fiery storm 7700 years ago. Views open up to the south across Klamath Lake's flats to the blue silhouette of the Mountain

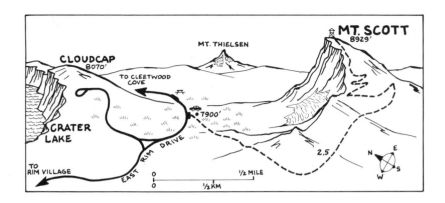

Lakes highland and the white tip of Mt. Shasta. To the right, Mt. McLoughlin's snowy cone rises above the summits of the Sky Lakes Wilderness. Wildflowers along the way include red paintbrush, purple penstemon, and the fuzzy seed stalks of western pasque flower.

The Crater Lake panorama from the summit is breathtaking, but so is the view north to Mt. Thielsen's spire and the distant Three Sisters. Mt. Scott itself was named for Levi Scott, an 1844 Oregon Trail pioneer who founded Douglas County's Scottsburg and helped scout the Applegate Trail to Southern Oregon.

Crater Lake from Mt. Scott's lookout tower.   Opposite: Clark's nutcracker.

25   The Watchman

Easy (to Watchman Lookout)
1.6 miles round-trip
413 feet elevation gain
Open mid-July through October
Map: Crater Lake West (USGS)

Easy (PCT around Hillman Peak)
4 miles round-trip
250 feet elevation gain

High on Crater Lake's western rim, The Watchman's lookout tower commands an eagle's-eye view across the amazingly blue lake to Wizard Island. The steep little climb up The Watchman is one of the most popular paths in the national park. It's also short enough that you might want to extend the hike by trying a new 2-mile stretch of the Pacific Crest Trail around Hillman Peak. Pets are banned on all park trails.

The Watchman won its name in 1886, when the U.S. Geological Survey set up a watch point here while surveyors in a boat sounded the lake with a reel of piano wire. Other names that stuck from that 1886 expedition are Cleetwood Cove (for the boat) and Dutton Cliff (for its captain). The survey recorded a maximum lake depth of 1996 feet—a figure that has since been corrected by sonar to 1932 feet.

The Watchman Trail begins at a large, rail-fenced parking area and viewpoint on Crater Lake's Rim Drive. The parking area is not well marked, but you'll find it by driving 4 miles north of Rim Village or 2.2 miles south of the junction with the north entrance road. From the parking area, follow a paved sidewalk along the highway 100 yards to the actual trailhead. Look here for the fuzzy seedheads of western pasque flower and the blue trumpets of penstemon.

The wide path—a portion of the long-abandoned 1917 rim road—traverses a rockslide of giant cream-colored boulders. These rocks are dacite, originally part

Crater Lake from The Watchman.   Opposite: Phlox.

of a 50,000-year-old lava flow on Mt. Mazama's shoulder. After Mazama's cataclysmic decapitation 7700 years ago, the old lava flow was left as The Watchman, a crest on the gaping caldera's rim.

At the 0.3-mile mark, a snowfield lingers across the trail until August. Turn left at a junction just beyond the snow and climb 0.4 mile amid struggling mountain hemlock, white lupine, and patches of pinkish 5-petaled phlox. The summit tower, built in 1932, is staffed each summer with friendly rangers who help spot fires and answer hikers' questions. Soak in the view from the lookout's stone patio before heading back to your car.

If you'd like more exercise and different views, hike right on past your car and up a sandy ridge to find a section of the Pacific Crest Trail that opened in 1995. This route skirts Hillman Peak for 2 miles, passing wildflower meadows, snow patches, rockfields with cat-sized marmots, and views across the Pumice Desert to the Three Sisters.

If you can't arrange to shuttle a car to the far end of the section—a lakeview pullout 2.2 miles from The Watchman's parking lot—turn back when the trail reaches a dramatic Crater Lake viewpoint beside the Devils Backbone. This craggy wall protruding from the lake's rim is a volcanic dike, formed when magma squeezed into a vertical crack inside ancient Mt. Mazama.

26 Lightning Spring

Easy (to Discovery Point)
2.6 miles round-trip
380 feet elevation gain
Open July through October
Maps: Crater Lake West (USGS)

Difficult (to Lightning Spring)
13.1-mile loop
1900 feet elevation gain

Explore the shattered flank of Crater Lake's ancient Mt. Mazama on these 2 very different hikes along the Pacific Crest Trail from Rim Village. The first is an easy view-packed stroll to Discovery Point. The second hike continues on a much longer loop that descends past Lightning Spring and returns through forests. Backpackers must pick up an overnight permit at a national park office. Pets are banned on all national park trails.

Start in Rim Village at the huge paved parking area between the gift shop and visitor center. Take the sidewalk back along Crater Lake's rim, heading clockwise around the lake. The pavement and the tourist crowds end just beyond the parking lot. After another 200 yards you'll briefly follow the Rim Road's shoulder. Then the path swerves back to the caldera rim for 0.8 miles of glorious views.

The picture-postcard setting features cone-shaped Wizard Island below the massive dacite cliffs of Llao Rock, with a frame of gnarled whitebark pines and mountain hemlocks. Look for lavender cushions of 5-petaled phlox along the path and raucous gray-and-black Clark's nutcrackers in the trees.

At the 1.2-mile mark the trail switchbacks down to cross a highway parking pullout. Then it climbs 200 yards to Discovery Point, where a bronze plaque

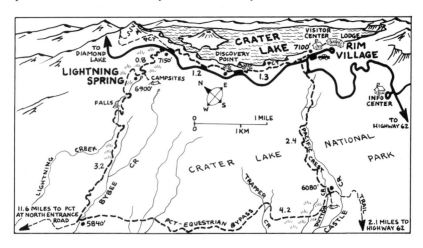

Crater Lake from Discovery Point.   Opposite: Scarlet Gilia.

commemorates the viewpoint from which John Wesley Hillman's prospecting party may have first spotted the lake in 1853.

For the easy hike, turn back here. If you're ready to tackle the longer loop, however, continue 1.2 miles along the rim-edge trail. When you reach the third highway parking pullout touched by the route, cross the road and walk 100 yards along it to the gravel Lightning Springs trailhead on the left. This path—actually a long-abandoned roadbed—descends a dry, sandy slope in sweeping curves. Mt. Mazama's pumice and ash fell so deep here 7700 years ago that only a few lupine, phlox, and dogbane plants have yet taken hold. After 0.8 miles you'll pass Lightning Spring, where a deliciously cold, 3-foot-wide creek emerges from the dry slope.

Beyond the spring the trail/road descends a wooded dale for 3.2 miles, passing a 15-foot falls along the way. Then you'll meet the old Pacific Crest Trail—now used as an equestrian bypass route because horses aren't allowed on Crater Lake's rim. Turn left on this level but relatively dull route through lodgepole pine woods for 4.2 miles. Finally, at an X-shaped trail junction by scenic little Dutton Creek, turn left for the 2.4-mile climb back to Rim Village. This last trail segment starts amid lovely meadowed openings of blue lupine, scarlet gilia, green hellebore, and chattering songbirds before crossing 6-foot-wide Castle Creek and climbing more seriously through mountain hemlock woods to your car.

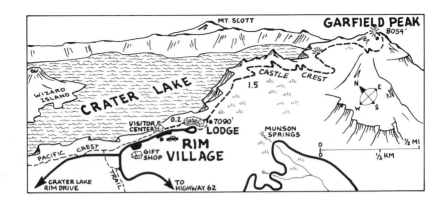

Garfield Peak from Crater Lake Lodge.   *Opposite: Crater Lake from Garfield Peak.*

27   Garfield Peak

Moderate
3 miles round-trip
970 feet elevation gain
Open mid-July through October
Map: Crater Lake W and E (USGS)

Perhaps the prettiest trail in Crater Lake National Park follows the lake's craggy rim from the historic lodge to the wildflowers and views of Garfield Peak. As on all park trails, pets and flower-picking are banned.

The path starts from the back porch of the grand old Crater Lake Lodge. To find it, follow signs to Crater Lake's Rim Village and continue straight through this beehive of tourists 0.3 mile to a turnaround at road's end.

Truth be told, the lodge here wasn't always grand. Built from 1909-1915 at a cost of just $50,000, the building originally opened with tarpaper on its outside walls and flimsy beaverboard between rooms. Years of makeshift maintenance and harsh winters left the building slated for demolition in the 1980s. But a public outcry pushed the Park Service to renovate it instead. After a $35 million makeover, the lodge reopened in 1995 with elegant woodwork in the Great Hall, a modern bath in each guestroom, and its rustic ambience remarkably intact.

Walk behind the lodge and turn right on the paved pathway along Crater Lake's rim. Pavement soon yields to a broad trail through meadows of pale blue lupine, bright orange paintbrush, yellow groundsel,**purple** daisy-shaped flea-bane,   and white pearly everlasting. Views improve with each switchback. The trail climbs past cliffs of *breccia*—welded volcanic rubble from Mt. Mazama's early mountain-building eruptions. The breccia here was long buried with lava flows, but these were stripped away by glaciers. The glaciers, in turn, vanished after Mt. Mazama lost its summit in a cataclysmic blast 7700 years ago.

Snow patches linger across the trail until August near the top. At this elevation, only gnarled, 5-needle whitebark pines survive. These trees' limber limbs, so flexible they can be tied in knots, help the pines bend rather than break in winter gales.

Garfield Peak was named for the Interior Secretary of Teddy Roosevelt, who created the national park in 1902. When you reach the peak's summit, the glowing blue of Crater Lake gapes below like a 4-cubic-mile pool from a high-dive tower. If you're quiet you might see foot-long marmots and guinea-pig-sized pikas watching from cliff-edge rocks 100 feet north of the summit. To the east, Mt. Scott looms above Phantom Ship's small craggy island. To the south stretch the distant flats of Klamath Lake, with the tip of Mt. Shasta and the cone of Mt. McLoughlin to the right.

Crater Lake Nature Loops

Easy (Castle Crest Wildflowers)
0.4-mile loop
70 feet elevation gain
Open mid-June through November
Maps in booklets at each trailhead

Easy (Godfrey Glen)
1-mile loop
100 feet elevation gain

Easy (Annie Creek Canyon)
1.7-mile loop
280 feet elevation gain

Wildflowers, tumbling brooks, and strange ash pinnacles highlight these short loop trails in Crater Lake National Park. Although not connected, the 3 paths are just few miles apart on the road between Rim Village and Highway 62, so it's easy to hike them all in a day. Note that pets are banned on park trails.

The shortest loop uses stepping stones to cross mossy springs in a natural wildflower garden below Castle Crest. To find its trailhead, drive north from Highway 62 for 3.7 miles (or south from Rim Village 2.7 miles). Almost opposite the park's headquarters and visitor information building, turn east on Rim Drive for 0.4 mile. Park on the left after a "Congested Area" sign.

The Castle Crest path crosses a 10-foot-wide creek and climbs to a mossy slope of springs and flowers. The pink blooms here are trumpet-shaped monkeyflowers and dart-shaped shooting stars. The blue flowers are pea-like lupines, tiny forget-me-nots, and elephant heads—stalks clustered with scores of tiny blooms that really look like elephant heads. The white ball-shaped flowers are American bistort, but their smell explains another common name: dirty socks. The loop back to your car crosses the creek twice more.

To try the 1-mile loop hike to Godfrey Glen's weird ash pinnacles, drive back to the junction near the visitor information center, turn left toward Highway 62 for 2.1 miles, and turn off at a "Godfrey Glen Nature Loop" sign for 200 yards to the trailhead. (If you're coming from Highway 62, drive 1.6 miles to find this

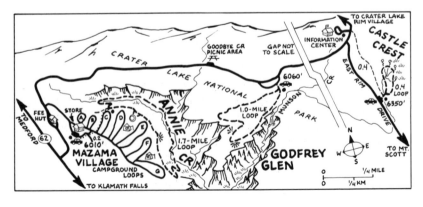

Godfrey Glen.   Opposite: Golden-mantled ground squirrel.

turnoff.) The trail here promptly forks for the loop; keep left for the quickest route to the astonishing overlook of Godfrey Glen, a green oasis 300 feet below in a box canyon flanked by fluted spires of beige ash. Watch children near this dangerously unrailed viewpoint.

The story behind the pinnacles begins in the Ice Age, when glaciers scoured U-shaped valleys through Godfrey Glen and adjacent Annie Creek Canyon. After the ice retreated, the eruption of Crater Lake's Mt. Mazama filled both valleys to the brim with glowing avalanches of hot pumice and ash. When the loose debris stopped moving, superheated gas rose through it, welding ash into solid rock along the vents. Since then streams have cut narrow V-shaped canyons into the softer ash, exposing the old vents as spires.

The 1.7-mile loop through Annie Creek Canyon is the longest of these 3 nature paths, but it features the attractions of the other 2 combined—and it starts conveniently in the national park's only campground. From the Godfrey Glen trailhead, drive 1.4 miles toward Highway 62, turn left into the Mazama Campground entrance, and park in 0.2 mile in front of the Mazama Village store. (If you're coming from Highway 62, drive 0.3 mile to the campground entrance and keep right to the store.) Then walk through the campground to the end of camping loop C, where you'll find the trailhead behind site C-11.

The loop starts to the right, following the wooded rim of Annie Creek's canyon along the edge of the campground. Black bears do visit these woods daily, looking for campsites with obvious cooler chests, but you're unlikely to see these unaggressive bears. On the other hand, you're almost certain to spot 3 species of squirrels and chipmunks. The lively, orange-bellied Douglas squirrels have no stripes and often chatter in trees. Golden-mantled ground squirrels have striped sides and scamper into burrows. Genuine chipmunks are smaller and have side stripes that extend all the way past their eyes.

After 0.5 mile the Annie Creek trail switchbacks down into a canyon with several ash pinnacles. Then the path follows the lovely cascading stream up through wildflower meadows a mile before climbing back to the loop's start at campground site C-11.

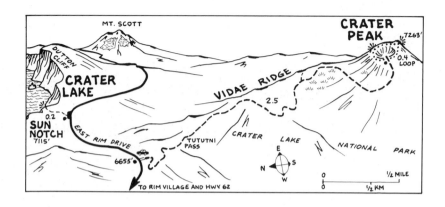

29   Crater Peak

Easy (to Sun Notch)
0.4 mile round-trip
150 feet elevation gain
Open July to early November
Maps: Crater Lake East, Maklaks Crater
   (USGS)

Moderate (to Crater Peak)
5.4 miles round-trip
880 feet elevation gain

These 2 uncrowded hikes on the south side of Crater Lake reveal the difference between a crater and a caldera. The 0.2-mile Sun Notch Trail climbs to a spectacular Crater Lake viewpoint above Phantom Ship's craggy little island. But the astonishingly blue, 6-mile-wide lake you see here is not in a crater at all—it fills a caldera, a giant pit created by a mountain's collapse. To see a true volcanic crater, take the nearby 2.5-mile path to Crater Peak, a cinder cone with a wildflower meadow in a cute little summit bowl. Pets are not allowed on either trail.

Start at the national park headquarters and visitor information building located halfway between Crater Lake's Rim Village and Highway 62. Drive 200 yards down the road toward Highway 62, turn left at a "Rim Drive (East)" sign, and follow this road 4.3 miles to the Sun Notch Trailhead on the left. Then hike the short path up through mountain hemlock woods to the cliff-edge viewpoint.

Much of Crater Lake's geologic story is exposed at Sun Notch's viewpoint. When eruptions started building Mt. Mazama 400,000 years ago, they began near here. Phantom Ship is a fragment of the volcanic plug from those early eruptions. As Mt. Mazama grew to an estimated height of 12,000 feet, the volcanic vents moved farther north, finally pouring out a thick dacite flow to create Llao Rock, the largest cliff visible across the lake. By then, glaciers were

Lupine atop Crater Peak.   *Opposite: Phantom Ship from Sun Notch.*

scouring deep U-shaped valleys into the mountain's flanks. Sun Notch is a remnant of one of the largest of these glacial troughs, amputated when the mountain exploded 7700 years ago.

If you'd like to see a genuine crater after visiting Sun Notch, drive 2 miles back on Rim Drive (and 0.6 miles past Vidae Falls) to a barricaded gravel road on the left with a small "Crater Peak Trailhead" sign. This abandoned road promptly narrows to a pleasant trail through mountain hemlock woods with patches of blue lupine, scarlet gilia, and golden currant bushes. After 2 mostly level miles the path climbs 0.5 mile to the mouth of the summit crater. Pumice and ash that rained down from Mt. Mazama's eruption filled this little crater halfway to the top. Since then lupine, dogbane, and grass have colonized the bowl, making it a popular grazing spot for elk; look for their hoofprints and sign. A patch of snow lingers in the crater until August.

For a view-packed 0.4-mile loop, walk clockwise around Crater Peak's rim. To the north, note Mt. Thielsen's distant spire above Sun Notch. To the east is Mt. Scott; to the west is Union Peak's spire; and to the south are Klamath Lake, distant Mt. Shasta, and snowy Mt. McLoughlin.

Union Peak from the Pacific Crest Trail junction.   Opposite: Elk.

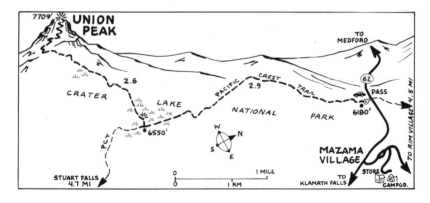

30 Union Peak

Difficult
11 miles round-trip
1600 feet elevation gain
Open mid-July through October
Map: Union Peak (USGS)

The oldest mountain in Crater Lake National Park, Union Peak's rocky volcanic plug affords a view across ancient Mt. Mazama's forested flanks to Cascade peaks from Mt. Thielsen to Mt. Shasta. The panorama comes with a price, however—the hike's first 4.7 miles are a trudge through viewless woods, while the final 0.8 mile is an invigorating climb up 3 dozen switchbacks. A few other cautions: backpackers must pick up an overnight permit at a national park office, pets are not permitted, and there is no water.

Start by driving 72 miles east of Medford (or 1 mile west of Crater Lake National Park's Mazama Village) to the summit of Highway 62. At a "Pacific Crest Trail Parking" sign, turn south to a dirt turnaround. The nearly level trail—actually, a long-abandoned fire road— sets off through a sparse forest that alternates between stands of almost pure lodgepole pine and groves of almost pure mountain hemlock. The pumice that fell here 10 feet deep during the eruption of Crater Lake's Mt. Mazama 7700 years ago is responsible for the utter lack of underbrush.

In an open pumice plain at the 2.9-mile mark, turn right at a sign for the Union Peak Trail and gain a first glimpse of Union Peak ahead. The path now climbs gradually through meadow openings with blue lupine and lots of elk sign. Once hunted nearly to extinction, elk were restocked here from Yellowstone National Park in the 1960s and are thriving.

Suddenly the trail emerges from the woods at the base of Union Peak—a gigantic rockpile surmounted with a fortress of black crags. As you switchback up, look for the dishmop-shaped seedheads of western pasque flower and the purple trumpets of penstemon. The final short switchbacks are so rugged you may need to use your hands as you climb.

The summit's black boulders have shiny spots of melted rock where lightning has struck, proving this is no place to be in a storm. On a clear day, however, distant Mt. Shasta floats ghost-like on the southern horizon above Devils Peak, with the cone of Mt. McLoughlin to the right. To the west is the Rogue Valley's haze. To the north, it's easy to imagine Mt. Mazama's former shape, although the mountain's forested flanks now rise to a broken hole. Crater Lake itself is hidden inside but Llao Rock's cliff, on the lake's far shore, peeks out above Rim Village.

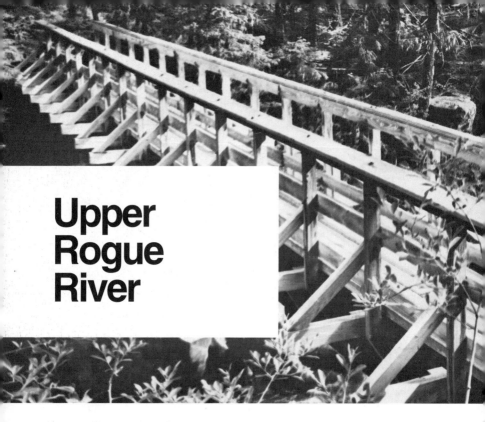

Upper Rogue River

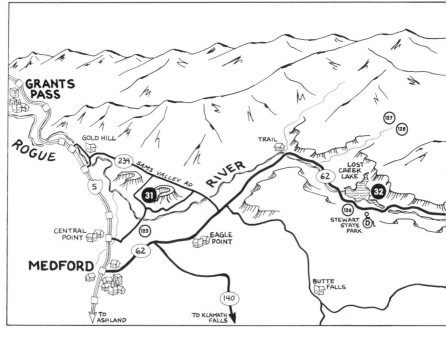

Above: Rogue Gorge on the Upper Rogue River Trail (Hike #34).

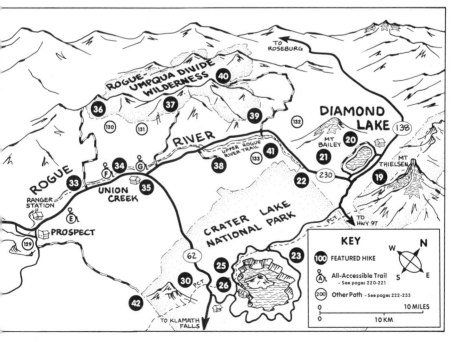

TO ROSEBURG

ROGUE-UMPQUA DIVIDE WILDERNESS

40

36

37

39

132

DIAMOND LAKE

138

130

131

RIVER

UPPER ROGUE RIVER TRAIL

MT BAILEY

20

21

230

MT THIELSEN

19

41

133

38

22

ROGUE

33

F

34

G

35

UNION CREEK

E

PROSPECT

RANGER STATION

129

PCT

TO HWY 97

CRATER LAKE NATIONAL PARK

62

23

25

26

30

PCT

42

TO KLAMATH FALLS

KEY

N W E S

100 FEATURED HIKE

A All-Accessible Trail
— See pages 220-221

200 Other Path — See pages 222-233

0   10 MILES

0   10 KM

31 Upper and Lower Table Rocks

Easy (Upper Table Rock)
2.8 miles round-trip
720 feet elevation gain
Open all year
Map: Sams Valley (USGS)

Moderate (Lower Table Rock)
5.4 miles round-trip
780 feet elevation gain

Once a sanctuary for Takelma Indians, today these cliff-edged mesas near Medford are a haven for hikers and endangered wildflowers. Views from the cliffs extend across the Rogue River to the Siskiyous and the Cascades. Visit in spring to catch the best flower displays and to avoid summer's merciless heat. Dogs, horses, fires, and flower picking are banned on both Table Rocks trails.

The 125-foot-thick andesite rims capping these U-shaped mesas are remnants of a lava flow that snaked down the Rogue River Valley 9.6 million years ago from vents east of Prospect. Since then, erosion has worn away the softer surrounding rock, leaving the hard andesite perched 800 feet above the plain. Why are the mesas U-shaped? Geologists propose that the curves were originally bends in the river channel where the lava flowed.

An 1850 gold strike at Jacksonville attracted so many miners and settlers to the Rogue Valley that the local Takelma Indians launched an attack in 1853 to reclaim their homeland. When the U.S. Army retaliated, the Takelmas retreated to Upper Table Rock, a natural fortress that long defied capture.

Today each mesa has its own trail, but the path to Upper Table Rock is shorter and slightly easier. To find its trailhead from Interstate 5 take Central Point exit 32 (just north of Medford), drive east on Biddle Road 1 mile, turn left on Table Rock Road for 5.2 miles to a curve, and turn right on Modoc Road for 1.5 miles to the trailhead parking lot on the left, just opposite an electric substation.

The Upper Table Rock Trail climbs through a scrub oak grassland ablaze with spring wildflowers. In April expect blue camas and pink fawn lilies. In May look for pink, 4-petaled clarkias (alias "farewell to spring"), California blue-eyed grass (with 6 small petals), and elegant brodiaea (with 6 long purple petals). By June, orange paintbrush and purple crown brodiaea are blooming too. In all seasons, beware of triple-leafleted poison oak.

At the 1.1-mile mark, after a final steep pitch, the trail suddenly emerges onto the table's amazingly flat, grassy summit. In 200 yards the path crosses an old road. Here you can either turn left along the road to a viewpoint at the table's southern tip or continue straight without a trail to a dramatic viewpoint west—both good destinations before heading back to your car.

The trail to Lower Table Rock, though longer and rockier, climbs through shadier woods and leads to a viewpoint atop a taller cliff. Most of Lower Table Rock was dedicated as a nature preserve in 1979 by The Nature Conservancy, the public-spirited non-profit organization that built the trail.

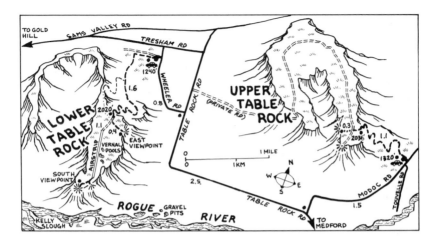

To find this trailhead get back in your car, continue driving on Table Rock Road north of Medford to milepost 10 and turn left on Wheeler Road 0.8 mile. The trail sets off along a fenceline through grasslands with the same profusion of flowers as at the other mesa. Listen for the musical warble of redwing blackbirds and the squawks of ring-necked pheasants.

The path climbs, steeply at times, through a dry forest of madrone and black oak. After 1.6 miles the path suddenly crests at the plateau and becomes an old road. The quickest route to a viewpoint is to walk the road 200 yards and fork left on a trail that deadends in 0.3 mile at a 200-foot cliff. From here you can see your car far below. The snowy rim of Crater Lake rises above Upper Table Rock. The Rogue River, like a great green snake, curves across a quilt of orchards, ranches, and gravel pit ponds toward the distant white cone of Mt. McLoughlin. Turkey vultures soar on updrafts.

For the best view of all, however, hike back to the road and follow it a mile across the mesa. The road becomes an old grassy airstrip bordered by vernal pools—ponds that dry up by May, leaving a haze of flowers. Look here for dwarf meadowfoam, a subspecies that exists only on the Table Rocks. At the airstrip's end, continue right on a path to a viewpoint overtowering the Rogue River.

Lower Table Rock.   *Opposite: Clarkia ("farewell to spring").*

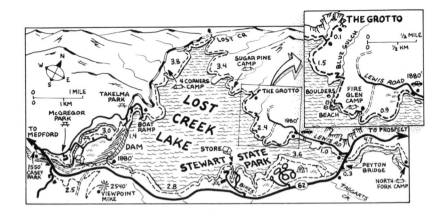

32 Lost Creek Lake

Easy (to The Grotto)
5 miles round-trip
100 feet elevation gain
Open all year
Maps: McLeod, Cascade Gorge (USGS)

Moderate (north shore, with shuttle)
9.6 miles one way
200 feet elevation gain

Difficult (entire lakeshore)
18.7-mile loop
400 feet elevation gain

Waterskiers and fishermen are familiar with this reservoir on the upper Rogue River, but surprisingly few hikers have discovered its shoreline trail. The path is nicest in spring when the reservoir is full, the wildflowers are blooming, the birdlife is at its most active, and the powerboats aren't yet too noisy.

Most visitors to Lost Creek Lake cluster around the dam's outlet (with picnic areas and the nation's third-largest steelhead hatchery) or Joseph Stewart State Park (with a campgound, swimming beach, boat ramp, marina, cafe, and store). But trails in those areas are mostly paved. For a wilder walk on the quieter side of the lake, head for The Grotto, a box canyon of colored ash formations.

To find the trailhead, drive Crater Lake Highway 62 east of Medford 35.5 miles. Just after crossing the bridge at the far end of Lost Creek Lake, turn left on Lewis Road for 1 mile to the Lewis Road Trailhead on the left. The path starts in an open forest of Douglas fir, ponderosa pine, and black oak. Watch out for poison oak here. Also notice orange paintbrush, pink 5-petaled geraniums, blue lupine, and yellow salsify. Lizards run through the dust. Fish-hunting osprey soar above the lake. Look back to the east to see Needle Rock, a lava-capped mesa with a window arch.

After 0.9 mile the trail passes a gravel boat ramp and crosses a footbridge to Fire Glen Camp, a cluster of walk-in sites commemorating a 50-acre blaze in 1979. The best swimming spot of the hike is 0.3 mile farther, at a small beach.

At the 2.4-mile mark, just before a footbridge over an inlet, turn right at a "Grotto" sign and climb to a viewpoint of a secluded gulch where a tiny creek drips 40 feet. The soft greenish rock here is ash from Crater Lake's volcano, and the hard basalt layer atop it is lava from the same source. In June, The Grotto is abloom with *pretty face,* a delicate, 6-petaled yellow amaryllis.

If you're not yet ready to turn back—and if you can arrange a car shuttle—continue onward around the lake's roadless north shore 7.2 miles to Takelma Park's boat ramp.

If you can't arrange a shuttle and you're up to an athletic challenge, trek 18.7 miles around the entire lake. Along the way you'll cross the reservoir's dam, follow 2 miles of paved paths in busy Stewart State Park, and finally hoof 1.3 miles along the Highway 62 bridge and Lewis Road to your car.

Other Hiking Options

Long-distance hikers are supposed to be able to follow the Upper Rogue River Trail from Lost Creek Lake to the river's source near Crater Lake. But if you hike from Peyton Bridge along the reservoir's upper arm, you'll find the trail peters out after 4.7 miles, where government property ends. Rather than bushwhack the next 4 miles, skip to the Forest Service trailhead near Prospect. To find it from the Prospect Ranger Station, drive 0.4 mile south on Highway 62 and turn right on a gravel road beside a canal for half a mile.

Lost Creek Lake.   Opposite: Balsamroot.

33   Takelma Gorge

Easy (to Takelma Gorge)
3.2 miles round-trip
No elevation gain
Open March to mid-December
Maps: Whetstone Point, Prospect
    North (USGS)

Easy (to River Bridge, with shuttle)
4.6 miles one way
160 feet elevation loss

Tormented by an ancient lava flow, the Rogue River twists around a hairpin curve, rages down a chute, and foams for nearly a mile through Takelma Gorge's 150-foot-deep rock slot. Several thousand years ago, Crater Lake's volcano filled the Rogue's valley with 650 feet of lava and ash. Through Takelma Gorge the river follows a crack in the lava—a weak spot where water eroded a canyon.

The gorge is named for the Upland Takelma (or Latgawa), a tribe native to this area. A warlike band, they often raided the Lowland Takelma in what is now the Grants Pass area for food and slaves. In their Penutian language—unrelated to the languages of other Southern Oregon tribes—Takelma means "those who live by the river." Early French trappers called them *coquins* ("rogues"), and later white settlers dubbed them Rogue River Indians. Today the Upper Rogue River Trail wends through an old-growth forest along the gorge's rim.

To hike here, start by driving east from Medford on Crater Lake Highway 62. Between mileposts 51 and 52 (past the Prospect Ranger Station 6 miles) turn left onto paved Woodruff Meadows Road. After 1.7 miles turn left into the Woodruff Bridge picnic area. Park at the far end of the turnaround.

The path curves left to the riverbank among 7-foot-thick Douglas fir. In early summer look here for tiny white starflower, the delicate double bells of twinflower, 5-petaled white anemone, and yellow Oregon grape blooms. In fall, vine

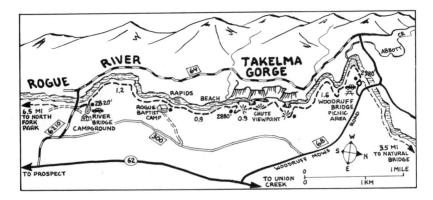

Takelma Gorge.   Opposite: Anemone.

maple lines the river with scarlet pinwheel-shaped leaves.

After 1.6 miles the trail reaches the first Takelma Gorge viewpoint, on a clifftop above the spectacular, churning chasm. Hikers with small children could turn back here, but it would take willpower, because the next 0.9 mile of trail follows the gorge's rim past a succession of stunning viewpoints. Finally the trail switchbacks down to a tamer stretch of river. In another 0.3 mile the path passes a small sandy beach suitable for sunning or wading—another possible turn-around point.

If you'd like to hike the entire 4.6-mile trail section from Woodruff Bridge to River Bridge one way, plan to leave a shuttle car at the far end. To find that trailhead, turn off Highway 62 a ways south of milepost 51. Take gravel Road 6210 west 1 mile, turn right into the River Bridge Campground entrance, and keep left for 0.2 mile to a trail sign at the day-use parking area.

Other Hiking Options

Long-range hikers can continue along the Upper Rogue River Trail for days. If you're walking downstream, it's 6.5 miles to trail's end at North Fork Park. (To find this trailhead, drive 0.4 mile south of the Prospect Ranger Station on Highway 62 and turn right on a gravel road beside a canal for half a mile.) The trail is prettier upstream, however. From Woodruff Bridge it's 3.5 miles to Natural Bridge (see Hike #34) and 36.8 miles to the Crater Rim Viewpoint trailhead near the Rogue River's source (see Hikes #41 and #22).

34 Natural Bridge

Easy (to Natural Bridge)
2.4-mile loop
300 feet elevation gain
Open mid-March through November
Map: Union Creek (USGS)

Easy (Rogue Gorge and Union Creek)
2.2-mile loop
No elevation gain

The upper Rogue River puts on its 2 most spectacular performances in the popular Union Creek resort area: a disappearing act where the river vanishes underground and a daredevil act where it squeezes through a rock chasm. Easy loop hikes visit each of the attractions. If you'd like to see both, a moderate 8-mile hike combines the 2 loops in one.

The secret behind both of the river's stunts is its use of lava tubes. Several thousand years ago Crater Lake's volcano filled this canyon with a long basalt lava flow. When the lava's crusted surface stopped moving, the molten rock underneath kept on flowing, leaving long caves. At Natural Bridge the Rogue River funnels through one of these tubes like water through a hose. At Rogue Gorge the river has ripped open the cave's roof, leaving a slot of raging whitewater.

For the Natural Bridge loop, drive Crater Lake Highway 62 east from Medford 55 miles (or west of Union Creek 1.1 mile), and turn off the highway at a "Natural Bridge Campground" sign near milepost 55. Then keep left for 0.7 mile to the Natural Bridge parking area. The trail starts at an information kiosk at the far right-hand end of the lot.

The paved path crosses the river on a long footbridge. Pavement ends in 0.2 mile at a railed viewpoint of the natural bridge. Below, the frothing river appears to be sucked into solid rock. Water pressure in the 200-foot lava tube is so great

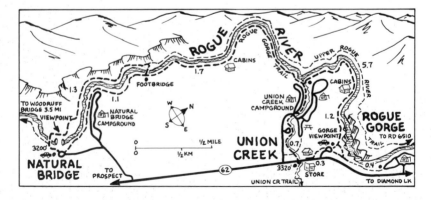

that spray sputters out from cracks in the cave roof.

Most tourists turn back here. But a lovely, quiet portion of the Upper Rogue River Trail continues upstream. In early summer, large patches of 5-petaled white anemones bloom here beneath old Douglas firs. Also look for vanilla leaf, with 3 big leaves and a stalk of tiny white flowers.

A mile beyond Natural Bridge take a fork to the right, cross the river on a footbridge over a churning chasm, and come to a T-junction with the Rogue Gorge Trail. Only turn left if you're interested in the 8-mile hike combining both loops. To complete the first short loop, turn right and hike 1.1 mile to your car.

The other easy loop hike, to Rogue Gorge, is a more civilized tour, passing summer cabins, campgrounds, and an ice cream shop in the village of Union Creek. To start, drive Highway 62 to Union Creek at milepost 56. A few hundred yards north of town, follow a "Rogue Gorge" sign to a parking lot. First take a minute to explore a paved 0.2-mile loop trail that visits fenced viewpoints of the 100-foot-deep gorge. This is all most tourists will see. For a more thorough, 2.2-mile tour of the Union Creek area, however, follow the fence downstream and continue on the unpaved Rogue Gorge Trail.

After 1.2 miles along the wooded riverbank, cross a footbridge over Union Creek to a trail junction. To the right the Rogue Gorge Trail continues 1.7 miles along the river to the Natural Bridge loop described above. For the short loop back to your car, however, turn left along Union Creek. This creekside path actually goes through a few campground sites, but the campers know they're beside a trail and don't seem to mind passersby. After stubbornly following the creekbank 0.7 mile upstream, turn left along Highway 62. Just beyond the ice cream shop, angle left beside a propane tank on a short trail back to your car.

Rogue River footbridge on Natural Bridge loop.   Opposite: Vanilla leaf.

35 Union Creek

Easy (to falls from Road 610)
0.6 mile round-trip
120 feet elevation loss
Open April through November
Map: Union Creek (USGS)

Moderate (to falls from Highway 62)
8.2 miles round-trip
330 feet elevation gain

A nearly level trail from the rustic resort village of Union Creek follows a cool mountain stream through old-growth woods to a small, mossy waterfall. This 4.1-mile path is lovely, but if you're pressed for time, a backdoor route will take you down to the falls in just 0.3 mile.

Begin by driving Crater Lake Highway 62 east from Medford. At milepost 56, in the hamlet of Union Creek and immediately before the Union Creek bridge, park on the right at a pullout with a small trailhead sign. This is the start of the longer, prettier route to Union Creek Falls.

The path heads upstream 200 yards and crosses the creek on a 50-foot bridge made of a single log. Then turn right and continue upstream. The Douglas firs in these woods are as much as 7 feet thick. The scraggly, flat-needled trees along the creek are yew; its bark yields the cancer drug taxol, and its resilient wood was once used by Indians for bows. Bracken fern and vanilla leaf add greenery to the forest floor. Star-flowered smilacina blooms in June with sprays of tiny stars.

The farther you hike, the livelier the creek becomes, bubbling through mini-

Union Creek.   Above: Footbridge near start of trail.

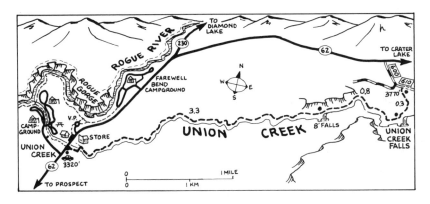

ature waterfalls and gorges. Watch for ouzels near an 8-foot cascade at the 3.3-mile mark. These dark gray, robin-sized birds dive underwater and flap their wings, "flying" along the creekbed in search of insect larvae.

Union Creek Falls is only 10 feet tall, but it tops a dramatic series of water slides, chutes, and rock channels—a nice lunch spot. Beyond the falls, the trail leaves the creek and climbs through smaller woods 0.3 mile to Road 610. To start your hike here (or to leave a shuttle car here for a one-way hike), drive Highway 62 north of Union Creek 1.3 miles, veer right on Highway 62 toward Crater Lake for 2 miles, turn right on gravel Road 600 for 0.2 mile, and fork left on dirt Road 610 for 200 yards to the trailhead on the right.

36 Abbott Butte Λ

Moderate (to Abbott Butte)
7.2 miles round-trip
1500 feet elevation gain
Open July through October
Use: hikers, horses
Map: Rogue-Umpqua Divide
   Wilderness (USFS)

Difficult (to Elephanthead Pond)
9.8 miles round-trip
1950 feet elevation gain

Right: Cascade lilies at Abbott Butte.

Wildflowers and vistas line this spectacular, often overlooked portion of the Rogue-Umpqua Divide Wilderness's ridgecrest. The chief destination here is Abbott Butte, where an abandoned lookout tower straddles a small cabin. But an equally interesting goal is Elephanthead Pond, in the shadow of an enormous, elephant-shaped cliff.

To drive here from Medford, head east on Crater Lake Highway 62. Between mileposts 51 and 52 (past the Prospect Ranger Station 6 miles) turn left onto paved Woodruff Meadows Road 68. Stick to Road 68 through numerous well-

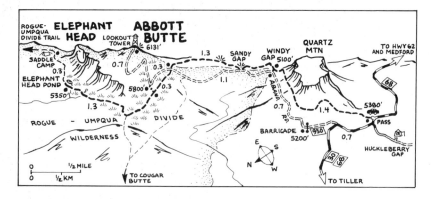

marked junctions for 4.9 miles of pavement and another 7.4 miles of 1-lane gravel road. At a pass, just before a large "Umpqua National Forest" sign, park in a gravel pullout on the right by a sign for the Rogue-Umpqua Divide Trail.

If you're coming from Roseburg, you'll want to take Interstate 5 south 25 miles to Canyonville exit 98. Following signs for Crater Lake, drive into Canyonville and turn east on 3rd Street—which becomes the Tiller-Trail Highway—for 23.3 miles to Tiller. On the far side of this hamlet, fork left onto Road 46 at a South Umpqua Falls pointer for 5.3 miles; then turn right on Jackson Creek Road 29 for 12.5 miles and finally turn right at a "Huckleberry Gap" sign for 15 gravel miles to the trailhead on the left, just beyond a pass.

The trail sets out through a mountain hemlock forest full of beargrass (with blooms in early July), blue huckleberries (ripe in late August), and a host of woodland wildflowers, including anemones and inside-out flowers. After 1.4 miles, at Windy Gap, the path dips to within 30 feet of the abandoned road to the Abbott Butte lookout, and 0.4 mile later at Sandy Gap the path briefly touches the old road. The views from Sandy Gap's pass stretch from Mt. Scott to Mt. McLoughlin and distant white Mt. Shasta. The sand in this pass is strewn with the sunny wildflowers one might expect in the Siskiyous, including

Abbott Butte's abandoned lookout and cabin.

Elephant Head from Elephant Lake.

sunflower-like balsamroot and blue crown brodiaea. Beyond the pass is a cliffy rock garden of stonecrop, yellow monkeyflower, and red paintbrush.

At the 2.7-mile mark the path crosses the old road and enters a lush meadow of white lupine, green hellebore, purple larkspur, and black coneflower. After hiking 0.3 mile into this meadow, look for a rock cairn and a view of Abbott Butte's lookout on the right. Leave the trail here, hike uphill 100 yards cross-country, and then follow the old lookout road up another 0.7 mile to Abbott Butte's summit. The 30-foot lookout tower lacks glass or stairs, but still shelters a 10-foot cabin where the lookout staff once slept. The view is a bit overgrown. Bunches of huge Cascade lilies brighten the slopes nearby.

If you're ready to head back, you can return on a loop by following the old roadbed 1.8 miles to Windy Gap. This route is not maintained, so expect to step over a few logs. Take the trail back from Windy Gap to avoid trudging along a trafficked gravel road the final stretch to your car.

If you'd like to visit Elephanthead Pond, walk down the lookout road 0.7 mile from Abbott Butte to the third switchback and hike cross-country 100 yards downhill to the trail. Turn right and follow this increasingly faint path as it contours across the meadow. Cairns and poles help mark the mostly level route 0.4 mile to an open pass with views of Mt. Bailey and Mt. Thielsen. From here the trail descends 0.9 mile through profuse wildflower meadows to a boardwalk at the marshy outlet of Elephanthead Pond, a shallow lake with a surprising view of a 300-foot rock cliff sporting a natural bas-relief sculpture of an elephant's head, complete with trunk, ear, and eye.

Other Hiking Options

Backpackers can continue along the Rogue-Umpqua Divide Trail beyond Elephanthead Pond 12 miles toHershberger Mountain (see Hike #37), 13 miles to Highrock Meadows (Hike #10), or 19 miles to Fish Creek Valley (Hike #40).

37   Hershberger Mountain

Easy (to Rabbit Ears and lookout tower)
0.5 mile round-trip
160 feet elevation gain
Open July through October
Map: Rogue-Umpqua Divide Wlds. (USFS)

Moderate (to Cripple Camp shelter)
4.8 miles round-trip
840 feet elevation loss
Use: hikers, horses

Short paths lead to 2 spectacular landmarks of the Rogue-Umpqua Divide high country: the historic Hershberger Mountain lookout and the 400-foot rock spires of Rabbit Ears. (Some summers Rabbit Ears is off-limits until August 15 to protect endangered falcons nesting on the spires.) To round out the day with a longer hike, try the nearby trail to Cripple Camp's shelter, in a wildflower meadow surrounded by huge Douglas firs.

To start, drive east from Medford on Crater Lake Highway 62 for 57 miles, veer left onto Highway 230 toward Diamond Lake for 0.9 mile, and turn left across a Rogue River bridge onto Road 6510 for 1.6 miles.

If there's no sign warning of a Rabbit Ears closure, fork to the right on gravel Road 6520 for 0.5 mile, and then turn left on Road 6515 for 5.6 miles to a sharp left bend at a ridge end. Park at an unmarked pullout here and follow a trail to the right along the wooded ridgecrest 300 yards to its end at the base of Rabbit Ears—a pair of huge, overhanging spires. The eroded remnants of a volcanic plug, these pillars were first scaled in 1921 and still attract technical rock climbers. Even from the base, the view extends south to snowy Mt. McLoughlin and distant Mt. Shasta. After inspecting Rabbit Ears, return to your car, continue driving up Road 6515 exactly one more mile, and turn right on Road 530 for 2.3 steep miles to road's end on Hershberger Mountain.

If the road to Rabbit Ears was gated closed, you can still drive to Hershberger

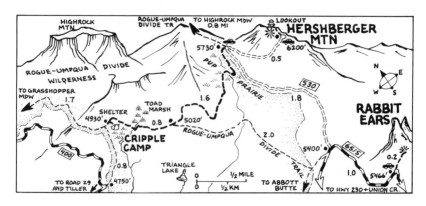

Hershberger Lookout and Rabbit Ears.   Opposite: Columbine.

Mountain by a longer route. From Medford, drive Highway 62 past Union Creek, fork left on Highway 230 for 0.9 mile, turn left (and *keep left*) on Road 6510 for 6.2 miles, turn right on Road 6515 for 9.2 miles, and turn left on Road 530 for 2.3 miles to its end.

Either way, park at the road's end. From here a metal staircase and 100-foot trail climb to the Hershberger lookout. Built in 1925, the 12-foot-square building has an inside ladder to a cupola—a small second story full of windows. Views sweep from Mt. Bailey to Mt. Shasta. The lookout is being restored for overnight rental (for details, call the Tiller Ranger District at 541-825-3201) but until the final touches are complete it remains unlocked and open to the public free.

For the more substantial hike to Cripple Camp shelter, drive 0.5 mile down from the lookout and park at the road's switchback. Two trails start here, but take the Acker Divide Trail down to the left. It descends through Douglas fir woods 0.5 mile to Pup Prairie, an astonishingly lush wildflower meadow with head-high stalks of purple larkspur. Also look for green hellebore, mountain bluebells, red paintbrush, fuzzy-topped mint flowers, red columbine, and petalless brown coneflower. Expect a few mosquitoes when the flowers are at their peak in late July and early August.

Continue a mile past Pup Prairie to a junction and go straight 0.6 mile to Toad Marsh, a former lake that really does foster toads. Fist-sized and warty, the khaki amphibians stumble across the trail. Hike another 0.2 mile to Cripple Camp, a meadow with large orange tiger lilies and a leaky shake-roofed shelter built in 1937. Droopy incense cedars and 8-foot-thick Douglas firs add to the ambience.

Other Hiking Options

Backpackers can continue past Cripple Camp shelter on a grand 13.4-mile loop to Buckeye Lake (see Hike #11), Fish Lake (Hike #10), and Highrock Meadow before returning to the Hershberger Mountain trailhead. The Rogue-Umpqua Divide Trail offers other long-distance choices. If you follow this path south along the crest of the Wilderness you'll reach Abbott Butte in 13 miles (see Hike #36). Follow it north instead and you'll reach Fish Creek Valley beside Rattlesnake Mountain (Hike #40) in 7 miles.

National Creek Falls. *Opposite: Fawn lilies in Muir Creek's upper meadow.*

38   National Creek Falls

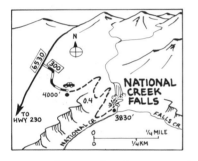

Easy
0.8 mile round-trip
170 feet elevation loss
Open mid-April through November
Map: Hamaker Butte (USGS)

This very short hike to a cool, misty waterfall glen makes a good family outing for a hot summer day. National Creek was a favorite stop for travelers as early as the 1860s, when miners and stockmen blazed a route past here on their way from Southern Oregon to the newly discovered John Day gold fields.

Drive Crater Lake Highway 62 east of Medford 57 miles and fork left onto Highway 230 toward Diamond Lake. After 6 miles, near a sign marking the Jackson County line, turn east on paved Road 6530 for 1.3 miles. Then fork left to keep on Road 6530 for another 2.4 miles and finally turn right on gravel Road 300 for a few hundred yards to the trailhead at road's end.

The trail sets off through woods of mixed Douglas fir, hemlock, flat-needled grand fir, and white pine. Look on the trail for spiny golf-ball-sized "porcupine eggs"—the seeds of the broadleaf chinkapin trees that form a scraggly understory here. In May, Oregon grape has clusters of yellow flowers and vanilla leaf puts up fuzzy white flower stalks resembling bottle brushes.

After ambling 0.2 mile the trail passes the top of the falls. Don't venture near the cliffs for a view. Instead continue down the trail another 0.2 mile to its end at the base of the falls, a side-by-side pair of 80-foot fans that spray out over a basalt cliff. The rock is actually the broken edge of a lava flow from Mt. Mazama, Crater Lake's ancient volcano.

39 Muir Creek

Easy (Highway 230 to Muir Falls)
5.4 miles round-trip
250 feet elevation gain
Open May through November
Use: hikers, horses
Map: Rogue-Umpqua Divide
 Wilderness (USFS)

Moderate (Road 400 to Upper Mdw)
5.6 miles round-trip
500 feet elevation gain
Open June to mid-November

Elk and deer love the brushy meadows along this mountain stream so much that early morning hikers almost always see them. If you're not an early riser, you'll still be able to see Muir Falls, wildflowers, and plenty of elk tracks. The 2 easy hikes recommended here sample the trail's highlights. More ambitious trekkers can connect these trail segments or continue for a backpack trip into the beautiful, uncrowded Rogue-Umpqua Divide Wilderness. Be aware that cows graze these meadows from July to early October.

The flattest and most accessible trail in this area leads from Highway 230 to Muir Falls. To find it, drive east from Medford on Highway 62 for 57 miles and veer left onto Highway 230 (toward Diamond Lake) for 10.3 miles. Immediately before a bridge labeled "Muir Creek", pull into an unmarked parking area on the left. (If you're coming from Diamond Lake, drive 0.6 mile past milepost 11 and park just after the Muir Creek bridge.)

The trail promptly leaves Muir Creek and sets off through a forest of hemlock

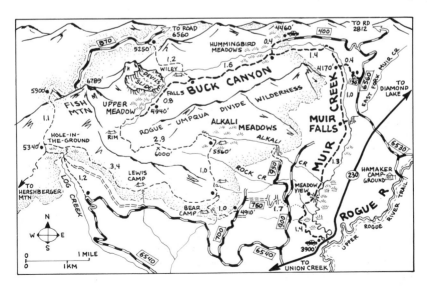

Leaves of green hellebore (corn lily).

and Douglas fir with low huckleberry bushes and princes pine plants. After crossing 2 bridgeless side creeks (look for logs up or down the stream), the path finally returns to Muir Creek at the 1.4-mile mark. A lovely viewpoint by the creekbank here overlooks the brushy, marshy meadows popular with elk and songbirds. Mosquitoes can be a problem the last half of June.

Continue another 1.3 miles—along a trail muddied in places by hooves—until you hear (and glimpse) Muir Falls to the right. Bushwhack 50 yards through alder brush to the creekbank for a closer look at this cascade, a series of 10-foot falls where Muir Creek forks. Turn back here unless you're ready to connect the 2 short hikes in a single long trek.

The second short hike along Muir Creek climbs through prettier wildflower meadows to a subalpine bowl dammed by an ancient landslide. To find this trail from the first trailhead, drive Highway 230 north 1.9 miles. Shortly after milepost 12, turn west on gravel Fish Creek Road 6560 for 1.9 miles. Then turn left on Road 400 for 1.3 miles to its end at the Hummingbird Meadows trailhead.

This path sets off through high-elevation woods with incense cedar, 5-foot-thick Douglas fir, and the white blooms of trilliums. In between are meadowed slopes with huge-leaved hellebore (corn lily), purple larkspur, and delicate yellow fawn lilies. There's also lots of cattle and elk sign. After 0.3 mile, hop across Muir Creek on rocks. Shortly afterwards, turn right on the Buck Canyon Trail.

In another 1.6 miles, keep left at a fork and climb through lichen-draped woods to a 10-foot waterfall beside the Devils Slide. This half-mile-long rock-slide dammed the canyon several thousand years ago, creating the waterfall and a quarter-mile-long lake. Since then, the lake has filled with silt and become a subalpine meadow traced with the meanders of the clear, swift, deep-pooled creek. In June look for marsh marigolds and fawn lilies in the meadow. Also listen for the *meep!* of pikas, the rabbit-like denizens of the nearby rockslide.

This upper meadow makes a good turnaround point. Beyond, the trail climbs 1000 feet to a broad pass before gradually descending to Alkali Meadows, with a spring, a campsite, and more wildflowers.

Other Hiking Options

Backpackers with map and compass can complete a 15.5-mile loop from the Muir Creek trailhead on Highway 230. Hike up Muir Creek and continue through Alkali Meadows to the Road 700 trailhead. The trail once continued east, but has been supplanted by logging Road 760. Follow it to its end and bushwhack downhill to the Muir Creek Trail.

Buck Canyon, Muir Creek's upper meadow.

40 Rattlesnake Mountain

Easy (to Windy Gap)
3.2-mile loop
740 feet elevation gain
Open July through October
Use: hikers, horses
Map: Rogue-Umpqua Divide Wlds. (USFS)

Moderate (to Rattlesnake Mountain)
6-mile loop
1750 feet elevation gain

Right next door to the popular Diamond Lake area, but overlooked by tourists, the Rogue-Umpqua Divide Wilderness is a hidden haven of subalpine wildflower meadows, viewpoints, and quiet trails. One of the best hikes starts from a gravel road that sneaks into the heart of the wilderness. For an easy loop, hike to Windy Gap and the flowers along Fish Creek. For a longer trip, climb to the views atop Rattlesnake Mountain—a snakeless summit with a meadow.

From Medford, take Crater Lake Highway 62 east for 57 miles, and then veer left onto Highway 230 for 12.2 miles, following a "Diamond Lake" pointer. At the Hamaker Campground junction shortly after milepost 12, turn left onto Fish Creek Road 6560. Follow this gravel road 4 miles to a pass where it becomes Road 37. Continue another 0.5 mile, fork left onto Incense Cedar Loop Road 800 for 2.8 miles, and then turn left on Fish Creek Valley Road 870 for 4.2 miles. This increasingly rough road passes 3 other trailheads before you reach the one you want—a small "Rogue-Umpqua Divide Trail" sign on the right, 100 yards before a parking pullout and a spur road to Happy Campsite, a primitive tent spot.

If you're driving to this trailhead from Roseburg, it's quicker to head east on Highway 138. Between mileposts 60 and 61 turn right on Fish Creek Road 37 for 13 miles. Then turn right on Incense Cedar Loop Road 800 for 3.5 miles and

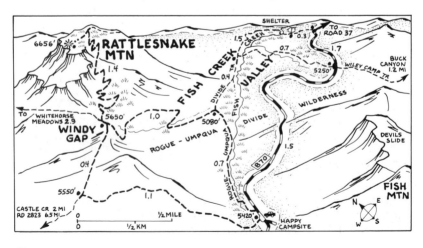

Rattlesnake Mountain from Fish Creek Valley.   *Opposite: Coneflower.*

finally turn right on Fish Creek Valley Road 870 for 4.2 miles.

The trail sets off downhill through a meadow with a rainbow of summer wildflowers. Look for goldenrod, red paintbrush, white yarrow, purple aster, blue lupine, black coneflower, and sweet-smelling mint. From late August to early October you may also find cows grazing here. The path follows Fish Creek, a splashing mountain brook, 0.7 mile to a junction. Turn left and climb 1 mile to Windy Gap, a wooded saddle where 4 trails meet.

For the easy loop, turn left on a faint path along the wooded ridgecrest, past a sign for Trail 1576 and Hummingbird Camp. In another 0.4 mile, turn left on an abandoned roadbed with views west to Castle Rock's plug-shaped lava knob. After 1.1 mile, the road/trail ends at Road 870 a few yards from your car.

If you like views, however, don't miss the side trip up Rattlesnake Mountain. When you first reach Windy Gap, go straight 50 feet to find the trail. It forks uphill to the right and promptly starts switchbacking up through meadows of lavender owl clover, bracken, aster, white lupine, and scarlet gilia. The path is faint, but maintained and not extremely steep. The only switchback that's easy to overlook is the second one, in a meadowed gully with a view of Fish Mountain.

When you reach a steep meadow near the summit, turn left at a trail junction. After another 100 yards the trail ends at a large rock cairn, but continue straight across the meadow 150 yards to a clifftop viewpoint virtually overhanging Castle Creek's broad wilderness valley. To the left, your view of the horizon's peaks sweeps from forested Fish Mountain, past the tip of Mt. McLoughlin, Union Peak's steep pyramid, Crater Lake's rim, flat-topped Mt. Scott, pointy Mt. Thielsen, and broad Mt. Bailey.

Other Hiking Options

The Rogue-Umpqua Divide Trail extends 23.8 miles in all. Hike it east 1.9 miles to Fish Creek Shelter, or head west to Highrock Meadow, Hershberger Mountain, and Abbott Butte (Hikes #10, #37, and #36).

41   Upper Rogue River

Easy (to No Name Falls)
3.4 miles round-trip
200 feet elevation gain
Open mid-May to mid-November
Map: Hamaker Butte (USGS)

Moderate (to Rough Rider Falls)
7.8 miles round-trip
650 feet elevation gain

Moderate (Highway 230 to Road 6530)
8.6 miles one-way
1200 feet elevation loss
Open June to mid-November

Near its headwaters the Rogue River churns through a rarely visited canyon of waterfalls. For an easy hike, take a nearly level stroll through the woods to an unnamed 40-foot S-shaped falls. For a longer hike, continue upstream to roaring, 50-foot Rough Rider Falls. Better yet, arrange a car shuttle and hike this entire 8.3-mile stretch of the Upper Rogue River Trail one way.

If a car shuttle isn't in the cards, start at the lower trailhead. From Medford, take Highway 62 east for 57 miles and continue straight on Highway 230 toward Diamond Lake 12.2 miles. At a "Hamaker Campground" sign shortly after milepost 12, turn right onto gravel Road 6530. In another 0.5 mile, keep left at a fork to stay on Road 6530. Then drive 0.2 mile, *watching closely for a small "Upper Rogue River Trail" sign on the left.* Park on the shoulder here. (If you're driving here from Diamond Lake, take Highway 230 toward Medford 11.4 miles and keep left on Road 6530 for 0.7 mile to the small trail sign on the left.)

The trail sets off through a quiet forest of big Douglas fir (up to 6 feet in diameter), flat-needled grand fir, droopy-limbed incense cedar, white pine, and chinkapin brush. The trail briefly swings beside the Rogue River after 0.4 mile, but then returns to the woods until the just before the unnamed waterfall. This

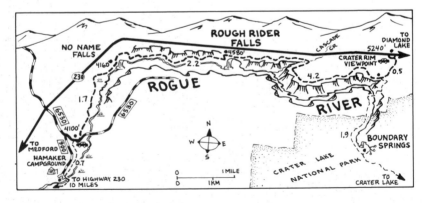

long cascade churns through 2 curves before frothing into a 120-foot-wide pool. White lupine and 4-petaled bunchberry bloom here.

If you decide to continue past the unnamed falls you'll follow the glassy river through the most remote and scenic part of its canyon. At a switchback 2.2 miles farther up the trail, bushwhack straight ahead 100 yards to reach a scenic river islet at the base of Rough Rider Falls. This turnaround spot affords a fine view of the cascade pounding down onto mossy boulders.

If you have access to 2 cars you can hike the trail one way—all downhill. After leaving one car at the lower trailhead on Road 6530, drive the other back to Highway 230 and turn right for 6.4 miles to the Crater Rim Viewpoint parking pullout, where the Upper Rogue River Trail begins. Follow this path 0.5 mile, keep right at a junction, and head downstream 8.1 miles to the first car.

The upper 4.2 miles of this trail is often within earshot of the highway, but follows the scenic rim of a 200-foot-deep canyon. The Rogue carved this chasm out of the vast ash layer deposited when Crater Lake's Mt. Mazama erupted 7700 years ago.

Other Hiking Options

Backpackers and equestrians can follow the Upper Rogue River Trail downstream even farther. From the lower trailhead at Road 6530, it's 0.7 mile to Hamaker Campground, 10.7 miles to Highway 230, 24.7 miles to Natural Bridge (Hike #34), and 39.3 miles to trail's end near Prospect.

Rough Rider Falls.   Opposite: Bunchberry.

Southern
Cascades

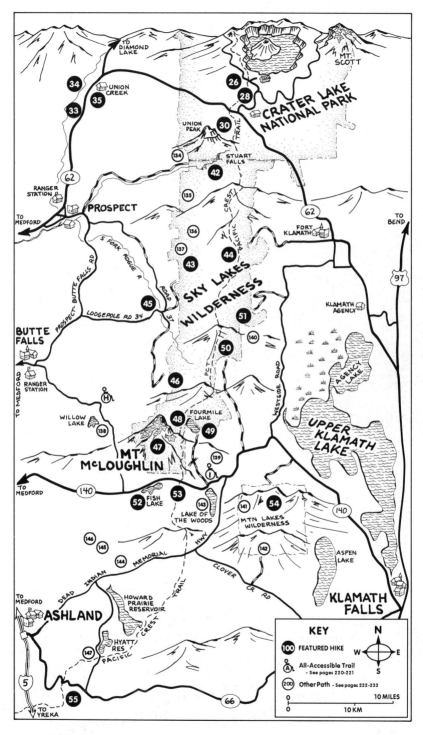

Opposite: Devils Peak from Grass Lake (Hike #44).

Red Blanket Falls.   Opposite: Stuart Falls.

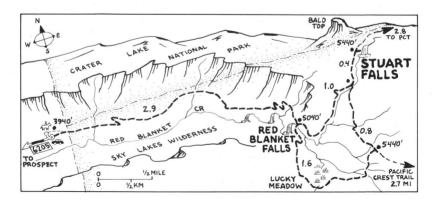

42   Stuart Falls

Moderate
8.6 miles round-trip
1500 feet elevation gain
Open mid-June to mid-November
Use: hikers, horses
Map: Sky Lakes Wilderness (USFS)

Waterfalls and huckleberries draw hikers to this canyon between the Sky Lakes Wilderness and Crater Lake National Park. In addition to Stuart Falls—a 40-foot fan on a columnar basalt cliff—the route passes Red Blanket Falls and several unnamed cascades. Blue huckleberries along the way ripen in profusion by late August. Expect some mosquitoes during the first 3 weeks of July.

To find the trailhead, take Crater Lake Highway 62 east of Medford 45 miles to a turnoff for Prospect and turn right for 0.7 mile to the center of this village. Just beyond the Prospect Hotel turn left onto Butte Falls Road, and 1 mile later turn left again on Red Blanket Road. In another 0.4 mile fork left on gravel Road 6205 for 11.4 miles to its end at a large parking turnaround.

The path begins in a park-like stand of Douglas fir, hemlock, and grand fir, with an understory of dogwood and hazel. The shiny leaves of holly-like Oregon grape and tiny twinflower serve as ground cover. After 100 yards the trail enters the official Wilderness near one of the corner markers for Crater Lake National Park. These monuments were built in 1902 to warn sheepherders and timber cutters away from the newly created reserve.

After 2 miles of well-graded but viewless climbing, the trail follows a canyon rim with glimpses of roaring waterfalls. The best view is of Red Blanket Falls, which tumbles 40 feet into a bubbling pool. The falls and creek are named for the red blankets early Prospect-area settlers used to purchase this area from the Takelma tribe.

At the top of Red Blanket Falls, keep left for 1.4 miles along a lovely mountain brook to a lodgepole pine forest at the base of splashing Stuart Falls. Look for water ouzels here, the robin-sized dippers that can "fly" underwater. Backpackers are directed away from this heavily used area to a camping area downstream and saddle stock are limited to an area away from the creek.

Other Hiking Options

If you're willing to add 1.4 miles to your trip back, you can return on a loop through the area's best huckleberry fields. Walk back from Stuart Falls 0.4 mile and fork left at a "Pacific Crest Trail" pointer. In 0.8 mile, after crossing 3 creeks, look carefully for a "Lucky Camp Trail" sign to the right. This rockier path, crowded with huckleberry bushes, descends past Lucky Meadow (a grassy bog with hellebore and columbine) and crosses 30-foot-wide Red Blanket Creek (on a log just above the falls) before rejoining the trail to your car.

43   Seven Lakes West

Moderate (to Alta Lake)
8.4 miles round-trip
1750 feet elevation gain
Open early July through October
Use: hikers, horses
Map: Sky Lakes Wilderness (USFS)

Difficult (to Cliff Lake)
10.4 miles round-trip
2300 feet elevation gain

Difficult (to Devils Peak)
13.7-mile loop
3050 feet elevation gain

From Devils Peak's lofty summit, the pools of the forested Seven Lakes Basin look like pips on a pair of green dice. Up close, each lake has its own character. Half-mile-long Alta Lake, for example, is so narrow you can throw a rock across it. Cliff Lake has a mountain view and a diving rock popular with swimmers.

The Seven Lakes Trail is the shortest route to this popular basin, but it climbs across a high ridge. For a gentler route from the east, see Hike #44. In either case, be warned that mosquitoes are a problem from mid-July to mid-August. Backpackers must tent at least 100 feet from lakeshores and are encouraged to use the 4 signed camp areas. Equestrians are required to use the 8 designated horse camps. In addition, horses are not allowed within 200 feet of lakeshores (except on trails or at designated watering spots) and grazing is usually banned.

To find the Seven Lakes Trailhead, take Highway 62 east from Medford 14.5 miles, turn right on the Butte Falls Highway for 15 miles to the town of Butte Falls, continue straight for another 1 mile, turn left at a sign for Prospect for 9 miles, turn right onto Lodgepole Road 34 for 8.5 miles, continue straight on Road 37 for 0.4 mile, and then veer right onto gravel Road 3780 for 4.1 miles.

The trail starts behind a guardrail and climbs steadily up a broad forested ridge. The path is a bit dusty and rocky from heavy use by horses and hikers, especially on summer weekends. Fork to the right at the 0.7-mile mark, and after another 1.5 miles take a break beside Frog Lake, a shallow pool rimmed with heather and lodgepole pine. Then continue 1.3 miles to a pass with a trail junction and a view ahead to Devils Peak. The thumb-shaped outcrop on the peak's left shoulder is the old volcano's original plug, stripped bare by the vanished Ice Age glacier that carved the lake basin below.

Go straight down the far side of the pass 0.2 mile to a second trail junction— this one for Alta Lake. For a moderate hike, turn left half a mile to this amazingly straight, skinny pool, aligned on the crack of a major north-south fault. Before turning back, be sure to follow a "Camping" pointer right 100 yards to the cliffy lip of Violet Hill and a view across the Seven Lakes Basin.

If you're up to a more difficult hike, skip the Alta Lake side trail and continue straight 1.5 miles to Cliff Lake. Along the way you'll descend through subalpine meadows with the tiny blooms of pink heather and white partridge foot. Pause at the rockslide between South Lake and Cliff Lake to watch for pikas, the round-eared "rock rabbits" that *meep!* at passing hikers.

The Seven Lakes Basin from Devils Peak.   Opposite: Alta Lake.

If you're backpacking, or if you can manage an even longer day hike, continue on a spectacular loop to Devils Peak. Go straight past Cliff Lake 0.4 mile, turn right on the Pacific Crest Trail, take this well-graded route 2.5 miles to a pass, and turn right on an unmarked path up a rocky ridge 0.2 mile to Devils Peak's summit. The panorama here spins from Mt. Thielsen and the Crater Lake rim to Klamath Lake and Mt. McLoughlin's snowy cone. On the way down, keep right at trail junctions for 1.9 view-packed miles. Then turn left on the Seven Lakes Trail for 3.5 miles to your car.

Other Hiking Options

Experienced hikers can return from Alta Lake on a different, 9.6-mile loop that passes the coneflower meadows and giant Engelmann spruce trees at King Spruce Springs. From the far, north end of Alta Lake, head left on a faint, rocky path. After half a mile this infrequently maintained route briefly vanishes in a meadow, but follow the field's left edge to keep on track. At the 1.4-mile mark, watch closely for a small trail sign on a tree to the right. Turn left here for 2.7 miles to return to the Seven Lakes Trail, just 0.7 mile from your car.

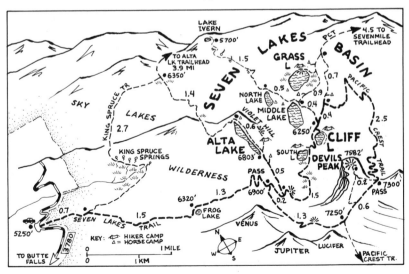

44   Seven Lakes East

Difficult (to Cliff Lake)
11.4-mile loop
900 feet elevation gain
Open early July through October
Use: hikers, horses
Map: Sky Lakes Wilderness (USFS)

Difficult (to Devils Peak)
17.3-mile loop
2150 feet elevation gain

This eastern "back door" route to the popular Seven Lakes Basin may be a trifle longer than the official Seven Lakes Trail from the west (Hike #43), but a delightful lack of elevation gain makes it seem easier. The popularity of the lake-dotted basin has brought a few rules. Backpackers must tent at least 100 feet from lakeshores and are encouraged to use the 4 signed camp areas. Equestrians are required to use the 8 designated horse camps. Horses are not allowed within 200 feet of lakeshores (except on trails or at designated watering spots) and grazing is usually banned. Also remember that mosquitoes are plentiful from mid-July to mid-August.

Start by driving to Fort Klamath, a hamlet near milepost 90 of Highway 62, east of Crater Lake 16 miles and 38 miles north of Klamath Falls. At an abandoned gas station in the middle of town, turn west on Nicholson Road. Follow this paved road absolutely straight 3.9 miles. Heeding "Sevenmile Trailhead" signs, fork left on gravel Road 3300 for 0.4 mile, and then fork to the right on Road 3334 for 5.6 miles to road's end. (A portion of this last road was so badly rutted by floods in 1996 that cars can just get through at a crawl. Call the Klamath Ranger District at 541-885-3400 to find out if it's been repaired.)

From the left side of the parking area, hop across a creek on rocks to find the start of the trail. Heavy horse use has left the path dusty in the dry lodgepole pine woods. After 1.8 miles, turn left on the Pacific Crest Trail in a cooler forest

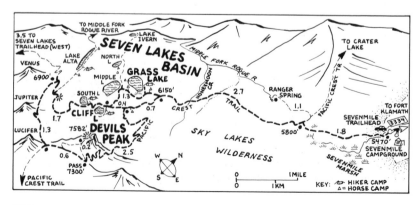

Devils Peak from Cliff Lake.   Opposite: Cascade toad at Grass Lake.

of mountain hemlock and Shasta red fir. The distant river roar audible in the canyon to the right is the Middle Fork Rogue, gushing from Ranger Spring.

At the 4.5-mile mark, fork to the right on the Seven Lakes Trail—the start of a delightful little loop tour. In another 0.3 mile, side trails branch off to the right to designated camp areas by Grass Lake. Take time for a detour here, ambling to the right along Grass Lake's shore to a viewpoint of the peaks rimming this basin. Along the reedy shore expect fuzzy pink spirea blooms, blue dragonflies, and zillions of thumbnail-sized Cascade toads.

Then return to the Seven Lakes Trail and continue the loop tour 1 mile to a junction, passing huckleberry patches, wildflower meadows, and sandy-bottomed Middle Lake along the way. At the junction, turn right 100 yards to find a short spur trail on the left to Cliff Lake. With a dramatic view of Devils Peak, a rockslide full of curious pikas, and a 30-foot diving cliff popular with daredevil swimmers, Cliff Lake is a popular destination. Heavy use has left much of its lakeshore closed for revegetation, but there's an approved camping area on a low ridge close by.

Day hikers will probably have to turn back here, completing the little loop tour by following signs back to the Pacific Crest Trail. Backpackers, however, can continue on a spectacular, larger loop to the top of Devils Peak. From Cliff Lake, continue west on the Seven Lakes Trail 1.7 miles to a forested pass, turn left for 1.3 view-packed miles to a junction in another pass, turn left on the Pacific Crest Trail along a slope for 0.3 mile, and take a steep unmarked side trail to the left 0.3 mile to Devils Peak's summit. The view here encompasses the entire route of your hike—and most of the Sky Lakes Wilderness from Crater Lake to Mt. McLoughlin. The shaley rock of the summit provides a foothold for wind-bent whitebark pines and dishmop-shaped western pasque flowers.

On the way down from Devils Peak, fork left to find a different route to the PCT. Then go left on this well-graded trail to complete the loop.

45   South Fork Rogue River

Moderate (upper portion)
6 miles one way
450 feet elevation gain
Open May through November
Use: hikers only
Map: Butte Falls Ranger District (USFS)

Moderate (lower portion)
6.8 miles one way
550 feet elevation loss
Use: bicycles, hikers, horses

A well-built trail follows the brawling, bouldery South Fork Rogue River more than 12 miles through old-growth woods. Access is easy: a middle trailhead divides the path into an upper half that's open only to hikers, and a lower, bicycle-approved portion that serves hikers and equestrians too. It's most fun to explore these routes one-way from the middle trailhead, but if you can't arrange a shuttle, start at the middle trailhead anyway. In either direction, you'll find good turnaround points for shorter hikes.

To drive to the central trailhead on Road 34, take Crater Lake Highway 62 east from Medford 14.5 miles, turn right on the Butte Falls Highway for 15 miles to the town of Butte Falls, continue straight for another 1 mile, turn left at a sign for Prospect for 9 miles, and turn right onto Lodgepole Road 34 for 8.5 miles. Half a mile past South Fork Campground, turn right at a hiker-symbol sign to the parking area.

The upper, hiker-only portion of the trail (on the right half of the map) visits quieter woods with bigger trees. To try it, start at the trail sign at the end of the parking area. The path crosses a forested flat and a cattle-proof fence before joining the 30-foot-wide river. Oregon grape, twinflower, pathfinder plant, and princes pine form a green carpet beneath the Douglas firs. If you're hiking with small children, you might make your destination Big Ben Creek at the 0.7-mile mark. A side trail to the left follows a cascading creek up toward Big Ben

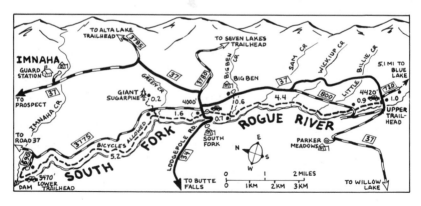

South Fork Rogue River.   Opposite: Sugarpine cone.

Campground, while the main trail crosses the creek on a 70-foot, railed log. Small gravel bars and logs along the river here make for good exploring.

If you decide to follow the main trail upriver, you'll cross 3 more large side creeks and gravel Road 800 before reaching the upper trailhead on Road 37. Douglas firs 7 feet in diameter line the upper part of the path. These ancient woods also host a remarkably dense understory of yew—a gnarly, shaggy-barked tree with flat needles, poisonous red berries, and a mystique dating to the days when its tough wood was used for bows. To shuttle a car here from the middle trailhead, drive 100 yards east on Road 34 and turn right on Road 37 for 5.3 miles to a parking area on the right, just before a river bridge. If you don't have a second car to shuttle, leave a bicycle at the upper trailhead for a quick ride back on the paved road.

If you've brought a bicycle, however, you might prefer to try the lower portion of the South Rogue River Trail instead. To find it from the middle trailhead, walk back to the parking area's entrance, cross Road 34, and look for an unsigned trail into the woods. This newly built path follows a very scenic part of the river's canyon , crossing 2 side creeks on bridges in the first 1.6 miles. For a short trip, turn right after the second bridge on a side trail that crosses Road 3775 and climbs 0.2 mile to a giant sugarpine tree. If you continue down the lower portion of the South Rogue River Trail, you'll see many more sugarpines, with tall, column-like trunks and foot-long cones dangling from the tips of long upper branches. Douglas firs 4 feet thick are common here, too.

At the 6.7-mile mark the trail passes an overlook of a diversion dam, where most of the river is shunted into a canal for power production. Just beyond is the Road 690 trailhead. To drive (or bike) here from the middle trailhead, go 100 feet up Road 34, turn left on gravel Road 3775 for 5 miles, and turn left on narrow Road 690 for 0.4 mile to its end.

Other Hiking Options

A much rockier, steeper portion of the South Fork Trail begins at Road 720 and traces the river to its headwaters at Blue Lake. This wilderness path fords the river on the way, and is not recommended for horses. An easier route to the Blue Lake Basin is described in Hike #46.

46   Blue Lake Basin

Easy (to Blue Lake)
4.6 miles round-trip
640 feet elevation loss
Open early July through October
Use: hikers, horses
Map: Sky Lakes Wilderness (USFS)

Moderate (to Horseshoe Lake)
6.2 miles round-trip
700 feet elevation gain

Difficult (to Island Lake)
11 miles round-trip
1300 feet elevation gain

The high lakes in this corner of the Sky Lakes Wilderness have been popular destinations since at least 1888. That's the year Judge John Waldo of Salem led a party of 5 horsemen from Willamette Pass to Mt. Shasta, becoming the first to trace the route of the present-day Pacific Crest Trail through Southern Oregon. While camped at Island Lake, Waldo's group carved their names in a large Shasta red fir. Today hikers who trek 5.5 miles along the Blue Canyon Trail can still read the inscription. But it's tempting to turn back at one of the smaller, prettier lakes along the way.

The area's popularity has brought a few rules. Backpackers must tent at least 100 feet from lakeshores. Equestrians are required to use designated horse camps. Horses are not allowed within 200 feet of lakeshores (except on trails or at designated watering spots) and grazing is usually banned. Also remember that mosquitoes are a problem from mid-July to mid-August.

To find the Blue Canyon Trail, drive Highway 62 east from Medford 14.5 miles, turn right on the Butte Falls Highway for 15 miles to the town of Butte Falls, continue straight for another 1 mile, turn left at a sign for Prospect for 9 miles, turn right onto Lodgepole Road 34 for 8.5 miles, turn right on Road 37 for 5.3

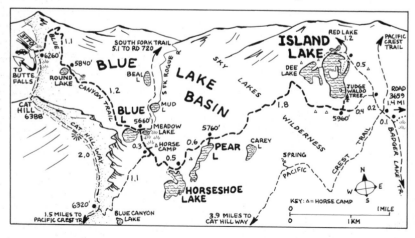

miles of pavement and an additional 2.1 miles of gravel, and finally turn left on gravel Road 3770 for 5.3 miles to a large parking pullout on the right.

The trail heads downhill into a forest of Shasta red fir with blue lupine blooms in late July and ripe blue huckleberries in late August. After 1.1 mile the path passes Round Lake—a scenic pool, but no match for Blue Lake, another 1.2 miles down the trail. Backed by a rockslide from a dramatic 300-foot cliff, Blue Lake is filled with deep green water suitable for swimming. From the mountain hemlock woods along the shore, you can watch dragonflies zoom or listen to the *meep!* of pikas scampering about the rockslide.

Hikers with children may want to turn back here. To continue, however, turn right at a trail junction near Blue Lake's outlet and then go straight 0.8 mile to Horseshoe Lake. The trail only touches the small end of this lopsided horseshoe. To find the prettier end, backtrack 100 yards on the trail and take a side path out to the lake's peninsula—off-limits to tenters, of course.

If you're headed for more distant lakes, note that neither Pear Lake nor Island Lake is visible from the main trail. Beyond Horseshoe Lake 0.6 mile, look for a short spur on the right that leads to Pear Lake, obviously named before bananas were common. Another 1.8 miles along the main trail, a large unmarked fork leads 140 yards to Judge Waldo's railed tree and the only grassy bank along the shore of large, brush-rimmed Island Lake.

To return on a loop through the area's best huckleberry fields, consider taking the somewhat rockier and steeper trail over forested Cat Hill. Look for the turnoff between Blue and Horseshoe Lakes. Follow this path up 1.1 mile to a crest and turn right on Cat Hill Way for 2 miles to your car, passing the area's only full view of Mt. McLoughlin along the way.

Blue Lake.   Opposite: Restoration site on Horseshoe Lake's shore.

Mount McLoughlin

Difficult
10.6 miles round-trip
3915 feet elevation gain
Open July through October
Map: Sky Lakes Wilderness (USFS)

Mt. McLoughlin overlooks half the state—and a good share of California, too. For years there was no official trail to the summit, so climbers spread out on a maze of scramble paths, spray-painting dots on rocks to help them find the route back. In the mid-1990s, however, Forest Service crews laid out a single clear route and chipped away the ugly, misleading markings. The hike is still one of the most demanding—and rewarding—in Southern Oregon. Only set out in good weather, bring sunscreen, and carry plenty of water.

From a distance, Mt. McLoughlin's relatively smooth cone suggests it is one of the youngest Cascade volcanoes. Climbers, however, can see massive gouges left by Ice Age glaciers on the peak's hidden north face, exposing a thumb-shaped lava plug. The most recent eruption, 12,000 years ago, poured blocky basalt from a vent low on the mountain's south slope.

The tallest peak in Southern Oregon has had many names. Klamath Indians called it *Kesh yainatat*, home of the dwarf old woman who commanded the west wind. The Takelma tribe dubbed it *Alwilamchaildis* after a mythic hero of their

The final pitch to the summit.   Above: Mt. McLoughlin from Lake of the Woods.

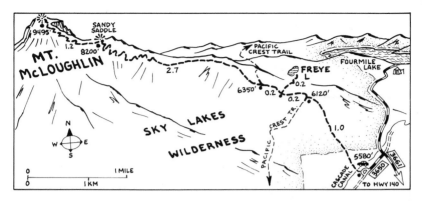

legends, and thought it was the home of Acorn Woman, who made oaks bear fruit each year. In 1838, the first map to show the peak labeled it Mt. McLoughlin in honor of the influential Hudson's Bay Company leader at Fort Vancouver. After Rogue Valley settlers began calling the peak Mt. Pitt (for California's Pit River), the Oregon legislature resolved in 1905 to restore the McLoughlin name.

To find the trailhead from Medford, take Highway 62 east 6 miles and turn right toward Klamath Falls on Highway 140 for 36 miles. Just beyond the Lake of the Woods Visitor Center, turn left at a "Fourmile Lake" pointer onto gravel Road 3661 for 2.9 miles, and then turn left on Road 3650 for 0.2 mile to a large parking lot. (From Klamath Falls, take Highway 140 west to milepost 36, turn right on Road 3661 for 2.9 miles, and turn left on Road 3650.)

The trail promptly crosses Cascade Canal, which shunts Fourmile Lake's outlet stream west toward Rogue Valley irrigators. Then the path marches steadily up through a mixed forest of Shasta red fir. After a mile, veer right onto the Pacific Crest Trail. In another 0.2 mile, an unmarked spur to the right leads over a rise to Freye Lake, a shallow pool with a view of the mountain's top half. To continue your climb, return to the PCT, follow it a few hundred yards uphill, and fork left on the Mt. McLoughlin Trail.

The next 1.5 miles are relatively easy, through boulder-strewn mountain hemlock woods. But then the route launches uphill with a vengeance to timberline, where only pinemat manzanita and gnarled whitebark pines survive. At the 4.1-mile mark the trail clambers to a sandy saddle where the sweeping view includes your first glimpse of Mt. McLoughlin's true summit. The final 1.2 miles gain a staggering 1300 feet along a craggy ridgecrest.

A crumbling rock wall at the top remains from the foundation of a vanished 1929-vintage lookout. On a clear day, the panorama includes every major Cascade peak from South Sister to Mt. Lassen. Even with a bit of haze you'll be able to spot snowy Mt. Shasta to the south and pointy Mt. Thielsen above Crater Lake's rim to the north. To the east, Upper Klamath Lake floods the Cascade foothills. Whale-shaped Fourmile Lake swims through the wilderness forests at the mountain's base, with Squaw Lake a calf at its side. To the southwest, beyond Howard Prairie Reservoir and the Rogue Valley, rise the peaks of the Siskiyous.

When you hike down, stick to the ridgecrest trail you followed on the way up. Don't be tempted to romp down a snowfield (or by August, a scree slope) to the right of the ridge. Nearly every year, search parties are organized for hikers lured far south of the trail by this "shortcut."

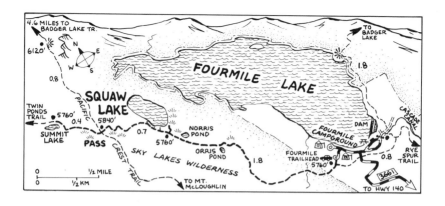

48   Squaw Lake

Easy (to Squaw Lake)
3.6 mile round-trip
100 feet elevation gain
Open July through October
Use: hikers, horses
Map: Sky Lakes Wilderness (USFS)

Easy (to Summit Lake)
5.8 miles round-trip
260 feet elevation loss

In early days, Indians crossed the Cascade Range through a high pass north of Mt. McLoughin, avoiding the rugged lava flows in lower passes. By the 1860s the U.S. Army was using this "Rancheria Trail" as the main military link between Fort Klamath and the Rogue Valley. Today hikers can follow a nearly level remnant of the old path—now dubbed the Twin Ponds Trail—to pristine wilderness lakes on either side of the pass. Expect mosquitoes from mid-July to mid-August.

To find the trailhead from Medford, drive Highway 62 east for 6 miles and turn right onto Highway 140 toward Klamath Falls for 36 miles. Just beyond the Lake of the Woods Visitor Center, turn left at a "Fourmile Lake" pointer onto gravel Road 3661 for 5.7 miles to the lake, and then keep left through Fourmile Campground to the trailhead parking turnaround. If you're coming from Klamath Falls, head west on Highway 140 to just beyond milepost 36, turn right on Road 3661 for 5.7 miles, and keep left to the trailhead.

The trail soon forks (keep right), enters the Sky Lakes Wilderness, and crosses a creek lined with flowers: fuzzy pink spirea, blue aster, and white marsh marigolds. For the next mile, however, the path traverses a viewless forest of lodgepole pines and rocks. Then the level landscape becomes more interesting, with odd hummocks, hidden ponds, and tiny meadows where lakes used to be.

At the 1.8-mile mark, beyond shallow, mud-ringed Norris Pond, take a large right-hand spur trail 100 yards to a lovely meadow at the tip of Squaw Lake. Hikers often startle ducks up from this large, wild lake. The ducks beat their wings against the water and then arc about the lake's rim of lodgepole pines in tight formation, their wingtips shivering.

If you decide to continue past Squaw Lake, you'll climb 0.7 mile to a pair of small, meadowed former lakebeds in a forested pass. If you cross the Pacific Crest Trail and descend 0.4 mile you'll reach shallow Summit Lake, strewn with rocks from a nearby slide. This makes a good turnaround point.

Other Hiking Options

For a challenging 14-mile loop hike, turn north at the pass and circle Fourmile Lake on the Pacific Crest and Badger Lake Trails (see Hike #49).

Squaw Lake.   Opposite: Shasta red fir cone opened by squirrels for seeds.

49 Badger and Long Lakes

Easy (to Badger Lake)
3.6 miles round-trip
200 feet elevation gain
Open early July through October
Use: hikers, horses
Map: Sky Lakes Wilderness (USFS)

Moderate (to Long Lake)
7.4 miles round-trip
360 feet elevation gain

Difficult (around Fourmile Lake)
14-mile loop
680 feet elevation gain

Mt. McLoughlin rises like an Egyptian pyramid above the driftwood-jammed shores of Fourmile Lake. Although the Sky Lakes Wilderness surrounds this mountain, surprisingly few other lakes in the area offer views of it. The next best view is a glimpse from cute, swimmable little Badger Lake. Catch both of these vistas on an easy, nearly level walk from the Fourmile Campground. Or continue past a wildflower meadow to skinny Long Lake. Or tackle a 14-mile loop hike that uses the Pacific Crest Trail to complete a grand circuit around Fourmile Lake.

To start, drive east of Medford on Highway 62 for 6 miles and turn right onto Highway 140 toward Klamath Falls for 36 miles. Just beyond the Lake of the Woods Visitor Center, turn left at a "Fourmile Lake" sign on gravel Road 3661 for 5.7 miles to Fourmile Campground. (If you're coming from Klamath Falls, head west on Highway 140 to just beyond milepost 36, and turn right on Road 3661 for 5.7 miles.)

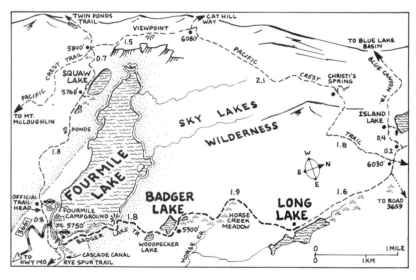

Mt. McLoughlin from Fourmile Lake.   Opposite: Fourmile Lake from the PCT.

Once you reach Fourmile Campground, signs point you left to an official trailhead parking turnaround—and if you're towing a horse trailer, that's where you should park. But if you're planning to *hike* toward Badger Lake, you can save 0.8 miles by turning *right* through the campground instead. Park at the free "Day Use Only" pullout beside the boat ramp's picnic area. From here, hike 100 yards to the end of the campground's loop road and walk past a gate with a "Road Closed" sign. Beyond the gate, go straight 100 yards on the largest dirt road to a sign for the Rye Spur Trail by a canal. Continue straight on the road another 100 feet and turn left onto the Badger Lake Trail.

The trail parallels Fourmile Lake's shore for nearly a mile through lodgepole pine woods with red and blue huckleberry bushes. The best viewpoint and shore access is at the 0.9-mile mark, just before the trail turns inland. From here it's painfully obvious that this mountain lake has been converted to a reservoir. Bleached snags and drift logs line the barren, rocky shore. The lake once drained east toward Klamath Lake, but now a concrete dam and canal near the campground divert its water west to irrigate Medford orchards.

After leaving Fourmile Lake, the trail passes shallow Woodpecker Lake before skirting Badger Lake at the 1.8-mile mark—an excellent goal, especially if you're hiking with children. If you decide to continue on the trail, you'll pass a lilypad pond and a long meadow. Look here for white marsh marigolds in July and bulbous yellow Bigelow's sneezeweed in August. Then the path crosses a low ridge to the densely forested edge of Long Lake.

If you hate to backtrack, consider marching onward on a 14-mile loop. Although the route ahead offers only one good viewpoint (across a forest to Fourmile Lake) and touches the shore of only one lake (Squaw Lake), the nearly level trail is so well built that joggers sometimes do the loop just for exercise. Simply follow the Badger Lake Trail 1.6 miles past Long Lake, turn left on the Pacific Crest Trail for 5.4 miles, and turn left on the Twin Ponds Trail for 2.5 miles to the Fourmile Trailhead. Of course, if you didn't park at the official trailhead, you'll have to continue 0.8 mile, following a "Badger Lake Trail" pointer on a bypass trail to the far end of the campground.

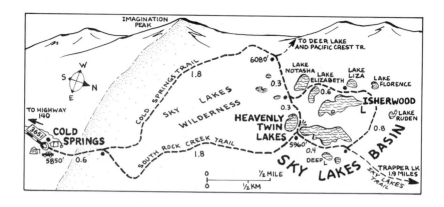

50   Sky Lakes via Cold Springs

Easy
6.9-mile loop
400 feet elevation gain
Open early July through October
Use: hikers, horses
Map: Sky Lakes Wilderness (USFS)

By far the easiest route into the famous lake-dotted high country of the Sky Lakes Wilderness, this loop passes half a dozen pools in a nearly level, forested basin. The drawbacks? The area's easy access draws crowds on summer weekends, mosquitoes are a nuisance from mid-July until late August, and the basin has few mountain views.

To find the trailhead, drive east of Medford 6 miles on Highway 62, turn right on Highway 140 toward Klamath Falls to milepost 41, and turn left at a "Cold Springs Trailhead" pointer onto Road 3651. Follow this gravel road 10.1 miles to its end at a turnaround with a primitive campground and a rickety shake-sided shelter beside a cold, piped spring. (If you're coming from Klamath Falls, take Highway 140 west to milepost 41 and turn right on Road 3651.)

The broad, dusty trail sets off amid mountain hemlocks and Shasta red firs up to 4 feet in diameter. White woodland flowers here include large, 3-petaled trillium, sprays of tiny star-flowered smilacina, and solitary queens cup. By late August, expect ripe blue and red huckleberries along the way.

After 0.6 mile the trail forks. Both paths traverse relatively tedious lodgepole pine and mountain hemlock woods to the lake basin, but the right-hand fork gets there a bit quicker, so branch right on the South Rock Creek Trail. In another 1.8 miles you'll reach a delightful isthmus between the Heavenly Twin Lakes.

This is a great place to let kids explore the shores of these shallow lakes, and it offers the area's only mountain view—of Luther Mountain and Devils Peak at the far northern end of the Sky Lakes Basin. If you're backpacking, remember that tents are banned within 100 feet of lakeshores, so this isthmus is off limits.

When you're ready to continue the loop, backtrack from the isthmus and veer left along the shore of the larger Heavenly Twin for 0.4 mile. At the far end of this lake, turn left on the Isherwood Trail for 0.8 mile to reach the shore of dramatic, half-mile-long Isherwood Lake. The smooth, curved bedrock shore was polished by glaciers that capped the Cascade Range during the Ice Age. Look closely for scratch marks showing the direction the ice flowed as it slowly carved the Sky Lakes Basin. Then continue along the trail 0.6 mile, passing lima-bean-shaped Lake Elizabeth and deep, blue-green Lake Notasha.

At a junction just beyond Lake Notasha, turn right for 0.3 mile. Then complete the loop by forking left onto the Cold Springs Trail for the final 2.4-mile walk back to your car.

Other Hiking Options

Backpackers can continue north from the Heavenly Twin Lakes for 1.9 miles to Trapper Lake, and from there explore a different part of the long Sky Lakes Basin, described in Hike #51.

Luther Mountain from Heavenly Twin Lakes.   *Opposite: Cold Springs Trailhead shelter.*

51 Sky Lakes via Nannie Creek

Easy (to Puck Lakes)
4.8 miles round-trip
760 feet elevation gain
Open mid-July through October
Use: hikers, horses
Map: Sky Lakes Wilderness (USFS)

Difficult (to Marguerette Lake)
12.8-mile loop
1560 feet elevation gain

Difficult (around Luther Mountain)
16.7-mile loop
2240 feet elevation gain

This lake basin deep in the heart of the Sky Lakes Wilderness is dominated by the cliffs of Luther Mountain—a landmark named to provide a religious opponent for nearby Devils Peak. For an easy hike, head for the large but shallow Puck Lakes. If you continue to deep, picturesque Marguerette Lake, you can return on either of 2 loops: a short tour to Trapper Lake or a much longer trek around Luther Mountain for a grandstand view of the entire basin. Note that visitors in the Wilderness are limited to a group size of 8 people and 12 stock animals. Mosquitoes can be plentiful in late July and early August.

To start, drive east of Medford 6 miles on Highway 62 and turn right on Highway 140 toward Klamath Falls for 43.5 miles. (If you're coming from Klamath Falls, head west on Highway 140 for 25 miles.) Between mileposts 43 and 44, turn north on paved Westside Road for 12.2 miles, and then turn left on gravel Road 3484 for 5.2 miles to a parking lot at road's end.

The Nannie Creek Trail switchbacks up through a forest of mountain hemlock and Shasta red fir for 1.6 miles, and then descends slightly for 0.8 mile to an unmarked Puck Lakes turnoff on the right. This side path leads 100 yards to a

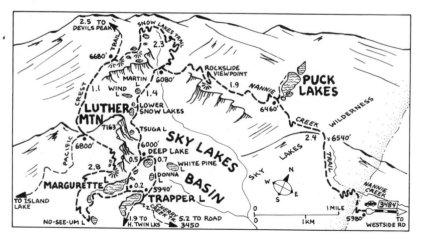

Luther Mountain from Lower Snow Lakes.   *Opposite: Margurette and Trapper Lakes.*

shaley beach. It's a great place to lounge in the pink heather below the shore's lodgepole pines while the kids look for tiny Cascade toads or wade in the relatively warm lake. A fainter trail continues left around the shore 0.3 mile to the northern Puck Lake. All that's missing at these lakes is a mountain view.

If you're continuing on the Nannie Creek Trail, you'll descend gradually for 0.9 mile to an open rockslide with a view that sweeps from Pelican Butte (on the left) to Mt. McLoughlin (above Luther Mountain's shoulder), and Devils Peak (on the right). After another downhill mile, veer left at a junction. Nearly level, the next 1.9 miles to Margurette Lake pass a series of scenic pools reflecting Luther Mountain's cliffs. Blue and red huckleberries ripen here by late August.

When you reach a T-shaped trail junction beside Margurette Lake you'll face a decision. For the shortest loop back, turn *left* 0.2 mile to large but less dramatic Trapper Lake and turn left again past shallow Donna and green Deep Lake, where you'll rejoin the route back to your car.

For a longer loop with better views, however, turn *right* at the Marguerette Lake junction. This route climbs past 2 small lakes to a dramatic, glacier-smoothed clifftop overlooking Margurette Lake, Trapper Lake, and distant Upper Klamath Lake. Scratches in the bedrock here reveal the direction Ice Age glaciers moved while scouring this lake basin from the mountainside. Continue up the trail to a pass and turn right on the Pacific Crest Trail for 1.1 mile to another cliff-edged viewpoint. Beside a large cairn where the PCT leaves the rim, turn right on the Snow Lakes Trail. This spectacular path passes a dozen rimrock tarns before switchbacking down through the woods to the Nannie Creek Trail, where a left turn will take you back to your car.

52 Fish Lake

Easy (to Fish Lake Resort)
6.6 miles round-trip
100 feet elevation gain
Open mid-May to mid-November
Use: hikers, bicycles
Map: Sky Lakes Wilderness (USFS)

Moderate (High Lakes Trail)
9.3 miles one way
500 feet elevation gain

A new bicycle-accessible trail links Fish Lake with Lake of the Woods, passing the lava flows of the Cascade summit on the way. The lakes on either end of the broad new High Lakes Trail are probably Southern Oregon's most popular—each has campgrounds, picnic areas, boat launches, and a rustic, old-timey resort. If the 9.3-mile, packed-gravel High Lakes Trail sounds too long, try the ungraveled 3.3-mile trail along Fish Lake's shore instead. Because the 2 trails connect end-to-end, adventurous hikers (or bicyclists) can do them both.

The Fish Lake Trail is easy enough for hikers with children. To find it, drive Highway 140 east of Medford 35 miles (or west of Klamath Falls 40 miles). Between mileposts 28 and 29, turn south on paved Road 37 at a "North Fork Campground" pointer. After half a mile turn left into the trailhead parking pullout, just opposite the campground entrance.

The Fish Lake Trail sets off along North Fork Little Butte Creek—a beautiful stream that begins as a glassy, meandering, meadow-edged river but soon shifts to a rushing whitewater torrent. Fir trees grow 4 feet thick along the path, with an understory of hazel and a few wildflowers. Look for white, 3-petaled trillium, fuzzy pink spirea, and lavender lousewort. At a trail junction after 0.6 mile, the main trail turns left away from the creek, but a spur continues straight 100 yards to the base of Fish Lake's dam. Arduously built in 1921-22 by men hauling rocks in horse-drawn railroad cars, the dam tripled Fish Lake's size. The original lake was created a few thousand years ago by a natural rock dam—the Brown Mountain lava flow visible across the creek. The Medford Irrigation District draws down the enlarged reservoir each summer to water orchards.

After leaving the creek, the Fish Lake Trail makes a tedious 0.8-mile detour to avoid private summer homes. But then the path sticks to the lakeshore for 1.9 miles, skirting 2 campgrounds and a picnic area before reaching the Fish Lake Resort. The dock, cafe, and general store here make a good turnaround point.

If you're planning to bicycle (or hike) the new High Lakes Trail to Lake of the Woods, it's probably best to start at the Fish Lake Campground. To find this trailhead, drive Highway 140 east of Medford 35 miles (or west of Klamath Falls 38 miles). Between mileposts 30 and 31, turn south at a "Fish Lake Recreation Area" sign and keep left for 0.4 mile to the start of the High Lakes Trail on the left. There's no room for parking here, however, and the nearby Fish Lake Resort has no parking for trail users either, so you'll have to drive on 100 yards to the Fish Lake Campground and pay a $2 day-use parking fee. Then walk (or ride

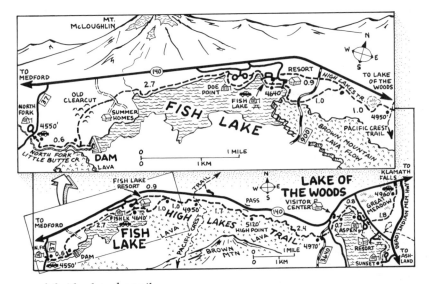

your bike) back to the trail.

From Fish Lake, the well-graded, 8-foot-wide High Lakes Trail climbs through ancient lava flows that have grown over with forest. The trail is often within 100 yards of noisy Highway 140. At the 1.8-mile the path skirts a sinkhole where water from the 20-foot-wide Cascade Canal vanishes underground. Irrigators built the canal to shunt Fourmile Lake's outlet creek toward the Fish Lake reservoir. To their chagrin, the canal's water vanished into a lava tube here. Then they realized the tube carries the water underground to Fish Lake anyway.

Brown Mountain from Fish Lake.   Opposite: North Fork Little Butte Creek.

Just beyond the sinkhole, the path crosses the Pacific Crest Trail (closed to bikes; see Hike #53). Then the High Lakes Trail climbs another 1.7 miles along the edge of a fresh-looking lava flow to the Cascade summit and descends 3.1 miles to the shore of Lake of the Woods, 200 yards behind the Forest Service's visitor center on Highway 140. If you continue 0.8 mile, you'll cross 2 bridges at the marshy end of the lake (with views, ducks, and mosquitoes) before reaching a trail junction at Aspen Point's north picnic area. A fee is charged if you park a car here. If you keep left at trail junctions and cross 2 roads, however, you'll follow the High Lakes Trail 1.8 miles around a vast, grassy plain to trail's end at the Great Meadow Recreation Site. To bring a shuttle car to this free parking lot, drive Highway 140 to between mileposts 37 and 38.

53 Brown Mountain Lava Flow

Easy (to view at high point)
5.8-mile loop
550 feet elevation gain
Open June to mid-November
Use: hikers, horses
Map: Sky Lakes Wilderness (USFS)

The lava flows on Brown Mountain are so rugged that trail builders had to dynamite the jumbled basalt surface and lay a tread of crushed red cinders. Perhaps the most expensive portion of the 2400-mile Pacific Crest Trail, this spectacular section is now easy to hike. From Highway 140, the path climbs gently to viewpoints of Brown Mountain, Fish Lake, and Mt. McLoughlin.

From Medford, take Highway 62 east 6 miles and turn right toward Klamath Falls on Highway 140 to the Cascade crest. Between mileposts 32 and 33, turn north at a "Summit Sno-Park" sign and drive to the far end of the huge paved parking area. The trail that starts here crosses a grassy, open fir forest for 0.2 mile and crosses a footbridge to the Pacific Crest Trail. Turn left, following the canal 0.4 mile to a crossing of noisy Highway 140. Of course you could start your hike at this unmarked crossing (Highway 140 does offer a small parking pullout at the end of a guardrail by milepost 32), but the walk alongside Cascade Canal can be quite pleasant. The canal was built to divert Fourmile Lake's outlet to the west side of the Cascade summit for Medford irrigators. When full, the rushing 20-foot creek provides a stark contrast to the lava ahead.

Beyond the highway crossing 0.2 mile, the PCT crosses the packed-gravel High Lakes Trail (see Hike #52). Shortly afterward, the PCT enters a moonscape of black boulders, with views ahead to Brown Mountain, the lava's source. Brown Mountain is called a shield volcano because of its low profile, built up by countless flows of runny black lava. About 2000 years ago a cinder cone erupted on the summit, adding a brown peak with a little crater. Shortly

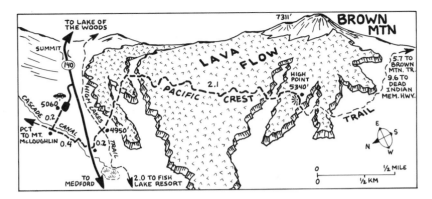

afterward, the lava you're crossing vented from the cinder cone's base. The flow's crust cooled first and jumbled when the lava underneath kept moving.

A surprising variety of life has gained a foothold here. Where the rocks aren't disturbed, they're crusted with gray, green, and black lichens—a combination of fungus and algae that gets all the nutrients it needs from the rain and the air. Another pioneer, chinkapin, forms 10-foot-tall bushes along the trail, with sprays of white flowers in summer and spiny fruit (known as "porcupine eggs") in the fall. Some animals live in lava to escape predators. Watch for orange-bellied Douglas squirrels and listen for the *meep!* of guinea-pig-shaped pikas.

At the 2.9-mile mark, by a cairn with the last best view of Mt. McLoughlin's huge cone, the PCT reaches a high point and begins heading downhill through Douglas fir woods. This makes a good turnaround point, although long-distance hikers can continue 5.7 miles to the Brown Mountain Trail crossing, 7.6 miles to a spring at the South Brown Mountain Shelter, or 9.6 miles to a parking area near milepost 27 of the Dead Indian Memorial Highway.

Mt. McLoughlin from the lava flow.   Opposite: Chinkapin flowers and fruit.

54   Mountain Lakes

Moderate (to Eb and Zeb Lakes)
9.6 miles round-trip
1230 feet elevation gain
Open mid-July to early November
Use: hikers, horses
Map: Mountain Lakes Wilderness (USFS)

Difficult (to Harriette Lake)
12.6 miles round-trip
1800 feet elevation gain

Difficult (Mountain Lakes loop)
17.1-mile loop
2720 feet elevation gain

Precisely 6 miles square, this pocket Wilderness towers above Upper Klamath Lake like a misplaced chunk of the High Cascades. In its center, a gorgeous 8.3-mile loop trail tours a string of hidden lakes and mountain passes. The price of admission is a 4.4-mile climb through the woods to the start of the loop.

Geologists once thought this isolated highland might be the remains of a huge volcano that exploded in Crater Lake fashion. But the area's outline is a lopsided square, not a circle, suggesting a cluster of at least 4 smaller volcanoes instead. Did one of them explode? It's hard to tell. Any caldera would have vanished in the Ice Age when 5 glaciers gutted these highlands, leaving lake basins, headwall cliffs, and several exposed lava plugs.

The Mountain Lakes Wilderness was one of 8 Oregon areas protected by the original 1964 Wilderness Act. All 7 of the other areas have been expanded since then, and more than 2 dozen new areas have been designated, but this preserve retains its original square boundary—exactly one township. The maximum group size for visitors here is 10 people and / or horses. Tents can't be closer than 100 feet to lakeshores, and horses can't be closer than 200 feet except on trails.

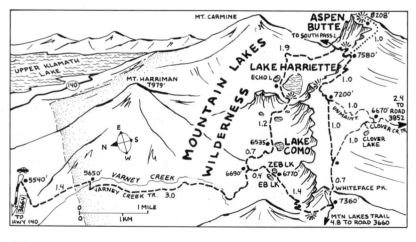

Lake Harriette.   Opposite: Eb Lake.

Three paths climb to the central loop, but the Varney Creek Trail requires the least elevation gain. To find it, drive Highway 140 east of Klamath Falls 21 miles (or east of Medford 54 miles). Between mileposts 46 and 47 turn south onto Road 3637 at a large green "Varney Creek Trailhead" sign. Follow this gravel road straight 1.8 miles and turn left on Road 3664 for 1.9 miles to the road's end.

The trail starts by contouring around a *lateral moraine*—a jumble of rocks and sand pushed aside by a valley glacier. Ponderosa pine and thickets of white fir now forest the slope. After 1.4 mile the path crosses mossy, gurgling Varney Creek and heads up the valley floor. Sparse lodgepole pine and Shasta red fir allow views of Mt. Harriman's broad, forested cone.

The trail forks at the 4.4-mile mark—the start of the central loop. If you're tired, turn right for 0.4 mile to make your goal Eb and Zeb Lakes, a pair of shallow but swimmable little lakes just 100 yards apart. The shores have pink heather, red huckleberries, and views of Whiteface Peak's bright rockslides. If you're up to a longer hike, however, skip Eb and Zeb. Instead turn left at the junction and descend 0.7 mile to Lake Como, a deeper, bigger, blue-green pool with better swimming and lots of small, jumping fish. But don't turn back yet. If you continue another 1.2 mile you'll climb to a rocky pass with a terrific view and descend to Lake Harriette—the largest, deepest, and prettiest lake of all.

Backpackers can complete the scenic central loop. Beyond Lake Harriette the path climbs 1.5 miles to a pass. If you've time for a detour, a spur trail to the left here deadends in 1.6 miles at South Pass Lake. Otherwise veer right and climb 0.4 mile to the crest of a cliffy rim. For a very dramatic detour, bushwhack left along the open ridgecrest 1 mile through stunted whitebark pines to the former fire lookout site atop Aspen Butte—the best viewpoint in the Wilderness. To continue, however, follow the loop trail right along the rim 1 mile, ignore an unmaintained left-hand spur trail (which heads toward small, disappointing Clover Lake), go straight through mountain hemlock woods 1.7 mile to a pass beside Whiteface Peak, and keep left 1.8 mile to complete the loop, passing viewpoints and the twin lakes of Eb and Zeb along the way.

Eastern
Siskiyous

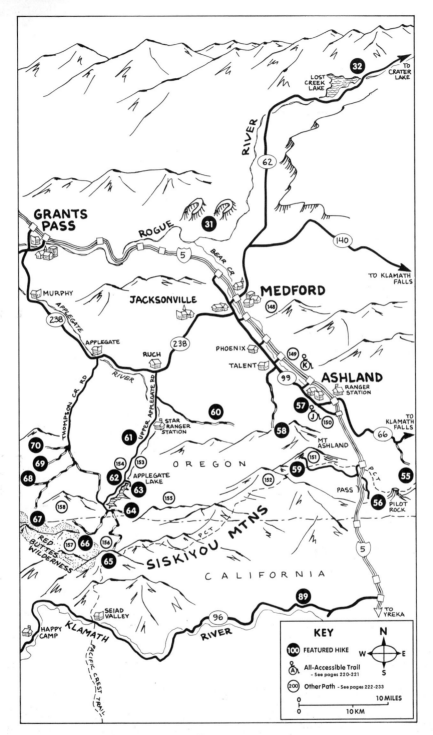

Opposite: Azalea Lake in the Red Buttes Wilderness (Hike #67).

55 Soda Mountain

Easy (to Hobart Bluff)
2.4 miles round-trip
340 feet elevation gain
Open mid-May through November
Use: hikers, horses
Map: Soda Mountain (USGS)

Moderate (to Soda Mountain)
4.2 miles round-trip
810 feet elevation gain
Open June to mid-November

This miniature wilderness near Ashland not only commands dramatic views, but it also contains an intriguing mixture of plants. Because Soda Mountain lies at the junction of 3 biologic regions, it mingles the Cascades' fir forests and the High Desert's sagebrush steppe with the droopy incense cedars and tough-limbed manzanita of the Siskiyous.

Hikers here can choose either of 2 easy trips on the Pacific Crest Trail—a walk north to cliff-edged Hobart Bluff or a hike south to the staffed lookout tower on Soda Mountain itself. For a full day's outing, visit both.

From Ashland exit 14 of Interstate 5, head east on Highway 66 toward Klamath Falls for 14.5 winding miles. Just 200 feet before the highway pass at Green Springs Mountain Summit, turn right on Soda Mountain Road 39-3E-32.3. Follow this one-lane gravel road 3.7 miles to a set of big powerlines in a grassy pass. Park on the right just beyond the powerlines. Small brown posts on either side of the road mark the Pacific Crest Trail's crossing.

For the short hike to Hobart Bluff, head left on the PCT. The path crosses a strangely mixed savannah of Oregon white oak, grand fir, and cedar—all flocked with bright yellow *Letharia* lichen. Spring flowers here include sweet-smelling mint, strawberry, and star-flowered smilacina. By summer, look for wild rose, edible blue elderberry, and inedible white snowberry. The brushy oak leaves along the path look alarming, but aren't poison oak.

After 0.9 mile turn left at a "Hobart Bluff Viewpoint" pointer and climb an arid slope of juniper, sunflower-like balsamroot (with June blooms), and mountain mahogany. Dip past a false summit to a rock outcrop with a magnificent view. From here the Bear Creek Valley resembles the inside of an enormous boat, with Interstate 5 as the keel, Medford as the stern, and Soda Mountain as the prow. Cascade landmarks include snowy Mt. Shasta to the south and Mt. McLoughlin's cone to the north.

If you're not yet tired after returning from Hobart Bluff, head for Soda Mountain by following the PCT south, straight past your car. This route climbs a sagebrush slope before entering a grand fir forest with grassy openings grazed by cows. When the trail levels off in the woods 1.1 mile from the powerline parking area, watch for an unmarked side trail that switchbacks up to the left. This unmaintained cow path climbs past 2 telephone poles for 0.2 mile to a dirt road. Go right on the steep road 0.8 mile to **Soda Mountain's** summit.

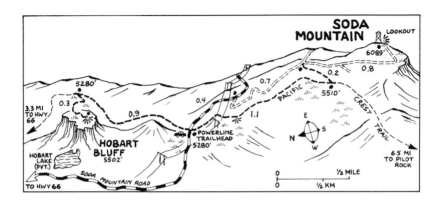

The 1933-vintage fire lookout tower atop the peak is staffed from early June to early October. Each year the staffer reports hundreds of smokes—once, he even called in a suspicious wedding barbecue at Callahan's Restaurant. Labels above the windows identify dozens of landmarks in each direction, but you won't need any help spotting snowy Mt. Shasta above the Klamath River canyon. Note the river's Irongate Reservoir, and broad Shasta Valley to the right. Farther to the right are Mt. Eddy (with a snow patch), the Trinity Alps, the Marble Mountains, and nearby Pilot Rock's knob.

On your way down it's slightly shorter—and less scenic—to follow the road all the way to your car. In fact, it's possible to drive this ungated service road up to the lookout in the first place. But most visitors choose the trail. The steep, badly rutted road is too rough for passenger cars. Besides, the trail is so pleasant it makes the walk worthwhile.

Hobart Bluff.   Opposite: Soda Mountain's lookout.

56 Pilot Rock

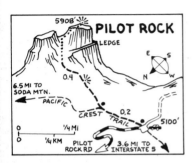

Moderate
1.2 miles round-trip
810 feet elevation gain
Open late May through November
Map: Siskiyou Pass (USGS)

Pioneers once looked to Pilot Rock to find the easiest pass across the Siskiyous from California to Oregon. Today Interstate 5 may miss this mountaintop Gibraltar by a few miles, but the landmark's sweeping viewpoints and dramatic columnar basalt cliffs are just a short hike away. The Pacific Crest Trail skirts the base of the crag. From there, agile hikers can tackle a very steep scramble route to the top.

Geologically, Pilot Rock is a remnant of a 30-million-year-old lava flow. Whenever basalt lava cools slowly enough, it fractures into hexagonal pillars perpendicular to the cooling surface. The sheer cliffs on Pilot Rock's south and west faces are entirely composed of these 6-sided stone columns. It's a popular practice spot for serious rock climbers.

The area also has a history as a wild hideout. Oregon's last grizzly bear, Old Reelfoot, was felled near the base of Pilot Rock in 1891. In 1923, after the D'Autremont brothers killed 3 men in a bungled train robbery at the end of the

Pilot Rock.

Mt. Shasta from Pilot Rock.

Siskiyou tunnel, they camped under a fallen log near Pilot Rock—and managed
to elude a 4-continent manhunt.

To find the trailhead from Interstate 5, take Mt. Ashland exit 6 and follow a
"Mt. Ashland" pointer onto old Highway 99, paralleling the freeway south.
After 0.7 mile go straight under the freeway, following the old highway another
1.2 miles. Beyond the Siskiyou summit 0.4 mile turn left onto Pilot Rock Road
40-2E-33. After 1 mile on this bumpy one-lane gravel road, ignore a Pacific Crest
Trail crossing. After another 1 mile, keep right past an old rock quarry. When
the road crests at the 2.8-mile mark, pull into an unmarked parking area on the
right.

From the parking area, walk across the road to find the PCT. This level path
passes small incense cedars, Jeffrey pines, and blue elderberry bushes. After 300
yards, fork to the right on a wide, unmarked path toward Pilot Rock. Wildflowers along this rocky, braided route include fuzzy mint, yellow Oregon grape,
gooseberry, wild rose, and strawberry.

If you're just out for an easy hike, declare victory at the base of Pilot Rock's
cliffs, where the view opens up across Shasta Valley to Mt. Shasta. If you're ready
for a scramble, head left up a dusty scree chute along the cliff's base. After
another 100 yards, you may be tempted to follow a ledge angling up to the
right—but that slippery route deadends at a cliff. Instead go straight up a very
steep chute, using hands and feet to climb past a tricky spot. Then continue
cautiously to the top. From here, the view of Mt. Shasta steals the show. Look
to its right to spot Mt. Eddy (with a patch of snow) and the jumbled, distant
peaks of the Trinity Alps. Close by to the west is Mt. Ashland, with the white
dot of a radar dome on top. If you face north you'll see I-5 snaking between
Ashland and Emigrant Lake, while Mt. McLoughlin's cone guards the horizon
to the right.

Ashland Creek

Easy (Lithia Park)
2.8 miles round-trip
260 feet elevation gain
Open all year
Use: hikers

Difficult (Ashland Loop Road)
28.5-mile loop
3180 feet elevation gain
Open April through November
Use: bicycles
Maps: Ashland, Mt. Ashland (USGS)

Before settling down to a play at Ashland's Shakespearean Festival, theater-goers often stretch their legs with a stroll through Lithia Park, a woodsy canyon with swan-filled lakes and the tumbling little falls of bouldery Ashland Creek. But there's room here for more than just a stroll. A hiking trail continues upstream 1.5 miles to a swimmable reservoir. And if you're on a mountain bike, you can tackle a challenging 28-mile loop that circles the entire Ashland Creek watershed to the edge of Mt. Ashland itself.

After gold rush miners found gold near Jacksonville in 1851, they found a different treasure here—water. By 1852, Southern Oregon's first lumber mill was using Ashland Creek's power to saw boards for the mines. In 1893, when the Chautauqua movement began bringing lectures and plays to rural areas of Oregon, the creek's campable woods became a regular stop. In 1908, the es-teemed architect who designed San Francisco's Golden Gate Park was hired to lay out the curving paths, pools, picnic lawns, and gardens of Lithia Park. In

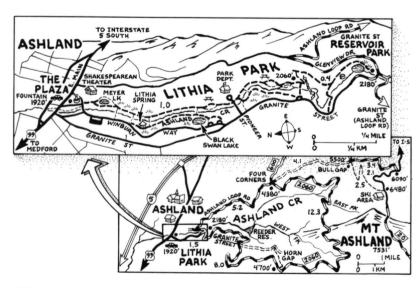

Ashland Creek.   Opposite: Swans in Lithia Park.

1935, local college professor Angus Bowmer converted an abandoned Chautauqua building into a replica of Shakespeare's open-air Globe theater and launched the tradition of performing plays beside the park.

To drive here from Medford, take Interstate 5 to Ashland exit 19 and follow signs 2.5 miles into town to a "Lithia Park" sign on the right. If you're driving here from the south, take Ashland exit 14 and turn left on Ashland Street for 2.7 miles. After crossing a bridge on the far side of downtown, turn left at a "City Center" pointer and curve back a block to the Plaza.

A fountain in the triangular Plaza serves up samples of Lithia Water—a bubbly, bitter combination of sodium, calcium, iron, bicarbonate, "and other healthful minerals" that emerges from natural springs up the canyon. After tasting this restorative drink, walk across Winburn Way to Lithia Park (see upper map). Footpaths meander everywhere here, but if you stick to the left-hand bank of Ashland Creek you'll follow increasingly quiet trails for a mile upstream, where a fence marks private land. To continue, take a small switchback trail uphill to the left. Then turn right on an upper path that leads 0.4 mile up to Granite Street Reservoir—a 200-foot-wide lake with a small sandy beach where swimming is allowed from 1pm-6pm if a lifeguard is on duty.

Hikers should turn back at the reservoir. To explore more of the park on the return trip, retrace your steps 0.2 mile, fork left across the creek, and then follow Lithia Park paths along the left-hand side of the creek where possible.

If you're tackling the 28.5-mile Ashland Loop Road by mountain bike (see upper map), remember that bicycles aren't allowed inside Lithia Park. So skirt the park, climbing from the Plaza along Winburn Way and then Granite Street for 1.5 miles to the Granite Street Reservoir, where the road turns to gravel. Turn left on Glenview Drive for 0.5 mile and then turn right on Ashland Loop Road for 4.7 grueling uphill miles to Four Corners, a 4-way road junction. (Many tourers skip the 2460-foot elevation gain of this first, difficult section by cajoling a friend to drive them to Four Corners in a shuttle car.) From there the loop route turns right, following gravel Road 2060 at a much easier, rolling up-and-down grade for 12.3 miles to Horn Gap, where a thrilling 9.5-mile downhill run shoots you back to the Plaza. To trim 1.1 mile off this final downhill stretch, take a marked shortcut trail from Horn Gap to a lower bend of the loop road.

The gravel, one-lane Ashland Loop Road is almost entirely within the watershed for Ashland's water supply, so camping, fires, off-road travel, and private vehicles are banned. Because Forest Service vehicles do use the road, however, bicyclists should keep an eye out for traffic.

58   Wagner Butte

Difficult
10.4 miles round-trip
2200 feet elevation gain
Open mid-June to mid-November
Maps: Siskiyou Peak, Talent (USGS)

The best view of the Ashland area isn't from Mt. Ashland, but rather from this lesser-known 7140-foot peak nearby. With binoculars, hikers atop Wagner Butte can pick out most of the individual buildings in Ashland, a vertical mile below. The demanding trail to the top offers other rewards as well—old-growth firs, an interesting landslide regrowing with wildflowers, a cold spring, sagebrush meadows, and an unusual quaking aspen grove.

The butte's name recalls Jacob Wagner, an early Talent settler who served in the 1853 Indian War and ran the flour mill at Ashland's Plaza. After a 1910 forest fire burned much of Ashland Creek's canyon and threatened Ashland, the Forest Service agreed to set up a fire lookout atop the butte. Staff made do with an open-air observation post until a cupola-style building could be built in 1923. Winter storms blew parts of the structure off the mountain. The building was finally replaced in 1961, but by then airplanes were taking over fire surveillance. Abandoned after just a few summers, the tower was intentionally burned by smokejumpers in 1972, leaving only foundation piers, melted glass, an iron railing, and the extraordinary view.

From Interstate 5 south of Medford, take Talent exit 21, head west on Valley View Drive for 0.4 mile, turn left on old Highway 99 for 0.4 mile, turn right on Rapp Road for 1.1 mile to a stop sign, and continue straight on Wagner Creek Road. After following this road for 2.5 paved miles and another 4 miles of one-lane gravel, veer left on Road 22 for the final 2 miles to the trailhead—marked by a trail sign on the left and a large parking area on the right.

The trail starts out climbing steeply for 0.9 mile through a second-growth forest with ponderosa pines, beargrass clumps, orange paintbrush, and speckled granite rocks. Then the path climbs more gently, traversing old Douglas fir woods with occasional meadowed slopes. The largest of these meadows is the Sheep Creek Slide, where a May 1983 thundershower sent 400,000 tons of soil, trees, and granite from Wagner Butte sliding 4 miles to the Little Applegate River. The Forest Service has since seeded the slide with grass and opened it to

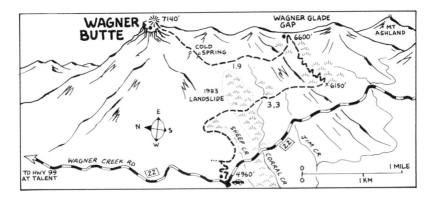

cattle grazing, but a wealth of native flowers also thrive here. In summer look for blue lupine, petalless brown coneflower, bulbous yellow sneezeweed, and sweet-smelling mint.

At the 2.4-mile mark the trail suddenly begins switchbacking up a steep sagebrush meadow for 0.9 mile to Wagner Glade Gap. Then the path ambles along for the final 1.9 miles, passing wind-gnarled mountain mahogany, white-barked quaking aspen, and a cold, piped spring before clambering up a stack of car-sized granite boulders to the summit. From here, the strip of urban development between Medford and Ashland looks like white confetti strewn along Interstate 5, with the dark squares of orchards on either hand. To the right stretch the forests of the Ashland's watershed valley, topped by Mt. Ashland and its white Doppler radar dome. Farther to the right look for snowy Mt. Shasta, the distant Marble Mountains, Red Buttes, flat-topped Preston Peak, and broad Grayback Mountain.

Ashland and Mt. McLoughlin from Wagner Butte.   Opposite: Sagebrush.

59 Mount Ashland Meadows

Moderate
6.8 miles round-trip
600 feet elevation gain
Open mid-June to mid-November
Use: hikers, horses
Map: Mt. Ashland (USGS)

There's no handier spot for a quick stroll through subalpine wildflower meadows than along the Pacific Crest Trail at Mt. Ashland. Starting from a paved road just 10 minutes from Interstate 5, this nearly level hike traverses the side of the Siskiyous' tallest peak, with views south to majestic Mt. Shasta. To make the trip even easier, you can shuttle a car or bicycle to Grouse Gap and hike this 3.4-mile section of the PCT one way.

To start, drive I-5 toward the Siskiyou summit and take Mt. Ashland exit 6. Following "Mt. Ashland Ski Area" pointers, parallel the freeway for 0.7 mile and turn right on Mt. Ashland Road 20. After 7.2 miles—and just beyond a huge entrance sign for the Rogue River National Forest—park at a pullout on the right. Then walk across the road to the trail, identified by a triangular Pacific Crest Trail marker on a tree.

The trail sets off through a forest of grand fir (with flat needles) and Shasta red fir (with upcurved needles). At the half-mile mark the path breaks into the first of 5 large meadows on the route. In July these slopes blaze with huge blue lupine, fuzy lavender mint, tall purple larkspur, and red paintbrush. By August the show includes yellow daisy-like Bigelow's sneezeweed, petalless brown coneflower, purple aster, white yarrow, and the tiny yellow trumpets of monkeyflower. Look for deer and even black bear in these fields during the early mornings and evenings.

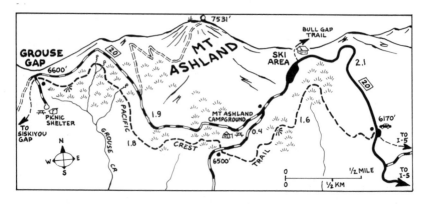

The Pacific Crest Trail near Grouse Gap. Opposite: Quaking aspen.

Beyond the second meadow the trail rounds a dry ridge where speckled granite bedrock has been weathered into rounded shapes. Yellow sulphur flower and 2 kinds of manzanita bushes grow here. After crossing a narrow gravel road at the 1.6-mile mark, you'll get your first views up to Mt. Ashland's summit. A white Doppler radar dome built atop the peak in 1995 resembles an eerie rising moon.

A mile beyond the gravel road the PCT enters a final, broad meadow that wraps around an alpine bowl to Grouse Gap. Joining the flower show here are a few surprising plant visitors from desert country—pungent sagebrush and white-barked quaking aspen. Turn back when the PCT crosses the road to the Grouse Gap picnic shelter. To bring a shuttle car (or bicycle) here from the first trailhead, simply drive 2 miles to Mt. Ashland ski area's huge parking lot and continue straight 2 miles on what becomes a narrow gravel road.

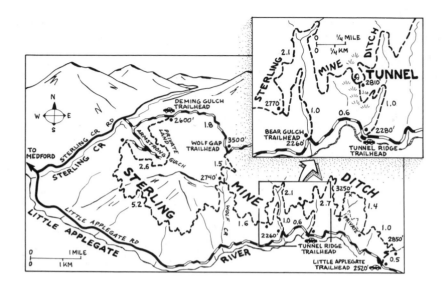

60   Sterling Ditch Tunnel

Easy (to tunnel)
4.7-mile loop
550 feet elevation gain
Open all year
Use: hikers, horses, bicycles
Map: Sterling Creek (USGS)

Difficult (entire trail)
17.1 miles one way
700 feet elevation gain

    Three years after the 1851 discovery of gold at Jacksonville, miners struck paydirt in Sterling Creek. After the easy ore was panned out, quite a bit of gold dust remained in the ancient river gravels stranded on dry slopes high above the creek. But how could miners get water up there to wash the gold loose?

    That question launched one of Southern Oregon's most remarkable engineering projects—a 26.5-mile ditch carrying water from the Little Applegate River to the Sterling Creek hills. Hand-dug by nearly 400 Chinese laborers in 1877, the 3-foot-deep ditch remained in use until the 1930s.

    Today the Sterling Mine ditch lives on as a 17.1-mile recreation trail winding through the oak grasslands and pine forests of the upper Applegate country. While much of this route is best appreciated from the saddle of a mountain bike or a horse, hikers can sample the trail's highlights on an easy, 4.7-mile loop to an explorable 100-foot tunnel where the ditch ducks through a ridge.

    To drive here from Medford, follow signs west to Jacksonville and continue straight on Highway 238 for 8 miles to the settlement of Ruch. (If you're coming from Grants Pass, follow signs south to Murphy and continue straight on Highway 238 to Ruch, between mileposts 25 and 26.) In Ruch, turn north at an "Upper Applegate" pointer for 2.9 miles. Then turn left on Little Applegate Road for 9.7 miles to the Tunnel Ridge Trailhead parking pullout on the right.

The trail climbs through oak woodlands mixed with Douglas fir, ponderosa pine, and Douglas maples. Expect wildflowers in May and June: pink clarkia, tall blue crown brodiaea, lilac-like deerbrush, and the pinkish, ball-shaped blooms of wild onion. Watch out for poison oak's triple leaflets. After 1 mile the path reaches the old ditch at the tunnel. Just 4 feet high, the tunnel is tight for adults but easy enough for children to hike through.

To continue the loop, walk left along the dry ditch's rim for 2.1 miles, passing huge madrone trees and a collapsed trestle along the way. Then turn left at a trail sign on a ridge end, take a 1-mile path down Bear Gulch to Little Applegate Road, and follow this gravel road left for 0.6 mile to your car.

If you're planning to tour the entire 17.1-mile ditch trail, you'll want to drive past the Tunnel Ridge Trailhead 1.8 miles to the Little Applegate Trailhead, marked by a sign on the left. From there, a trail climbs 0.5 mile before turning left on the ditch itself. After a mile, the ditch path detours up a hillside for 1.4 miles to avoid private land. Beyond that, it's 2.7 miles along the ditch to the tunnel and another 3.7 miles to Wolf Creek, where a side trail climbs 1.5 miles through a patch of old-growth Douglas fir to the Wolf Gap Trailhead. If you continue on the ditch, you'll contour 5.2 miles to an unmarked left-hand spur that leads to Armstrong Gulch Road. The main trail continues along the ditch another 2.6 miles (through private land and clearcuts) to trail's end at Deming Gulch Road.

To find the Deming Gulch Trailhead, drive back along Little Applegate Road to milepost 3, turn north on paved Sterling Creek Road for 2.1 miles, turn right on Armstrong Gulch Road 39-2-17 for 0.3 mile, and fork left on Deming Gulch Road for 0.7 mile to the ditch crossing where the trail begins. To find the Wolf Gap Trailhead, simply drive another 1.7 miles, keeping right at all junctions.

The Sterling Mine Ditch tunnel.   *Opposite: Giant madrone on the ditch's rim.*

61   Gin Lin Gold Mine

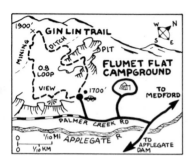

Easy
0.8-mile loop
200 feet elevation gain
Open all year
Map: brochure at trailhead

Tour the hydraulic gold mine of a Chinese pioneer on this short interpretive loop trail, conveniently located beside Flumet Flat Campground on the upper Applegate River.

Chinese nationals were not allowed to stake claims in the heydey of Jacksonville's 1851 gold rush. After the easy gold had been panned out of the Applegate River country, however, American miners sometimes sold their worn-out claims to men like Gin Lin—Chinese pioneers who realized that hard work and ingenuity might make these "worthless" claims surprisingly profitable.

Gin Lin relied on hydraulic mining. With this system it didn't matter that the placer miners had extracted all the gold from the riverbeds. Hydraulic miners looked instead at the hillsides, where ancient rivers deposited sand, gravel, and flakes of gold long ago. To wash the gold loose, the miners ditched water across the hillside from a high creek, funneled it into a long pipe to build up pressure, and sprayed it at the hill through a gigantic nozzle. Then they let the resulting slurry of dirt and sand run through a sluice box, where riffles on the bottom trapped the gold flakes.

Gin Lin opened his hydraulic mine here in 1881. His unexpected success made locals so jealous that they harassed Chinese miners with onerous taxes and discriminatory laws. Nonetheless, Gin Lin banked over $1 million in Jacksonville. Then he took his wealth back to China with him.

To find the trailhead from Medford, follow signs west to Jacksonville and continue straight on Highway 238 for 8 miles to the settlement of Ruch. (If you're coming from Grants Pass, follow signs south to Murphy and continue straight on Highway 238 to Ruch, between mileposts 25 and 26.) In Ruch, turn north at an "Upper Applegate" pointer for 9 miles. Beyond the Star Ranger Station 2.2 miles, fork to the right on paved Palmer Creek Road. After 0.8 mile, just past the campground, pull into the trailhead parking area on the right.

Pick up a brochure from the box at the trailhead. Then set out clockwise on the loop trail. A young forest of Douglas fir, ponderosa pine, madrone, and manzanita is struggling to grow over the devastation left by Gin Lin's mine more than a century ago. Hydraulic mining turns entire hillsides inside out, leaving scars that are slow to heal. The path passes former water ditches, a long pit excavated by Gin Lin's water jets, and vast tailing piles of cobbles before returning to the parking area.

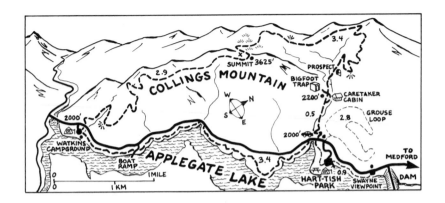

62 Collings Mountain

Easy (to Bigfoot Trap)
1 mile round-trip
200 feet elevation gain
Open all year
Use: hikers, horses, bicycles
Map: Carberry Creek (USGS)

Moderate (to Watkins Campground)
6.8 miles one way
1700 feet elevation gain
Open except in winter storms
Right: Bigfoot trap.

Hikers in this part of the Siskiyous have been reporting sightings of Bigfoot since 1895. So when a private research group resolved to catch the mythic apeman outright in 1973, they built their trap here.

Today an easy half-mile trail from Applegate Lake leads to the abandoned contraption and a ramshackle caretaker's cabin nearby. If you believe more in exercise than in Sasquatch, consider following the woodsy trail another 6.3 miles, across Collings Mountain to the far end of Applegate Lake's reservoir.

To drive here from Medford, follow signs west to Jacksonville and continue straight on Highway 238 for 8 miles to the settlement of Ruch. (From Grants Pass, follow signs south to Murphy and continue straight on Highway 238 to Ruch, between mileposts 25 and 26.) In Ruch, turn north at an "Upper Applegate" pointer for 15.9 miles. When you've driven 1 mile past Applegate Dam—and just 200 yards past the entrance to Hart-tish Park—look for a Collings Mountain Trail sign on the right by a guardrail. Park on the shoulder here.

The trail switchbacks down into a gulch and then follows a mossy creek up through a forest of Douglas fir, white pine, madrone, and bigleaf maple. Watch out for poison oak on the forest floor. After 0.5 mile the path splits around the dilapidated caretaker's cabin, a shake-sided 9-by-12-foot shack. From here, a spur trail to the left climbs to the Bigfoot trap, a formidable 10-foot-tall cell with thick walls and a guillotine-like steel door. Poison oak is thick here.

If you decide to continue, return to the main trail and follow it up the canyon 0.3 mile to a prospector's adit—a short tunnel built to check for ore. Beyond this the trail climbs steeply up a hillside of scrub oak and madrone, with glimpses out to Applegate Lake. Then the path follows a broad ridge 2 miles before switchbacking past a grassy opening that is Collings Mountain's summit. Although this mountaintop lacks views, the open woods host a surprising variety of June wildflowers: beargrass plumes, fuzzy white lupine, trumpet-shaped purple penstemon, tall crown brodiaea, pink clarkia, and white iris.

Beyond the summit, the trail descends 2.9 miles through the woods before crossing the paved road to the Watkins Campground parking area. Ideally you'll have left a shuttle car or bicycle here for a quick ride back to the starting trailhead. If not, walk to the far left end of the parking lot and take the Da-Ku-Be-Te-De Trail, a path that parallels the reservoir's shore (and the road) for 3.4 miles back to your car.

63   Applegate Lake

Easy (around peninsula)
6.4-mile loop
400 feet elevation gain
Open all year
Use: hikers, bicycles
Map: Applegate Lake brochure (USFS)

Difficult (around entire lake)
17.8-mile loop
300 feet elevation gain

This reservoir is wreathed not only by the forests of the Siskiyou Mountains, but also by a convenient network of trails. Admittedly, low water levels expose the brown bathtub ring typical of reservoirs, but noisy speedboats are banned and the overall setting remains fairly wild. Expect to see fish-hunting osprey, wildflowers in grassy openings, and glimpses of Siskiyou peaks. For an easy loop hike along the shore, explore the trails on a peninsula beside French Gulch. For a longer, level bike ride, circle the entire lake on a 17.8-mile route that's two-thirds on trail and one-third on paved roads.

To find the trailhead from Medford, follow signs west to Jacksonville and continue straight on Highway 238 for 8 miles to the settlement of Ruch. (From Grants Pass, follow signs south to Murphy and continue straight on Highway 238 to Ruch, between mileposts 25 and 26.) In Ruch, turn north at an "Upper Applegate" pointer for 14.9 miles. Then turn left across Applegate Dam for 1.2 miles to the French Gulch Trailhead parking area on the right.

The trail passes the walk-in campsites of French Gulch Campground and follows the lakeshore through a patch of June wildflowers. Look for pink clarkia, fuzzy white lupine, blue crown brodiaea, and the 6-petaled, yellow-and-purple-striped blooms of pretty face. Then the path sallies into the open, second-growth woods that ring the lake with Douglas fir, white pine, and madrone.

Applegate Lake.   Opposite: Pink stringflower.

Keep an eye out for the triple leaflets of poison oak.

After 0.7 mile the trail crosses the primitive Latgawa Cove Campground, accessible only by boat, bike, or foot. Just beyond, at a 5-way junction, ignore a "Viewpoint" pointer to the right that leads to a disappointing deadend. You'll find better views by simply continuing straight on the Payette Trail along the shore. In another 0.8 mile, at the tip of the peninsula, the Payette Trail becomes an old road. For much of the next 2.4 miles the path follows this abandoned chromium mining track around the lake, passing prospects of green ore. Then, to complete the peninsula loop, turn left on the Osprey Trail. This path climbs through an oak grassland 0.7 mile to the parking lot at the Dagelma Trailhead. Here, veer left onto the Calsh Trail for 0.7 mile. Then turn right on the Payette Trail to return to your car at French Gulch.

If you'd like to circle the entire lake on a mountain bike, start out from the

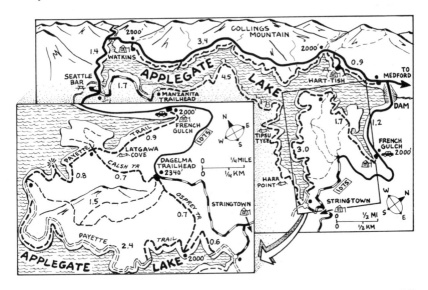

French Gulch Trailhead as described above, but follow the Payette Trail a total of 9.2 miles. When the trail ends at the Manzanita Trailhead, continue 1.7 miles on a gravel road to the Seattle Bar picnic area. Keep right for 1.4 miles on pavement, but then pull into Watkins Campground, where the Da-Ku-Be-Te-De Trail begins. Follow this path, wedged between the lakeshore and the paved road, for 4.3 miles to its end at the Swayne Viewpoint parking pullout just before Applegate Dam. Then cross the dam and follow the paved road 1.2 miles back to your car.

64   Stein Butte

Difficult
9.4 miles round-trip
2400 feet elevation gain
Open April through December
Use: hikers, horses, bikes
Map: Squaw Lakes (USGS)

Motorcycle trails rarely appeal to other users, but the well-built path to this lookout site above Applegate Lake is an exception. After a strenuous climb through the woods, the path traces a ridgecrest with strange knobcone pines and birds-eye views of a dozen Siskiyou peaks.

From Medford, follow signs west to Jacksonville and continue straight on Highway 238 for 8 miles to the settlement of Ruch. (From Grants Pass, follow signs south to Murphy and continue straight on Highway 238 to Ruch, between mileposts 25 and 26.) In Ruch, turn north at an "Upper Applegate" pointer for 18.8 miles. When you reach a T-shaped junction at the far end of Applegate Lake, turn left on Applegate Road for 0.9 mile to the Seattle Bar Trailhead and picnic area on the right. The entire driving route is paved.

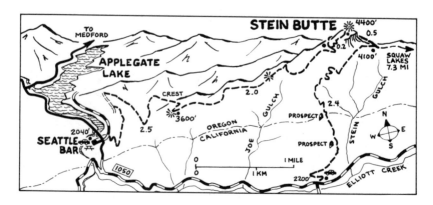

Applegate Lake from Stein Butte.   Opposite: Dead knobcone pine.

From the parking area, walk across a lawn and duck under the highway bridge to find the trail. The path promptly crosses a gravel road and launches uphill at a steady grade through a dry forest. Trees here include Douglas fir, long-needled Jeffrey pine, madrone (with red, peeling bark), black oak (with large, pointy leaves), and canyon live oak (with small, pointy leaves). Also watch for poison oak bushes (with leaflets in threes).

After a wearying 2.5 miles the path finally gains the ridgecrest. Look here for knobcone pine—an odd, spindly species with knobby cones clustered on its trunk. You're also likely to see black bear droppings. Bears like to eat the tough berries of the 12-foot-tall manzanita bushes on this ridge—and the manzanita prospers because its berries only sprout after being passed by a bear.

A scenic 2-mile walk along the ridge brings you to an 0.2-mile spur trail to Stein Butte's rocky summit. This final trail segment is open to hikers only.

The Civilian Conservation Corps built a lookout tower atop Stein Butte in 1936, but only the foundation and the view remain. On the horizon to the left of Applegate Lake rises the broad hump of Grayback Mountain. A string of rocky Siskiyou peaks extends to its left. The reddest and nearest of these is Red Buttes. Hovering farther to the east are the Cascade snowpeaks, Mt. Shasta and Mt. McLoughlin.

Other Hiking Options

A shorter, but steeper and less scenic route up Stein Butte starts from Elliott Creek Road 1050. This path passes a couple of 100-foot prospecting tunnels near the Oregon-California border. If you can arrange a short car shuttle, you can hike both trails one way. To find the other trailhead from Seattle Bar, continue on Applegate Road for 0.3 mile to a big gravel intersection. Then go straight on Road 1050 for 2.8 miles to a small sign on the left for the New London Trail.

65   Red Buttes

Moderate (to Lilypad Lake)
8.2 miles round-trip
1440 feet elevation gain
Open June to mid-November
Use: hikers, horses
Map: Red Buttes Wilderness (USFS)

Lakes are relatively rare in the Siskiyous, but the Pacific Crest Trail passes near 2 as it skirts this rocky, double-topped mountain—the ruddy landmark of the Red Buttes Wilderness.

The buttes are made of peridotite, a red, iron-rich rock created when seafloor sand and mud are baked together inside the earth. The 200 million-year-old rock tells a lot about the history of this range. The Siskiyous formed as the North American continent crunched westward over the Pacific plate, scraping off seafloor sediments and volcanic island chains like cake batter on a spatula.

Patches of white marble on the side of Red Buttes are the remains of seashells, cooked and contorted by pressure. Outcrops of greasy-looking, greenish-black serpentinite rock along the Pacific Crest Trail are the lubricant that formed between the sliding plates of continent and seafloor. An old road paralleling the PCT was built by miners searching for gold, chromium, and other heavy metals churned up by the titanic collision of crustal plates.

To find the trailhead from Medford, follow signs west to Jacksonville and continue straight on Highway 238 for 8 miles to the settlement of Ruch. (From Grants Pass, follow signs south to Murphy and continue straight on Highway 238 to Ruch, between mileposts 25 and 26.) In Ruch, turn north at an "Upper Applegate" pointer for 18.8 miles. When you reach a T-shaped junction at the far end of Applegate Lake, turn left on Applegate Road for 1.2 miles to a big gravel intersection. Continue straight on one-lane Road 1050 for 0.9 mile and then fork to the right on Road 1055. Follow this narrow gravel road for 10 miles, climbing to Cook and Green Pass and a trailhead parking area on the right.

Two trails start here, but head left on the PCT up a forested ridge. The shady woods of fir and tanoak soon give way to a rocky red scrubland of manzanita brush and beargrass with a few incense cedars and white pines. Expect views not only of Red Buttes, but also south across the Klamath River's dark canyon to the Marble Mountains and Mt. Shasta's ghostly white cone.

After 2.6 miles, at a trail junction in a brushy pass, detour 100 yards to the right to a spectacular viewpoint of green Echo Lake backed by red cliffs. If you have the time, scramble another 0.5 mile down this steep, rocky side trail to Echo Lake's shore and a wildflower meadow with blue gentians.

Then return to the PCT and continue 1.5 miles to another trail junction in Lilypad Lake's scenic alpine bowl. This smaller, shallower pond is packed with yellow pond lilies. The surrounding meadow has mint, yellow sneezeweed,

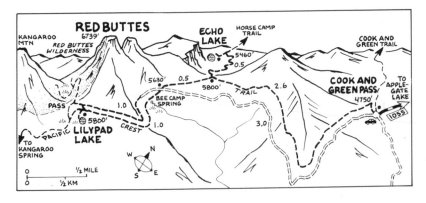

coneflower, and unfortunately, cow pies. As in the Swiss Alps, the background music here is often the tinny clank of cowbells.

From the junction near the lake, turn uphill to the right 100 yards to find the end of the old mining road in a pass overlooking much of the Red Buttes Wilderness. To return on a loop, follow this abandoned roadbed back 1 mile to a barricade near Bee Camp Spring. High clearance vehicles can drive to this point from Cook and Green Pass, but seldom do. Walking this drivable portion of the old road is no fun either, so angle left on the PCT for the final 3.1 miles back to Cook and Green Pass.

Lilypad Lake.   Opposite: Red Buttes from the Pacific Crest Trail.

66

Frog Pond

Easy (to Middle Fork Applegate bridge)
2.4 miles round-trip
400 feet elevation gain
Open except in winter storms
Use: hikers, horses
Map: Red Buttes Wilderness (USFS)

Moderate (to Frog Pond)
7.9-mile loop
1800 feet elevation gain
Open mid-May through November

The first of these 2 hikes is an easy stroll along the Middle Fork Applegate River to a swimmable pool, some log cabin ruins, and a scenic footbridge in an old-growth forest. The second, steeper trail loops past Frog Pond through subalpine Wilderness meadows. Backpackers can connect the 2 paths for a more challenging tour.

To drive here from Medford, follow signs west to Jacksonville and continue straight on Highway 238 for 8 miles to the settlement of Ruch. (From Grants Pass, follow signs south to Murphy and continue straight on Highway 238 to Ruch, between mileposts 25 and 26.) In Ruch, turn north at an "Upper Applegate" pointer for 18.8 miles. At the far end of Applegate Lake, turn left on Applegate Road for 1.2 miles to a big gravel intersection. Then turn right on one-lane gravel Road 1040 for 5.1 miles to a signed junction.

From this junction you can find the easy riverside trail by simply driving straight on Road 1035 for 300 yards to the Middle Fork Trailhead on the left. To drive to the upper Frog Pond Loop Trailhead instead, turn left at the junction and continue 6.9 miles on narrow Road 1040 to the *third* trailhead on the left, 0.2 mile after the road splashes across an easy ford in Frog Pond Gulch.

If you're setting out on the Middle Fork Trail, you'll start by tracing a canyon

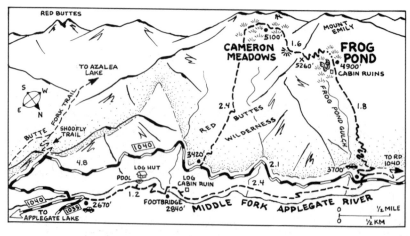

Middle Fork Applegate River.   Opposite: Dragonfly at Frog Pond.

slope above the river. Douglas firs grow up to 4 feet thick in these shady woods. Vine maple and alder dapple the riverbank with bright green. Tanoak and madrone strew the drier slopes with crackly leaves. After 0.6 mile a steep spur to the left scrambles 100 feet down to a chilly but swimmable green river pool below a little waterfall, with a primitive log hut on the far shore.

After another 0.6 mile the Middle Fork Trail crosses the river on an 80-foot bridge carved from a single log. Beside the bridge is a small gravel beach among riverside boulders. If you've brought children, this makes a good turnaround point—although you might want to continue 200 yards up the trail to explore a ruined log cabin on the left. Beyond this point the Middle Fork Trail mostly stays out of sight of the river for 2.4 miles to Road 1040 and the upper Frog Pond Loop Trailhead.

A pond may not sound like a spectacular Wilderness destination, but the Frog Pond Loop is actually one of the prettiest tours in the Red Buttes area. Unfortunately, it's not quite a loop. The path has 2 trailheads on Road 1040. To connect them you'll end up walking on the road 2.1 miles or shuttling a car.

Frog Pond.

Start the Frog Pond Loop from the upper trailhead. This wide spot in Road 1040 has a message board on the left reminding visitors that groups in this Wilderness are limited to 8 persons. Hike past this sign and keep left on a steep, uphill path through the woods. Look here for pink rhododendron blooms, foot-long sugarpine cones, and the dusty blue berries of Oregon grape. Also notice witch's broom, an odd tree affliction that has channeled the growth of some local Douglas firs into clumps of greenery.

After 1.8 miles the path enters a meadow of mint and asters at Frog Pond, a sinuous pool with lilypads, water boatmen, and dragonflies. Nearby is the ruin of a shelter built among the trunks of 8 large incense cedars. The trail peters out here, but angle to the right to the meadow's far upper end. There, a large "X" sign on a tree marks the resumption of the path. The trail then switchbacks over a ridge, ambles past viewpoints of Red Buttes and distant Mt. McLoughlin, descends through Cameron Meadows' grassy alpine bowl, and dives down a broad wooded ridge to Road 1040. If you haven't left a shuttle car at this lower trailhead, walk left 2.1 miles to complete a 7.9-mile loop.

67   Azalea Lake

Difficult
13 miles round-trip
2030 feet elevation gain
Open mid-June to mid-November
Use: hikers, horses
Map: Red Buttes Wilderness (USFS)

Showy pink mountain azaleas and white beargrass plumes fringe this lake deep in the Red Buttes Wilderness. The trail to the lake passes a Siskiyou crest viewpoint overlooking green Phantom Meadow and groves of 2 odd trees—knobcone pine and Brewer's weeping spruce.

To find the trail from Grants Pass, follow signs south 6.5 miles to Murphy and continue straight on Highway 238 another 11.5 miles to a green steel bridge just before the town of Applegate. (From Medford, follow signs for Jacksonville 5 miles west and continue straight on Highway 238 to the bridge at milepost 18.) At the Applegate bridge turn south on Thompson Creek Road for 11.9 miles of pavement and another 2.8 miles of gravel. Then, following "Azalea Lake" or "Fir Glade" pointers, turn right across a bridge, immediately fork left on Road 1030 for 5.1 miles, turn left on Road 400 (which becomes Road 1040) for 4.7 miles, and finally fork right onto rough, rocky Road 800 for 0.6 mile to a turnaround.

The trail starts in a second-growth fir forest with incense cedar, tanoak brush, and hazel. In the first 1.3 miles you'll pass a 40-foot pond, the California line, and several small meadows of brown coneflower, yellow sneezeweed, and grazing cows. Then the path switchbacks down beside Fir Glade, a larger meadow that also hosts blue lupine and red paintbrush. Next the path gradual-

Azalea Lake.   Opposite: Phantom Meadow.

ly climbs through sparsely wooded brushfields for 2.7 miles to a rocky pass above Phantom Meadow. Views here extend west to square-topped, snowy Preston Peak. Nearly all of the trees on the left side of this pass are Brewer's weeping spruces, whose cones dangle from strangely drooping branch tips. The trees on the drier, right-hand side of the pass are even odder—they're knobcone pines, whose cones cluster along skinny trunks like bumps on flagpoles.

After crossing a second pass the path switchbacks down to a 0.6-mile loop trail through the lodgepole pine and white pine around shallow Azalea Lake. Camping and fires are banned within this lakeshore loop. Backpackers are supposed to tent in the sloping area west of the loop, while equestrian campers are directed to the flatter area east of the loop.

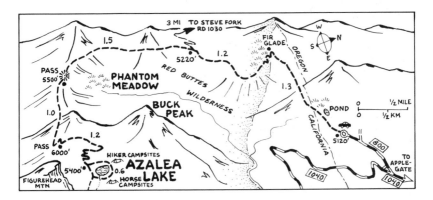

68 Sucker Creek Gap

Moderate
6.8 miles round-trip
1080 feet elevation gain
Open early June to mid-November
Use: hikers, horses
Map: Red Buttes Wilderness (USFS)

On one side of Sucker Creek Gap, a rustic shelter stands in a meadow ringed with huge incense cedars. On the other side, an unmarked trail leads to a hidden lilypad lake in a cliff-rimmed cirque valley.

This corner of the Red Buttes Wilderness won its gullible-sounding name in the 1850s gold rush, when miners from Illinois (proudly known to Midwesterners as the "Sucker State") christened both the Illinois River and its tributary Sucker Creek.

To drive here from Grants Pass, follow signs south 6.5 miles to Murphy and continue straight on Highway 238 another 11.5 miles to a green steel bridge just before the town of Applegate. (If you're coming from Medford, follow signs for Jacksonville 5 miles west and continue straight on Highway 238 to the bridge at milepost 18.) At the Applegate bridge turn south on Thompson Creek Road for 11.9 miles of pavement and another 2.8 miles of gravel. Then, following "Steve Fork Trail" pointers, turn right across a bridge and immediately fork left onto Road 1030 for 11 miles to a large trailhead parking lot at road's end.

Along the start of the trail, look on the floor of the fir forest for the tiny, shiny leaves of twinflower—a delicate double-belled bloom that opens in July. The much larger, irregular three-part leaves along the trail are vanilla leaf, which

Sucker Creek Shelter.   Above: Meadow at Sucker Creek Shelter.

Incense cedars at Sucker Creek Shelter.

puts up a little stalk of tiny white flowers. Its roots were sometimes mashed by pioneers as a vanilla substitute. Keep right at a fork, climbing very gradually to drier slopes with big sugarpines, beargrass, and views south to Buck Peak.

After crossing 2 side creeks (which are often dry) and switching back to the left through open pine woods, the trail suddenly turns to the right at the 2.8-mile mark. A rock cairn on a log here marks a very faint trail that goes straight instead. If you explore this unmaintained path 200 yards you'll find a lovely, secret lake, wedged between cliffs and a bunchgrass meadow with purple aster and yellow sneezeweed. Like nearly all lakes in the Siskiyous, this one fills a cirque—a high, bowl-shaped valley once carved at the head of a glacier's grinding river of ice. Siskiyou cirque lakes are small because only small glaciers formed in these sunny mountains during the Ice Age.

Beyond the turnoff for the cirque lake, the main trail climbs 0.3 mile over a low ridge to a 4-way trail junction in grassy Sucker Creek Gap. Veer slightly left to stay on the Sucker Creek Trail. After following this path just 100 yards, however, take a rocky side trail down to the right. This trail scrambles down 200 yards past gigantic 7-foot-thick incense cedars to a grassy meadow and the leaky but scenic shake-roofed Sucker Creek Shelter—a worthy turnaround point.

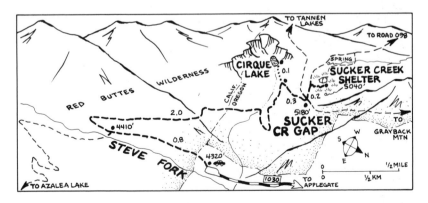

Upper Miller Lake and Grayback Mountain.   Opposite: Miller Lake.

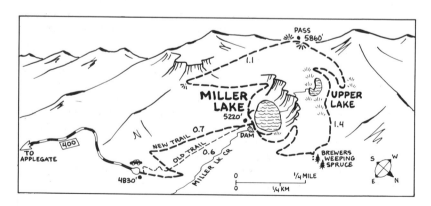

69 Miller Lake

Easy (to Miller Lake)
1.4-miles round-trip
390 feet elevation gain
Open June to mid-November
Use: hikers, horses
Map: Grayback Mountain (USGS)

Moderate (to upper lake)
3.9-mile loop
1030 feet elevation gain

This very deep mountain lake provides an easy destination for anglers and swimmers, but hikers will particularly appreciate a little-known loop trail that prowls up to a viewpoint in a pass and a rarely visited, shallow upper lake.

To find the trailhead from Grants Pass, follow signs south 6.5 miles to Murphy and continue straight on Highway 238 another 11.5 miles to a green steel bridge just before the town of Applegate. (From Medford, follow signs for Jacksonville 5 miles west and continue straight on Highway 238 to the bridge at milepost 18.) At the Applegate bridge turn south on Thompson Creek Road for 11.9 miles. Where pavement ends at a pass, veer right at a "Miller Lake Trail" pointer onto Road 1020 for 4.5 miles to a junction, and then go straight on Road 400 for 3.5 miles to its end.

Set out straight on a new, well-graded trail that climbs to Miller Lake in long switchbacks. Along the way you'll cross the old trail—a steep, abandoned roadbed that can be explored on the return trip, if you like. Both routes climb through a hillside forest of Douglas fir (up to 5 feet thick) and prim Shasta red fir. Also notice beargrass plumes, tanoak bushes, and blue huckleberries. The trails join just before an earthen dam that long ago converted this once-modest pool into a deep, steep-banked green lake.

When you cross the dam, the obvious lakeshore path simply deadends at a grassy campsite. To find the loop trail, walk 50 feet past the gully that serves as spillway and fork up to the right into the forest. This well-graded but infrequently maintained path switchbacks twice as it climbs a broad, wooded ridgecrest above the lake. Expect to step over a few logs along the way. A short side path to the right leads to a grove of unusually large Brewers' weeping spruce, an odd tree with tiny, spiny cones on the tips of droopy branches. Continuing up the loop trail, you'll pass the shallow upper lake. Full of lilypads and surrounded by a field of yellow sneezeweed, this shallow pool is caught halfway through the normal, slow transition from mountain lake to meadow.

Just beyond the upper lake, watch closely to follow the trail around 2 faint switchbacks as it climbs to an open pass. To the right of this rocky viewpoint, distant Mt. Shasta floats above the Siskiyou crest. To the left, the meadowed pyramid of Grayback Mountain rises above a checkerboard of clearcuts. Beyond the pass, the loop trail descends in 2 long switchbacks to the Miller Lake dam and the route back to your car.

Grayback Mountain

Moderate (to Krause log cabin)
2.6 miles round-trip
1100 feet elevation gain
Open mid-June to early November
Use: hikers, horses
Map: Grayback Mountain (USGS)

Difficult (to summit)
4.8 miles round-trip
1800 feet elevation gain

Two historic cabins and a glorious wildflower meadow adorn the slopes of this landmark peak. The steep trail ends short of the summit, but adventurers can scramble on to the panoramic view at the top.

This mountain may look like the broad, gray back of a sleeping elephant when viewed from the Applegate Valley, but it was named for a much smaller animal. Miners in Southern Oregon's 1850s gold rush christened the peak after their worst bugaboo—the omnipresent, itchy lice commonly called graybacks.

To drive here from Grants Pass, follow signs south 6.5 miles to Murphy and continue straight on Highway 238 another 11.5 miles to a green steel bridge just before the town of Applegate. (From Medford, follow signs for Jacksonville 5 miles west and continue straight on Highway 238 to the bridge at milepost 18.) At the Applegate bridge turn south on Thompson Creek Road for 11.9 miles. Where pavement ends at a pass, turn sharply to the right past an "O'Brien Creek Trail" sign onto Road 1005. Follow this gravel road 2.3 miles to the lower O'Brien Creek trailhead on the left. Stop here if you're towing a horse trailer; otherwise drive uphill another 1.7 miles to the road's rocky end at an upper trailhead.

From the upper trailhead, the path climbs along an ancient roadbed for 0.3 mile before charging steeply up through dense, cool woods of old-growth Douglas fir and incense cedar. At the upper end of a gully of wildflowers the path crosses O'Brien Creek. Keep left at a fork for the level path to the shelters.

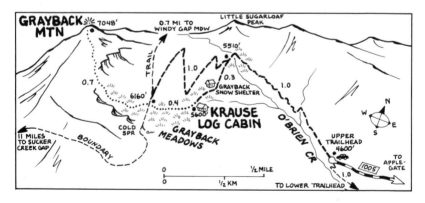

Krause Cabin and Grayback Meadows.   *Opposite: Grayback Mountain's summit.*

The first structure you'll see is Grayback Snow Shelter, a funky 10-by-14-foot cabin with a wood floor, rustic table, stump chairs, 3 glassless windows, and a massive unlocked door. The stove doesn't work, but the roof is tight and the loft has bunks for two. If you hike onward 200 yards, contouring into Grayback Meadows' purple aster, goldenrod, yellow sneezeweed, orange paintbrush, and big-leaved hellebore, you'll come to Krause Cabin. This 10-by-16-foot log structure has sagging floorboards, a rickety stove, and a leaky shake roof. But the view here is stupendous—up the meadow to Grayback Mountain and north to Little Sugarloaf Peak. Notes at this historic log cabin record that mid-April, 1992 visitors found no snow here, but that they could snowboard on a 3-foot pack down from the summit. Each year is different.

This meadow makes a good turnaround point, but if you're looking for views, get ready to scramble. From the log cabin, hike straight up Grayback Meadows for 0.4 mile, cross the Boundary Trail, and continue straight up, scrambling through a gap in the cliffs. Then follow the ridgecrest, pushing your way through the manzanita brush for 0.2 mile up to the rocky summit of Grayback Mountain. Here, a 360-degree panorama encompasses a startling shiny swath of the Pacific Ocean near Crestent City. To the right is the woodsy Illinois Valley with the peaked ridges of the Kalmiopsis Wilderness beyond. To the left are the spires of the Siskiyou Wilderness (with M-shaped Preston Peak the tallest). Farther left are Red Buttes, snowy Mt. Shasta, Mt. McLoughlin's cone, Crater Lake's rim (above Medford), Mt. Thielsen's spire, and the Applegate Valley's ranches.

Western
Siskiyous

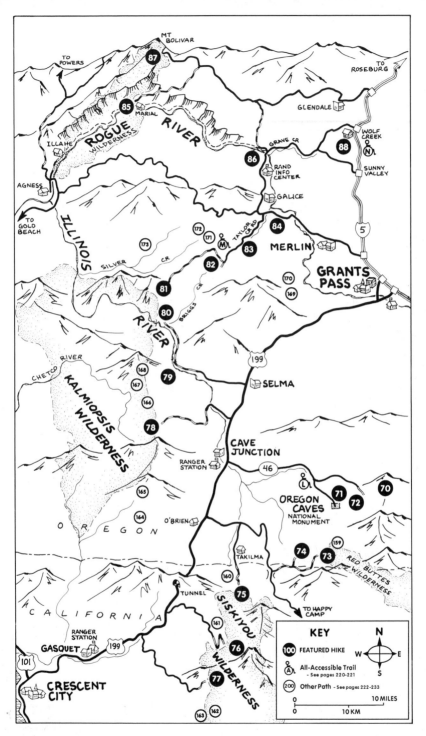

Opposite: Devils Punchbowl Lake (Hike #77).

71 Oregon Caves

Easy (cave tour)
1-mile loop
250 feet elevation gain
Open except Christmas and Thanksgiving
Map: Oregon Caves (USGS)

Moderate (to Big Tree)
3.8-mile loop
1120 feet elevation gain
Open late April to early December

Poet Joaquin Miller's praise of the "great Marble Halls of Oregon" helped win National Monument status for Oregon Caves in 1909. Visitors today can join a guided tour for about $6, exploring narrow passageways and stairs to hidden rooms of cave formations. For a free hike above ground try the Big Tree Loop, crossing a forested Siskiyou mountainside to one of Oregon's largest Douglas firs. Pets are banned on all park trails.

The caves' marble formed when this part of the Siskiyou Mountains was scraped up from the Pacific seafloor 190 million years ago and compressed by the advancing North American continent. At first the land here was so wet that percolating ground water dissolved parts of the marble, forming pockets. When the land rose and the caves drained, dripping water gradually deposited calcite inside—much as a dripping faucet can stain a sink. Drips in the cave first form "soda straws," thin tubes hanging from the ceiling. When the tubes get plugged, water runs down the outsides and forms thicker stalactites. If the drip is fast, it carries dissolved calcite to the cave floor to form a stalagmite.

Hunter Elijah Davidson discovered the cave in 1874 when his dog chased a bear into the entrance. Davidson lit matches to follow. When the last match died he found his way out of the darkness only by crawling along a cave-floor stream. After word spread of his find, early entrepreneurs damaged the cave by encouraging visitors to break off stalactites as samples, sign their names on the walls, and hug the white dripstone columns, darkening the rock. A cave operator who took over in the 1920s hoked up his tours with ghost stories, colored lights, and hidden growling men in lion skins—the origin of the Grants Pass caveman mascot. To preserve the cave, the National Park Service now urges visitors not to touch anything in the cave. Lighting is dim and bleach is sprayed on the dripstone to discourage the moss and algae that grow near artificial lights.

To drive here, take Highway 199 south from Grants Pass 29 miles (or north from Crescent City 57 miles) to Cave Junction and follow "Oregon Caves" pointers west on Highway 46 for 20 miles to a turnaround. Unless you have reservations at the lodge (for rates, call 541-592-3400), park here and walk up the road 0.2 mile to the gift shop and cave entrance on the left.

Cave tours leave at 9:30am, 11:30am, 1pm, 2:30pm, and 4pm in winter (October through April). In summer, tours are supposed to start whenever 16 people sign up, but on busy weekends you may have to wait an hour. Children under 6 must be 42 inches tall to join the tour. You don't need a flashlight, but

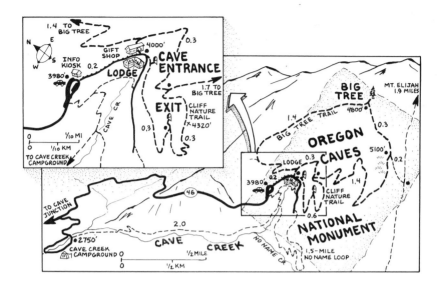

because it averages 41 degrees Fahrenheit in the cave year-round, you'll want warm clothes. The 75-minute tour climbs 0.3 mile through the cave to an upper exit. From there the quickest return route is a 0.3-mile trail to the right.

If you'd rather hike to Big Tree, walk through the gift shop's breezeway arch and fork to the left. This path climbs a slope of marble outcroppings and manzanita bushes before entering old-growth fir woods with rhododendron, vanilla leaf, and incense cedar. Expect lots of golden-mantled ground squirrels, chipmunks, and dark blue Stellars jays with pointy black topknots. At Big Tree (a Douglas fir over 13 feet in diameter) the loop trail switchbacks up to the right. Keeping right at junctions you'll pass high meadows of aromatic mint, orange paintbrush, purple larkspur, and cow parsnip before descending through a grove of Port Orford cedars to the gift shop by the cave entrance.

Other Hiking Options

For a longer hike, either start 2 miles below the cave at Cave Creek Campground (see map), or continue up from the Big Tree Loop 2.1 miles to Mt. Elijah (see Hike #72).

Big Tree.   Opposite: Entrance to Oregon Caves.

72   Mount Elijah

Moderate
4.1-mile loop
900 feet elevation gain
Open mid-June to mid-November
Use: hikers, horses, bicycles
Maps: Grayback Mountain, Oregon
       Caves (USGS)

This relatively easy loop crosses the panoramic top of a Siskiyou peak named for Elijah Davidson, discoverer of the nearby Oregon Caves. A short side trip through a wildflower meadow leads to shallow Bigelow Lake, full of lilypads. The loop ends with a 0.8-mile walk along a road, but with luck some kind soul in your group will volunteer to hike ahead and fetch the car.

Drive Highway 199 south from Grants Pass 29 miles (or north from Crescent City 57 miles) to Cave Junction and follow "Oregon Caves" pointers east on Highway 46 for 12 miles. Just 0.3 mile past Grayback Campground, veer left onto Grayback Road and follow this narrow, paved road for 7 miles. Then turn right on gravel Bigelow Lakes Road 070 for 3.3 miles and turn left to keep on Road 070 past an "End Maintenance" sign. After another 0.6 mile fork to the right on an unmarked, rough road for 1.4 miles to a trailhead sign on the left. Park by a horse hitching rack on the right.

The path climbs through a fir grove with wildflower meadows on either hand. In late June and July these subalpine fields brim with blue daisy-like fleabane, sweet mint, yellow sulphur flower, brown coneflower, orange paintbrush, and blue lupine. Unfortunately, cows graze here from late July to early October.

After 0.5 mile, when the main trail switchbacks left into the woods, go straight on a fainter path into the meadow. This side path soon peters out, but keep crossing the meadow, heading slightly to the right and slightly downhill for 0.2

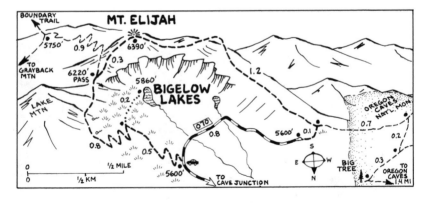

The larger of the 2 Bigelow Lakes.   Opposite: Mt. Elijah's summit.

mile to find the larger of the 2 Bigelow Lakes. Full of yellow pond lilies and polliwogs, the pond would be a more attractive goal if it weren't so frequently visited by cattle.

Return to the main trail, follow it 0.8 mile to a pass, and keep right for 0.3 mile to the rock-strewn summit of Mt. Elijah. The view here encompasses all the Siskiyou peaks from Red Buttes (a double hump on the eastern horizon) to Preston Peak (to the south, with snow patches). Across the Illinois Valley rise the dark ridges of the Kalmiopsis Wilderness.

After absorbing the view, continue on the loop trail down a ridge 1.2 miles to a junction, turn right for 250 yards to the end of Road 070, and—if you are the kind soul who volunteers—walk along the road 0.8 mile to fetch the car.

Tannen Lake.   Below: Tanoak acorns.

73   Tannen Lakes

Easy (to the lakes)
2.6 miles round-trip
350 feet elevation gain
Open late May through November
Use: hikers, horses
Map: Oregon Caves (USGS)

Difficult (to Tannen Mountain)
8.3-mile loop
1700 feet elevation gain
Open early June to mid-November

This pair of green mountain lakes set in side-by-side, cliff-rimmed cirques makes a clever destination for hikers with children. If the kids seem tired when they reach lake number one, declare victory there. If they're still antsy, push on to the huckleberry fields at lake number two. And if you're hiking without children, the ticket is to continue up Tannen Mountain for a birds-eye view of the lakes and the whole Siskiyou range.

To start, drive Highway 199 south of Grants Pass 35.5 miles (or north of Crescent City 50.5 miles). South of Cave Junction 7 miles, between mileposts 35 and 36, turn east on Waldo Road. Follow this route 5 miles to a crossroads, go straight on paved Happy Camp Road for 12.5 miles to a high pass, and turn left at a "Tannen Lakes" pointer onto a one-lane gravel road. Watch your odometer from here, because junctions are poorly marked. After 0.8 mile, fork to the right. After another 0.6 mile keep left at a fork. At a junction 0.4 mile farther on, turn right. In another 2.4 miles ignore the Bolan Campground turnoff, and instead keep right for 3.3 miles to a fork in Kings Saddle. Then keep left for 1.4 miles, watching for the trailhead's message board on the right. Park at a pullout on the left 100 feet farther down the road.

The trail angles up through a forest of big Douglas firs with orange paintbrush, blue Oregon grape, incense cedar, and acorn-bearing tanoak bushes. After a mere 0.4 mile you'll reach Tannen Lake, a large but fairly shallow round pool in a steep-walled, forested amphitheater. Several gaps in the shore's alder brush provide good lake access.

Head left across Tannen Lake's outlet creek to find a 0.9-mile trail through nice huckleberry patches to East Tannen Lake, a smaller but scenic twin with lots of small jumping fish. Thick alder brush allows only one small access path to the shore itself, where you can look across the lake to the cliffs of Tannen Mountain.

To climb Tannen Mountain, continue past East Tannen Lake for 2.1 nearly level miles to a ridge end, turn right on the Boundary Trail, and climb steeply 1.2 miles to the trail's crest in a small grassy meadow of yellow sulphur flowers. Leave the trail here and walk up through the meadow to the right 300 yards to Tannen Mountain's rocky summit. The view here includes (from left to right), East Tannen Lake, the Illinois Valley, a patch of Pacific Ocean, M-shaped Preston Peak, the crumpled canyons of the lower Klamath River, the Marble Mountains' highlands, snowy Mt. Shasta, and Red Buttes' double-humped summit.

To return on a loop, continue on the Boundary Trail 0.5 mile to a trailhead on Road 570. Ideally, a shuttle car will be waiting for you here. (To drive here from the other trailhead, simply return 1.4 miles to Kings Saddle, and turn left on Road 570 for 1.5 miles.) If you don't have 2 cars you could simply turn right and walk 2.9 miles along the road to your car. But if you've brought a compass and some route-finding skills, there's a shortcut. Walk just 0.9 mile along the road to a pullout at Sundown Gap, turn right past a boulder, and follow an abandoned roadbed 0.2 mile into a meadow. When the old road peters out, follow your compass due east down through the meadow (and some woods) for 0.4 mile to the Tannen Lake Trail. Then turn left to return to your car.

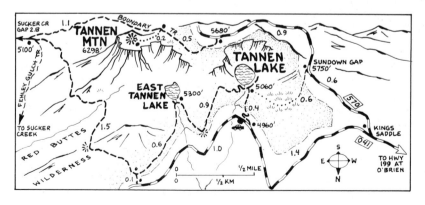

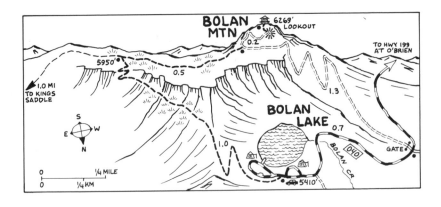

Bolan Lake from Bolan Mountain. Opposite: Bolan Mountain's lookout.

74 Bolan Mountain

Moderate
3.4 miles round-trip
860 feet elevation gain
Open early June to mid-November
Use: hikers, horses, bicycles (USGS)
Map: Oregon Caves (USGS)

A well-graded trail from a campground at a quiet mountain lake climbs past patches of wildflowers to a lookout atop this panoramic Siskiyou summit.

The names of Bolan Mountain and nearby Bolan Creek date to Southern Oregon's 1853 gold rush, when cagey entrepreneurs sought to lure gold dust from entertainment-starved miners by building a bowling alley at the confluence of Sucker Creek and *Bowling* Creek (as it was then called). Indians burned the entire establishment to the ground, but the determined bowlers returned in 1857, carrying 30 balls and 20 pins on their backs over a mountain trail.

To drive here, take Highway 199 south of Grants Pass 35.5 miles (or north of Crescent City 50.5 miles). South of Cave Junction 7 miles, between mileposts 35 and 36, turn east on Waldo Road. Follow this route 5 miles to a crossroads, go straight on paved Happy Camp Road for 12.5 miles to a high pass, and turn left at a "Bolan Lake Campground " pointer onto a one-lane gravel road. Take the uphill fork at the first 2 junctions you meet along this poorly signed road, but go downhill to the right at the 1.8-mile mark. After another 2.4 miles a "Bolan Lake Campground " arrow points left onto Road 040. Follow it 1.8 miles down to the lake and keep left through the campground for 200 yards to a trailhead message board on the left. Park just beyond at a wide spot in the road.

The trail climbs through a forest of flat-needled grand fir. Notice that the trunks are draped with 3 kinds of lichen: a shaggy black variety, the bright yellow *Letharia*, and the gray-green matted hair of *Usnea*, or old man's beard. Lichens don't sap trees, but instead collect nutrients solely from the air and rain. This explains why they cannot live below the winter snowpack—which must be 5 feet deep here, judging from the height of lichen on these trees.

After 0.4 mile the forest shifts to mountain hemlock. Small rocky meadows bloom with purple asters, orange paintbrush, and lavender penstemon. The trail switchbacks up a cliffy rim to a junction at the 1-mile mark in a field of yellow sulphur flowers. Turn right for a nearly level half mile to the Bolan Mountain Road and follow it 400 yards left to the summit lookout. The towerless cabin has a railed deck that makes a good lunch spot. The view includes not only Bolan Lake, but nearly all of the Illinois Valley, a large swath of Pacific Ocean, most Siskiyou peaks, and distant Mt. Shasta.

It's possible to drive to the lookout in late summer's fire season when the cabin is staffed. The rest of the year the access road is closed by a gate, but the cabin may be available for overnight rental. Call (541) 592-2166 to check.

75

Polar Bear Gap

Moderate (to Polar Bear Gap)
5.2 miles round-trip
1000 feet elevation gain
Open mid-June to mid-November
Use: hikers, horses
Map: Polar Bear Mountain (USGS)

Difficult (to Private Lake)
14.3-mile loop
3600 feet elevation gain

This corner of California's Siskiyou Wilderness is so remote it's accessed via Oregon. A well-graded trail traverses Black Butte' dry forests to Polar Bear Gap, a bare saddle strewn with bright red, green, and white rocks. Views extend west to Mt. Shasta. For a grander adventure, however, continue on a much rougher loop trail across Twin Valley to a rarely visited cirque lake surrounded by the crags of The Lieutenants. If you plan on using a campfire, be sure to pick up a permit from the Forest Service ranger stations in Cave Junction or Gasquet.

To find the trailhead, drive Highway 199 south of Grants Pass 35.5 miles (or north of Crescent City 50.5 miles). South of Cave Junction 7 miles (and between mileposts 35 and 36), turn east on Waldo Road. Follow this route 5 miles to a crossroads, turn right on Bridgeview-Takilma Road for 3.7 miles to the end of pavement, fork left on one-lane Road 4904 for 1.7 miles, fork to the right across a bridge on Road 4906, and keep right on this narrow gravel route for 5.4 miles. At a fork, veer left onto Road 053 for 4.5 miles. Then park on the shoulder beside a small message board on the right for the Black Butte Trail.

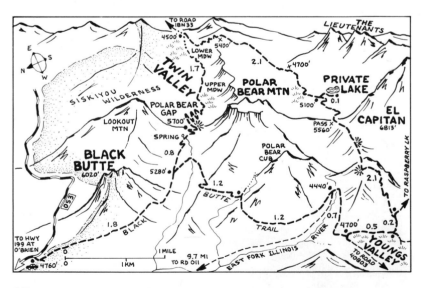

The Black Butte Trail.   Opposite: Private Lake.

The trail sets off along a broad, dry ridge of serpentinite—a shiny greenish rock that creates such mineral-poor soils that only a scattering of small Douglas fir, incense cedar, and Jeffrey pine can survive. Ahead looms the massive dark plug of Black Butte. Before long the trail traverses the mountain's slopes through cooler woods of Shasta red fir, droopy-limbed Brewer's weeping spruce, and Port Orford cedar. In all, this area is has quite an odd jumble of tree species.

After 1.8 miles keep left at a fork marking the start of the long loop. In another 0.4 mile you'll pass a patch of huge, blue gentian blooms and come to a miraculously cold, clear, delicious spring that gushes out of the ground 6 inches wide. Then continue 0.4 mile to Polar Bear Gap, a stark saddle beneath the craggy tower of Polar Bear Mountain. Far to the east, Marble Mountain looks like a white brick dropped onto the horizon beside Mt. Shasta.

Polar Bear Gap makes a good turnaround point, but if you're geared for a longer loop on faint, rugged trails, sally onward into the Wilderness. The path switchbacks gently downward 6 times before giving up and tumbling straight down the hill. Following feeble rock cairns, skirt Twin Valley's grassy upper meadow and continue down to the lower meadow, where the trail gives out altogether. Expect to search a bit for the continuation of the trail—and expect to be disappointed when you find it. From the right-hand side of the middle of this long, lower meadow, the path launches straight up a steep, rocky hillside to the right, as graceless as a bobsled run in a quarry.

After 2.1 more miles of up-and-down hiking—and just 250 yards beyond a meadow with a marshy pond—look for a large rock cairn. Here, veer left on a faint trail for 200 yards to lovely, swimmable Private Lake. The commanding crags surrounding this first-class pond are The Lieutenants, standing guard for El Capitan to the south.

To complete the loop, return to the main trail, turn left, and then keep right at all junctions. You'll cross a pass, descend to an old road , follow it right 0.2 mile, turn right for 0.5 mile alongside grassy Youngs Valley, and turn right at a "Black Butte Trail" pointer for a relatively easy 2.4-mile hillside tour back to the start of the loop. Then turn left for 1.8 miles to your car.

76

Raspberry Lake

Difficult
12.4 miles round-trip
2300 feet elevation gain
Open mid-June to mid-November
Maps: Broken Rib Mountain, Preston
  Peak, Devils Punchbowl (USGS)

Nestled against the cliffs of the Siskiyou Wilderness' highest peak, this deep lake is fringed with sweet-smelling mountain azalea blooms in July. A massive marble outcropping on one shore makes a dramatic base for fishing or chilly swimming.

Such a beautiful spot would be more crowded if the hike were easier. The first 5 miles of the route follow an ancient roadbed to the ruins of an old chrome mine. From there a rugged path scrambles 1.2 miles to the lake. Black bears are common, so remember to hang food 10 feet high at night. Permits are required only for campfires, and are available at the Gasquet Ranger Station 18 miles east of Crescent City.

To find the trailhead, drive Highway 199 south of Grants Pass 48 miles (or north of Crescent City 33 miles). South of the Siskiyou summit tunnel 3.5 miles (at milepost 30.12), turn east on Knopki Creek Road 18N07. Follow this one-lane, gravel road 13.7 miles to a T-shaped junction. Then turn right on Road 4803 for 1.6 rough miles to a parking area at road's end.

Start hiking down a barricaded old road to the left. Colorful rocks strewn along the route include green serpentinite, red peridotite, and white marble. Despite poor soils and the high elevation, the struggling forest here includes Douglas fir, grand fir, Shasta red fir, and white pine. The underbrush of tanoak and manzanita bushes is well adapted to tolerate fierce winters and bone-dry summers. Across the valley rise the landmarks of the Siskiyou Wilderness: El Capitan (on the left) and Preston Peak (on the right, with snow).

After a 2.3-mile downhill march, the road/trail curves around flat, grassy Youngs Valley for half a mile. Wild roses and incense cedar trees rim this broad field. The road forks at the meadow's far end. Veer left here and follow the increasingly rocky road another 2.2 miles as it climbs past the cliffs of El Capitan. Ignore small side trails to Twin Valley and Cyclone Gap.

The road ends at an old chrome mine with tailings piles, collapsed shacks, tunnel entrances, and ore cart rails. Keep left to continue on a narrow, rocky, up-and-down trail. After a mile on this maddeningly rugged path, listen for the gurgle of a spring just below the trail. Surrounded by big orange tiger lilies and lady ferns, an amazing, delicious fountain bubbles out of the ground and flows just 2 feet before vanishing without a trace.

Beyond the spring 0.2 mile the path crashes down to Raspberry Lake, a mountain paradise that makes it all worth while. Although no raspberries grow here, wild ones do ripen along the trail at Youngs Valley in September.

Raspberry Lake.   Opposite: Incense cedar at Youngs Valley.

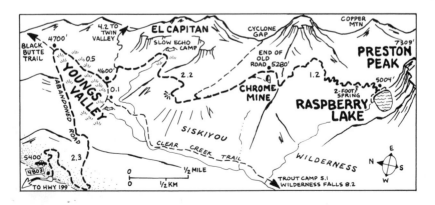

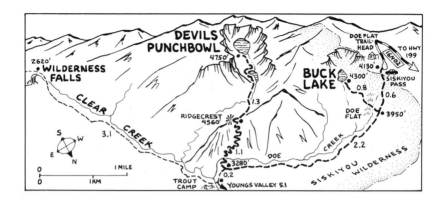

77   Devils Punchbowl

Easy (to Buck Lake)
2.8 miles round-trip
530 feet elevation gain
Open June to late November
Map: Devils Punchbowl (USGS)

Difficult (to Devils Punchbowl)
10.4 miles round-trip
2700 feet elevation gain

The color of sapphires and emeralds, Devils Punchbowl Lake is surrounded by a breathtaking, cliff-walled coliseum of stone. The trail to this Shangri-La, however, is breathtaking in other ways as well. After scaling a 1300-foot ridge in a single mile—a feat akin to climbing all the stairs in the Empire State Building—hikers have to follow cairns across an eerie, bedrock granite valley. This is why many visitors (especially those with children in tow) opt instead for the far simpler stroll to Buck Lake, a less dramatic goal.

If you insist on tenting in the Devils Punchbowl's bare granite basin, be sure to bring a stove so you're not tempted to scavenge scarce, scenic wood for a fire. Also bring plastic bags to pack out toilet paper, because it can't be buried in solid rock. As in all of the Siskiyou Wilderness, permits are only required for camp-fires. The permits are available at the ranger station in Gasquet, 18 miles east of Crescent City.

To find the trailhead, take Highway 199 north of Crescent City 28 miles (or south of Grants Pass 53 miles). South of the Siskiyou summit tunnel 9 miles (at milepost 24.85), turn east on Little Jones Creek Road. Stick to this one-lane paved road for 10 miles. Then turn left and keep left on gravel Road 16N02, following "Doe Flat" pointers 4.5 miles to a large gravel parking area with a few tiny campsites at road's end. The final 1.7 miles are rocky and rough.

The trail sets off down an old roadbed that has become a pleasant trail, shaded

Devils Punchbowl Lake.   Opposite: Glacier-polished granite in Devils Punchbowl.

by a dense forest of largish Douglas fir, Port Orford cedar, and vine maple. The ground cover includes vanilla leaf and twinflower. After 0.6 mile the trail forks at an old campsite. If your goal is Buck Lake, turn right. This 0.8-mile path crosses brushy Doe Flat, climbs through a forest of droopy Brewer's weeping spruce, and crests a glacially rounded rock lip to Buck Lake. This kid-friendly destination has a gravelly beach, sheltered campsites in the woods, small jumping fish, blooming mountain azaleas along the shore, and a cliffy backdrop.

If you're headed for the more spectacular scenery of the Devils Punchbowl, however, ignore the Buck Lake turnoff and follow the main trail straight another 2.2 miles down Doe Creek. At a fork, turn right on a path that crosses the creek and charges uphill with dozens of steep switchbacks. After a grueling 1.1 mile, the trail crests a ridge and sets off across bare landscape of speckled granite— much of it cooked by tectonic pressure to stripey gneiss and then polished smooth by Ice Age glaciers. Following rock cairns, you'll pass a small lake before reaching trail's end at a large lake that's so deep and clear the boulders in its depths look like looming whales.

Other Hiking Options

A longer but easier hike leads to a swimmable pool at the base of 50-foot Wilderness Falls. At the turnoff for the steep ridge trail to Devils Punchbowl, fork left for 0.2 mile and then turn right on the Clear Creek Trail. This path promptly crosses the bouldery creek (an easy hop in summer) and then ambles down through creekside woods 3.1 miles to the falls. Remember to save some energy for the 6.1-mile return trip to your car, because it's all uphill.

78 Babyfoot Lake

Easy (to Babyfoot Lake)
2.4 miles round-trip
360 feet elevation loss
Open May to mid-December
Use: hikers, horses
Map: Kalmiopsis Wilderness (USFS)

Moderate (to Road/Trail 1124)
5.3-mile loop
800 feet elevation gain

Difficult (to Emily Cabin)
20-mile loop
3700 feet elevation gain

A sprawling land of rugged canyons, rare plants, and ancient gold mines, the Kalmiopsis Wilderness is so remote that most of it is accessible only to backpackers. Here on its western rim, however, day hikers can sample some of the area's best scenery on short tours to Babyfoot Lake. Backpackers can continue on a longer loop to the Little Chetco River in the heart of the Wilderness.

To start, drive Highway 199 south of Grants Pass 24 miles (or north of Cave Junction 5 miles) and turn west on Eight Dollar Road at a pointer marked "Kalmiopsis Wilderness Area 17." This paved road narrows, turns into Road 4201, crosses the Illinois River, and then climbs for 11.4 gravel miles. At a fork in a pass, follow a "Babyfoot Lake" pointer left on Road 140. Then keep right for 0.7 mile to the trailhead.

The trail sets off through Douglas fir woods with Oregon grape, vanilla leaf, and beargrass. After 0.3 mile fork to the right, and in another 0.9 mile reach Babyfoot Lake. This green pool, ringed with cream-colored mountain azaleas

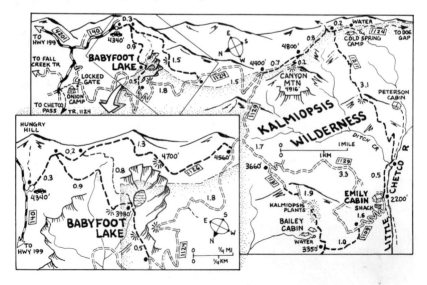

Babyfoot Lake.   Opposite: Scales of Port Orford cedar (left) and incense cedar (right).

in May, is set in an old-growth forest of strangely mixed tree species. Look for long-needled Jeffrey pine and the weirdly drooping branches of Brewer's weeping spruce. The lakeshore also hosts no fewer than 3 kinds of cedar trees. You can tell these cedar species apart by their needle-scales. The scales on incense cedars are twice as long as those on western red cedars, while Port Orford cedar scales have white X's on their undersides.

If you're not ready to turn back, continue on a 5.3-mile loop. Turn right along the lakeshore, following braided paths through overused campsites. The correct trail crosses the outlet creek 100 feet from the lake and traverses a hillside for 0.5 mile to a dirt road. Although this road is still occasionally used by miners with pre-1964 claims in the Wilderness, a gate at Onion Camp closes it to all other vehicles. Turn left along the road—known here as Kalmiopsis Rim Trail 1124. After 1.8 miles, watch for a rock cairn and an obscure sign on the left. To complete the 5.3-mile loop, turn left here on a path that climbs along a panoramic ridge (with views north to Babyfoot Lake and south to the snowy Siskiyous) before descending to your car.

If you'd prefer a 2- to 4-day backpacking loop, continue straight on Road/Trail 1124 past the cairn. After 1.5 miles, at a switchback in a pass, go straight on a small path that now takes over the "Trail 1124" designation. In another 0.7 mile, detour up a brushy side trail on the right to the former lookout site atop Canyon Mountain, where a 360-degree view sweeps from the Pacific Ocean to the distant white cone of Mt. McLoughlin.

From Canyon Mountain, keep right at all junctions to descend a steepish, spectacular open ridge of colorful rocks (red peridotite and green serpentinite) and colorful June flowers (lavender iris, red Indian paintbrush, and fuzzy cats ears) down to the bouldery Little Chetco River. Head downstream along the riverbank past Emily Cabin (a private, abandoned log cabin) and then a smaller plywood shack. From here, follow a mining road ("Trail 1109") uphill for 1.6 switchbacking miles to a cairn on the left. A sign on a big pine tree here marks a faint side path. Follow this trail up a ridge 1 mile to a junction in a pass. Then turn right on Trail 1131 for 0.2 mile to the Bailey Cabin ruin. The loop trail continues to the right, but first explore left 100 yards to a campsite beside a bog of *Darlingtonia*, an insect-eating pitcher plant that looks like a green baseball bat.

Back on Trail 1131, look for *Kalmiopsis leachiana*, a rare azalea-like shrub that blooms pink in early June and only grows inside this Wilderness. Beyond Bailey Cabin 0.8 mile, switchback up to an old cat road. Follow it left 0.2 mile to a pass, veer left on a ridgecrest path 0.2 mile to a prospect pit of green rock, and then veer right on a road for 0.5 mile to the junction of 2 roads (labeled Trail 1131 and Trail 1129). Keep left, following Road/Trail 1129 for 3.2 miles. At a cairn, turn right on a genuine trail for 1.8 miles to your car.

79   Fall Creek

Easy (to falls and copper mine)
1.8 miles round-trip
300 feet elevation gain
Open all year
Map: Kalmiopsis Wilderness (USFS)

Moderate (to Fall Creek forks)
7.2 miles round-trip
1000 feet elevation gain

After crossing a suspension footbridge 100 feet above the green-pooled Illinois River, this path passes a roaring river waterfall and follows a side creek up a canyon full of interesting old mining claims.

To find the trailhead from Grants Pass, follow "Crescent City" signs south on Highway 199 for 20 miles to Selma. At a flashing yellow light, turn right on Illinois River Road for a total of 11 miles. Along the way this road narrows to a single lane, turns into Road 4103, and becomes gravel. At an "End Maintenance" sign look for a gravel pullout on the left and a tiny "Camp McCaleb" pointer. Turn left here on Road 087, a rutted, rocky track that descends steeply toward the Illinois River. Park after 0.5 mile when you reach a switchback beside the 240-foot-long, railed suspension footbridge that marks the start of the trail.

While hiking across the footbridge, notice the cliff swallows zooming along the green river below. On the far shore, walk 200 feet straight across a rocky meadow to a trail sign on a post, and turn left on a path that follows the forest's edge. Poison oak crowds the trail in places, so wear long pants. Broadleaf trees here are madrone (with peeling red bark) and canyon live oak (with mossy, gnarled limbs). Conifers are Douglas fir and incense cedar. May/June flowers include purple daisy-like aster, wild rose, and long-stalked purple cluster lily.

At the mouth of Fall Creek it's worth detouring left a few hundred yards to Illinois River Falls, although the route to this frothy 10-foot drop is a cross-country scramble over bedrock and boulders. Then return to the Fall Creek Trail and follow it up a lovely 6-foot-wide stream full of little chutes and falls. The path is rough, with small washouts and more poison oak. After 0.2 mile, hop across

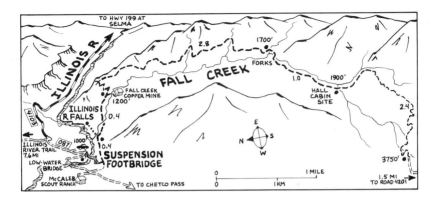

the creek on boulders. In another 0.2 mile the path reaches a cat road for the Fall Creek Copper Mine—a possible turnaround point.

If you'd like a longer hike, turn left on the cat road and follow it up 0.4 mile to a junction atop a dry ridgecrest amid ponderosa pine. Numerous prospect pits in this area expose quartz and green copper ore. Views extend across Fall Creek's canyon to Pearsoll Peak, a red, pointy mountain on the horizon, topped by a restored lookout cabin. Turn right at the pass and follow the ridgecrest 0.4 mile. From there the trail contours 2 miles along a wooded hillside before diving down to a campsite in a rugged canyon where the bouldery forks of Fall Creek join—a good goal for a moderate hike.

If you're determined to continue beyond the forks of Fall Creek, follow flagging and square, yellow metal signs to find single-log footbridges across both stream forks. The path then heads upstream another mile to the site of a mining cabin. After that the trail charges 2.4 miles up a steep, dry slope to an old mining road near Onion Camp (see Hike #78).

Suspension footbridge over the Illinois River.   Opposite: Catwalk along Fall Creek.

80 Illinois River

Easy (to York Creek)
5 miles round-trip
450 feet elevation gain
Open all year
Use: hikers, horses
Map: Kalmiopsis Wilderness (USFS)

Moderate (to Pine Flat)
10.6 miles round-trip
1650 feet elevation gain

Difficult (to Bald Mountain)
20.6-mile loop
4125 feet elevation gain
Open late April to early December

The Illinois River rages through a Wilderness canyon so rugged that the Illinois River Trail has to climb over a 3975-foot mountain just to get through. Following this trail up Bald Mountain is a classic backpacking adventure through some of the wildest country in Oregon. But day hikers can sample the trail's scenery, too—either with an easy walk to York Creek or with a longer hike to Pine Flat, where the green river boils over aptly-named Boat Eater Rapids.

To find the trail from Grants Pass, follow "Crescent City" pointers south on Highway 199 for 20 miles to a flashing yellow light in Selma. Then turn right on Illinois River Road 4103 for a total of 18.6 miles to the road's end and a primitive campground at the Briggs Creek Trailhead. Be warned that although this road starts out paved, it turns to gravel after 7 miles and becomes so rough after the 11-mile mark that passenger cars have to be driven quite slowly.

The trail begins with a 140-foot steel footbridge across bouldery Briggs Creek. Then the path crosses a flat of scrub oak, Douglas fir, long-needled ponderosa pine, and red-barked madrone. A rusting model T and a grassy opening remain from an old homestead. In May and June look for the blooms of pink clarkia (alias farewell to spring) and blue, 6-petaled elegant brodiaea.

After crossing Panther Creek on a footbridge, the path traverses a slope 300

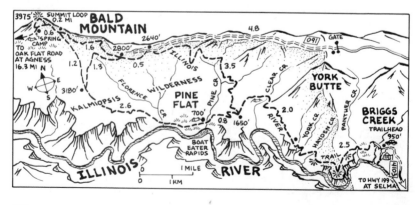

The Illinois River Trail.   *Opposite: Boat Eater Rapids at Pine Flat.*

feet above the Illinois River's roaring gorge. River viewpoints continue until the trail's 1.9-mile mark. In another 0.6 mile you'll reach York Creek in a red canyon that's full of sweet-smelling mountain azalea blooms in June. Explore 20 feet up the creek's first fork to find a patch of *Darlingtonia*, the insect-eating pitcher plants that resemble green baseball bats. This is a good turnaround point for hikers with children—except that the kids won't have gotten down to the Illinois River's shore to skip rocks. A good strategy may be to return to your car and walk 0.1 mile to the right through the campground to let the kids loose on a nice, gravelly river bar after the hike.

If you're continuing past York Creek you'll climb 2 miles through woods to a ridgetop junction. Turn left here on a steep trail that drops 0.8 mile to Pine Flat, a riverside bench forested with Douglas firs, gargantuan canyon live oaks, and big sugarpines that scatter foot-long cones along the path. The top attraction here is Boat Eater Rapids, where the Illinois splits around a granite island and drops 6 feet. To find it, strike off to the left 200 yards across a rock-strewn river bar. On hot days, green pools below the rapids invite swimming.

If you're headed to Bald Mountain, continue 0.7 mile to the far end of Pine Flat. After crossing Florence Creek, the path shoots uphill at a staggering grade, gaining 2300 feet in 1.5 miles. Then keep left to follow a ridge to a campsite and spring beside grassy Bald Mountain Prairie. From here a 0.2-mile loop trail visits the actual summit, a rocky area with 360-degree views. To complete the long loop back to your car on the well-graded Illinois River Trial, keep left at trail junctions as you descend from the summit.

Other Hiking Options

With a car shuttle you can hike the entire 27-mile Illinois River Trail one way. Beyond Bald Mountain the trail ambles past ridgetop bracken meadows for 3 miles before diving 4.7 miles down to a footbridge across scenic Silver Creek. Then the path traces a slope high above the river for 4.4 miles to Indigo Creek and climbs across craggy Buzzards Roost 4.2 miles to the Oak Flat Trailhead near Agness. To drive the 94-mile car shuttle route from Briggs Creek to Oak Flat (via Selma, Grants Pass, and Galice), bring a Siskiyou National Forest map.

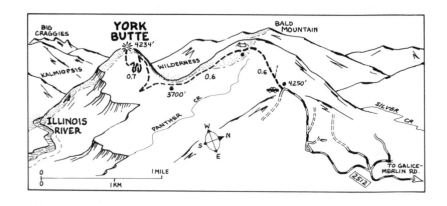

81   York Butte

Moderate
3.8 miles round-trip
1100 feet elevation gain
Open May to early December
Use: hikers, horses
Map: York Butte (USGS)

The trail atop pyramid-shaped York Butte, 3400 feet above the raging Illinois River, offers a rare panorama of the remote Kalmiopsis Wilderness—a vast, crumpled landscape where ancient forests cling to precipitous canyons of red rock. As everywhere in this Wilderness, groups are limited to 12 or fewer.

To find the trailhead from Interstate 5, take Merlin exit 61 just north of Grants Pass, follow signs 3.6 miles to Merlin, continue straight 8.5 miles toward Galice, and then turn left onto paved, one-lane Taylor Creek Road for 13.4 miles. A mile after Big Pine Campground, turn right on Road 2512 for 10.4 gravel miles. Choose the largest road at unmarked junctions and keep left for the final 2 miles. Finally, at a sharp left turn, park on the right beside a "York Butte Trail" sign.

The trail begins as an old mining road crowded with red-limbed bearberry and manzanita bushes. Summer blooms include white iris and plumes of beargrass. When the trail ducks into Douglas fir woods, look for the weird foot-high spires of snow plant, a leafless red saprophyte that grows in forest duff.

The big, long-needled pines near the start of the trail are ponderosa pine, but near the end they are a less common look-alike, the Jeffrey pine. The surest way to tell these 2 orange-barked pines apart is to look at their pine cones. On a ponderosa pine, the spines on a cone point out or up, while on a Jeffrey pine they point down. A less scientific way to distinguish the pines is to sniff the cracks in their bark. Some people swear these cracks smell like vanilla on a ponderosa pine while Jeffrey pine bark smells like pineapple.

After 0.6 mile the old road ends at a campsite on the right beside a miner's prospecting pit. Veer left along a ridgetop trail. This faint path descends 0.6 mile to a saddle. Then it switchbacks up York Butte amid a profusion of rhododendrons that bloom pink in early summer. The summit, fringed with a few rare, droopy Brewer's weeping spruces, yields a vista across the Illinois River to the Big Craggies and Bald Mountain.

Forest on York Butte.   Opposite: Snow plant's bell-shaped flowers.

82   Briggs Creek

Easy (to ford)
4.8 miles round-trip
210 feet elevation loss
Open all year
Use: hikers, horses, bicycles
Map: Chrome Ridge (USGS)

Moderate (to Onion Creek)
7.8 miles round-trip
Open except in high water
600 feet elevation loss

Starting at a gold mining ghost town, the trail along this mountain stream west of Grants Pass passes old hydraulic mines and crosses a flume ditch on its way to an abandoned miner's cabin. And yet this is not just a path for mining history buffs. The valley's old-growth forest and lovely creekside scenery have survived the area's rough-and-tumble gold rush era surprisingly well.

From Interstate 5 just north of Grants Pass, take Merlin exit 61, follow signs 3.6 miles to Merlin, continue straight 8.5 miles toward Galice, and then turn left onto paved, one-lane Taylor Creek Road for 13.4 miles. A mile after Big Pine Campground, turn right on Road 2512 for 0.3 mile. Then turn left into the Sam Brown Campground entrance and keep left for 200 yards. Just before the 2 picnic shelters, pull into a large trailhead parking lot on the right.

The meadow here is all that remains of Briggs, a gold mining boomtown that once boasted a hotel, barber shop, brothel, and bar. A gravesite near the picnic shelters commemorates one of the first black men in Southern Oregon, Sam Brown, a barkeeper who was shot for allegedly "messing with miners' wives."

From the parking area, the trail sets off through creekside Douglas firs and big ponderosa pines. In early summer expect a carpet of inside-out flowers (delicate white blooms dangling from 6-inch stalks) and tiny 6- or 7-pointed white starflowers. Also notice pathfinder plant, whose arrow-shaped leaves have a silvery underside that points the way any off-trail traveler has gone.

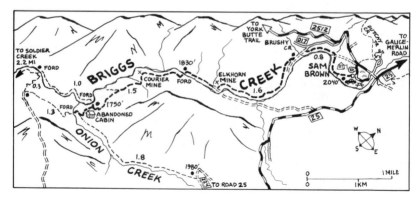

Briggs Creek ford.   Opposite: Abandoned cabin near Onion Creek.

After 0.4 mile hop across Dutchy Creek. In another 0.3 mile, join dirt Road 017 and follow it left for 600 yards. When the path resumes, it briefly crosses 2 old clearcuts before launching into uncut woods with 6-foot-thick Douglas firs, sweeping creekside red cedars, and twisted little yews. At the 2.1-mile mark, pass a campsite with rusty hydraulic mining equipment marking the Elkhorn Mine. Another 0.3 mile beyond, the trail fords Briggs Creek—a good turnaround spot if you don't want to take off your boots. The creek is cold, 30 feet wide, and calf-deep even in summer. After winter rainstorms, it's too deep to wade at all.

On the far shore, the trail climbs gradually through drier woods of tanoak and madrone for 1.3 miles before descending steeply past an abandoned flume ditch and several huge sugarpines to another ford of Briggs Creek. To the left 100 yards is a dilapidated one-room shake cabin—a good goal for a moderate hike. The mossy creekbank here, overhung with bigleaf maples, makes a nice lunch spot.

Other Hiking Options

Explorers will want to look behind the cabin's porch for a trail angling up the wooded hillside to the right. This path climbs 100 yards to a junction atop a rocky ridgecrest. To the left, orange dots on trees mark the Onion Creek Trail, which climbs to an abandoned flume ditch and follows it up the canyon 1.8 miles to Road 224, passing active placer claims along the way. To the right of the ridgecrest junction, the trail promptly switchbacks down to a ford of Onion Creek in a cool, hidden glen.

For a longer hike along Briggs Creek, cross the ford at the abandoned cabin. The trail goes downstream a mile, fords the creek again, and continues 2.2 miles before ending at gravel Road 4105 just beyond Soldier Creek.

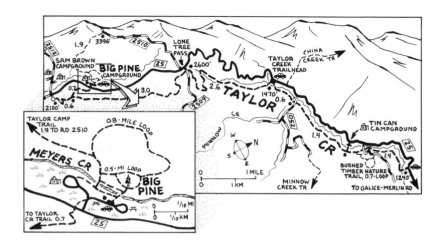

83   Taylor Creek

Easy (to Big Pine)
0.8-mile loop
60 feet elevation gain
Open all year
Use: hikers, horses, bicycles
Map: Chrome Ridge (USGS)

Moderate (to Lone Tree Pass)
5.2 miles round-trip
1130 feet elevation gain

Difficult (entire trail, with shuttle)
9.6 miles one way
1700 feet elevation gain

Conveniently near Grants Pass and open all year, this trail traces Taylor Creek up to a forested pass and then descends past Big Pine Campground, home of the world's tallest ponderosa pine tree. Although the entire path is 9.6 miles long, it touches the paved, one-lane Taylor Creek Road every few miles, so most visitors sample shorter segments.

For an easy introduction to the area, try Big Pine Campground's collection of little loop trails—all less than a mile long. To drive there from Interstate 5, take Merlin exit 61 just north of Grants Pass, follow signs 3.6 miles to Merlin, continue straight 8.5 miles toward Galice, turn left onto Taylor Creek Road 25 for 12.5 miles, turn right at the Big Pine Campground entrance, and keep right for 200 yards to a day-use parking area and map board on the left.

From here a packed gravel path crosses 15-foot-wide Meyers Creek on a footbridge (see inset map). Keep straight for 200 feet to find Big Pine. This ponderosa's double top soars 250 feet high. It was one of many pine seedlings that sprouted after a major fire some 300 years ago. Douglas firs later grew up beneath them, and the firs' cooler shade fostered a host of smaller plants, including vanilla leaf, pathfinder, Oregon grape, and wild hazel. Most of the large pines were logged in the 1970s. From Big Tree you can either go left for a 0.4-mile loop back to your car, or you can turn right for 0.5- or 0.8-mile loops.

For a more substantial hike, try the quiet middle portion of the Taylor Creek Trail to Lone Tree Pass. To start, drive as to Big Pine Campground, but only go up Taylor Creek Road 7.4 miles. Then turn left into the huge Taylor Creek Trailhead parking area. Take the trail on the right by a "Taylor Creek Trail West" sign. This path promptly crosses 2 rushing forks of the creek on footbridges. Anchored logs in the streams are part of a project to create pools for fish habitat. Placer mining claim notices tacked to creekside alders and maples prove that the area's 1800s gold rush isn't entirely dead.

For 0.5 mile the trail follows an abandoned wagon road that once supplied the gold mining boomtown of Briggs. Then the trail narrows, crosses patches of old-growth forest (with Douglas fir 5 feet thick and scraggly yew trees), crosses the head of Taylor Creek's south fork, and climbs more steeply through drier woods to a gravel road at Lone Tree Pass. To drive here from the lower Taylor Creek Trailhead, continue 3.2 miles up Taylor Creek Road to a pass and turn left on Road 2509 for 50 feet to a trail sign on the left.

To tackle the entire Taylor Creek Trail—a tour popular with equestrians and mountain bikers—you'll need to start at a less obvious trailhead. From the Galice-Merlin Road, drive up Taylor Creek Road only 3.8 miles to a curve and park at a gate on the left. The trail begins as a gravel road through a meadow before crossing the creek and heading upstream 3.8 miles to the larger, more obvious Taylor Creek Trailhead. Cross the huge parking area, continue on the 2.6-mile trail segment to Lone Tree Pass (described above), cross Road 2509, and follow the trail along a broad, wooded ridge for 3 miles to a junction. Either turn right for 0.7 mile to Big Pine Campground or go straight for 0.6 mile to a trailhead at the crossing of Roads 25 and 2512, near Sam Brown Campground.

Other Hiking Options

Four side trails connect with the Taylor Creek Trail. The 0.7-mile Burned Timber Nature Trail is an easy interpretive loop on a hillside of meadows and recovering forest near Tin Can Campground. Three more difficult side trails (the China Creek, Minnow Creek, and Taylor Camp Trails) scramble faintly up steep, dry ridges to gravel logging roads.

Taylor Creek.   Opposite: Big Pine.

84 Indian Mary Park

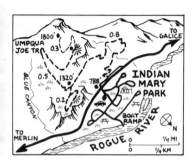

Easy (to viewpoint)
2.3 miles round-trip
850 feet elevation gain
Open all year
Map: Galice (USGS)

Expect spring wildflowers and views of the Rogue River's canyon while climbing the Umpqua Joe Trail from this popular Josephine County park.

In the 1850s Umpqua Joe leaked word to white settlers that his fellow tribesmen were planning an attack. In gratitude, the U.S. government gave his daughter Mary a piece of Rogue riverfront in 1894, creating the nation's smallest Indian reservation. Converted to a park after her death, the riverfront land has been developed with picnic lawns, a campground, and a boat ramp. The original wild landscape, however, survives on the trail's canyon slope.

To drive here from Interstate 5, take Merlin exit 61 just north of Grants Pass, follow signs 3.6 miles to Merlin, and continue straight 7 miles. Turn right at the park entrance, keep right, and park in a lot just before the campground fee booth. Then walk back across the highway to a trail signboard behind a weigh station building. Beware of shiny, 3-leaved poison oak here.

Steep at times, the trail switchbacks up a dry slope of Douglas fir and red-barked madrone. After 0.8 mile a viewpoint trail forks to the left. This short loop path visits a wooded ridge and a steep grassy meadow where pink, yellow, and purple wildflowers bloom from April through June.

Back on the main trail, continue up 0.5 mile through a black oak savanna to the trail's official end at a rock outcrop overlooking the park lawns and the twisting green river far below. Adventurers with boots and long pants (for poison oak) can continue 0.3 mile on a faint, unmaintained path up to a craggy, stonecrop-draped rock formation with lesser views.

View from the Umpqua Joe Trail.

Easy (Marial to Paradise Lodge)
6.6 miles round-trip
200 feet elevation gain
Open all year
Map: Kalmiopsis and Wild Rogue
   Wilderness (USFS)

Difficult (Marial to Illahe)
15 miles one way
950 feet elevation gain
Right: Kayakers at Inspiration Point.

At Inspiration Point, the trail through the Rogue River's wilderness canyon has been blasted out of sheer basalt cliffs. Hundreds of feet below, kayaks and rafts drift through green-pooled chasms toward the roar of Blossom Bar's whitewater. In other places the river trail ducks into forested side canyons with waterfalls. Sometimes the path emerges at grassy river bars with ancient ranch cabins and gnarled oaks. Hikers always share this wilderness gorge with the plentiful wildlife drawn by the river--kingfishers, black bears, deer, and eagles.

The eastern portion of the 40-mile Rogue River Trail is described in Hike #86. This western segment crosses the Wild Rogue Wilderness, with the river's wildest rapids and narrowest canyons. It also passes 2 commercial lodges where hikers can stop for a meal or a night—or catch a jet boat to Gold Beach. A few warnings: Avoid August, when the rocky, exposed slopes often shimmer with 100-degree heat. Poison oak is common. Backpackers should bring a stove because campfires are only allowed in no-trace firepans. At night, hang food bags at least 10 feet high and 5 feet from a tree trunk to discourage black bears.

The river's name comes from the Takelma and Tututni Indians, whom the early French trappers called *coquins* (rogues). When gold attracted white interlopers, the tribes retaliated in 1855 by massacring settlers. The Army pursued the Indians to this remote canyon, where the soldiers were besieged by a superior force of well-armed warriors. The Army's trenches are still visible above the trail at Illahe's Big Bend Pasture. Relief troops from the east turned back when Indians rolled rocks on them from the steep slopes above Solitude Bar. When soldiers from Gold Beach arrived, however, nearly 1200 Indians were taken captive and forcibly moved 150 miles north to the Siletz Reservation.

Today hikers can sample the Rogue River Trail's most dramatic scenery on an easy 3.3-mile walk from Marial to Paradise Lodge. To find the trailhead from Interstate 5, drive 22 miles north of Grants Pass (or 44 miles south of Roseburg) to Glendale exit 80, and head west 2.9 miles into Glendale. Opposite a small gas station, turn right on Brown Street (which becomes Reuben Road). After 12.3 miles turn left at a large brown signboard on the left. Following "Marial" pointers, take this paved side road for 8 miles. Then turn left on Road 32-9-14.2 for 3.8 miles of narrow pavement and another 9.5 miles of steep, bumpy gravel road to Marial. Ignore a turnoff for the Rogue River Ranch museum and go straight for 1.8 rough miles to road's end.

The trail west of Marial traces the edge of Mule Creek Canyon, a gorge so

Blossom Bar.   Opposite: Whisky Creek Cabin.

narrow that boaters sometimes bridge sideways or spin helplessly in a cylindrical maelstrom called The Coffeepot. After 0.7 mile the path crests at Inspiration Point, with a view across the chasm to Stair Creek's dramatic waterfalls. In another 1.4 miles the trail crosses Blossom Bar Creek, with campsites and a swimmable creek pool. Across a brushy lava flat to the left is the river's most treacherous rapids, a boulder field resembling a giant pinball game for boaters. Blossom Bar's rapids mark the upstream limit of jet boat traffic from Gold Beach.

In another mile the trail forks at Paradise Bar's grassy airstrip. The official trail skirts the woods to the right, but keep left along the river 0.2 mile to visit rustic Paradise Lodge, a good day-hike goal. Drop-in hikers are welcome at the bar and buffet restaurant. Book well in advance at 1-800-525-2161 if you want an overnight room (about $160 for 2, including meals). Jet boats from Gold Beach (about $80 round-trip) make scheduled stops here from May 1 to October 31.

If you're hiking onward from Paradise Lodge, rejoin the main trail at the upper west end of the airstrip and turn left 2.9 miles to Brushy Bar, a forested

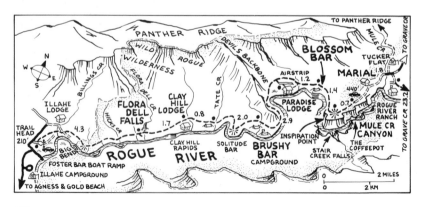

plain with a large, official campground. In the next 2.8 miles the trail skirts the scenic cliffs of Solitude Bar and reaches Clay Hill Lodge, an inn with the same price schedule and reservation phone number as Paradise Lodge. From Clay Hill Lodge, it's 6 miles to the Illahe trailhead, passing lovely 20-foot Flora Dell Falls along the way.

To drive a shuttle car to Illahe from Marial, go back up the Marial road 13.3 miles. At an "Oregon Coast" pointer, turn left for 5 miles. At Anaktuvuk Saddle's 6-way junction, go straight on gravel Road 32-8-31 (which becomes Road 3348) for 22 miles. Then turn left on Road 33 for 15.6 miles toward Agness, and turn left toward Illahe for 3.5 miles to the trailhead spur on the right.

86   Rogue River Trail East

Easy (to Whisky Creek)
7 miles round-trip
300 feet elevation gain
Open all year
Maps: Mt. Reuben, Bunker Hill
   (USGS)

Difficult (Grave Creek to Marial)
23.2 miles one way
2800 feet elevation gain
Additional maps: Kelsey Creek,
   Marial (USGS)

At times the irascible Rogue River idles along in lazy green pools, but elsewhere it's misty mayhem, plunging over Rainie Falls or boiling through Mule Creek Canyon's Coffeepot. During the peak whitewater season from May 15 to October 15, the 40-mile stretch between Grave Creek and Illahe has become such a popular float trip for kayakers and rafters that the Forest Service holds a lottery to issue 10,000 permits from 90,000 applications.

But why not hike through this spectacular river canyon instead? The 40-mile

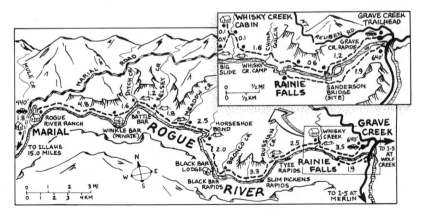

Rogue River Trail offers the same scenery without the crowds or the permit hassles.

This eastern section of the famous trail begins with a 3.5-mile jaunt that's easy enough for hikers with children. From Grave Creek, the route passes Rainie Falls' frothy 15-foot cascade and leads to the Whisky Creek Cabin, a gold miner's shack from 1880 restored as a rustic museum. Backpackers continuing west should bring stoves because campfires are only allowed within 400 feet of the river if they're kept in firepans. At night, hang food at least 10 feet high and 5 feet from a tree trunk to discourage black bears.

To find the eastern trailhead at the Grave Creek bridge, take Interstate 5 north of Grants Pass 18 miles (or south of Roseburg 48 miles) to Wolf Creek exit 76, drive half a mile to the Wolf Creek Tavern, turn off into town 2 blocks, go under a railroad overpass, turn left, and follow this paved road 15 miles. Just before the Grave Creek bridge, turn right to a boat ramp and trail parking area.

Mossy, gnarled canyon live oak trees provide spots of shade along the trail. Western fence lizards do push-ups on rocks, warning other lizards away from their territory. Expect tall blue wildflowers in May: cluster lily and 6-petaled elegant brodiaea. Beware of poison oak along the trail. At 0.2 mile the path overlooks Grave Creek Rapids, a rock-walled chute where boaters flail. After 1.2 miles, a trailside high-water mark commemorates the 1964 flood's crest, 55 feet above normal river level. Just beyond are the cement piers of Sanderson's Bridge, a miner's mule bridge from 1907 swept away by a 1927 flood.

In another 0.6 mile, a short fork to the left leads to the shore beside Rainie Falls. Most boats are lined around the falls on a channel blasted out of the rock for migrating fish. Daring souls in large rubber rafts sometimes run the falls without flipping. Continue on the main trail 1.6 miles, pass a cluster of popular campsites at a sandy beach, and then cross Whisky Creek on a footbridge. Here

Grave Creek Rapids.

a spur to the right leads up to the historic 2-room log cabin, with its collection of rusty mining memorabilia. Note the 1890 flume ditch just uphill.

Backpackers continuing to Marial will find the Rogue River Trail mostly traverses rocky slopes high above the river. Just 0.4 mile past Whisky Creek is Big Slide Camp, a quiet riverside tent area where a late 1800s landslide briefly dammed the Rogue, backing it up 15 miles. Attractions farther down the trail include Horseshoe Bend's dramatic river loop, Western author Zane Grey's (private) log cabin at Winkle Bar, and the restored 1903 Rogue River Ranch museum beside the Marial trailhead. To shuttle a car to Marial from the Grave Creek trailhead, turn left on the Mt. Reuben Road and follow signs 38.7 miles to Marial, mostly along narrow, winding gravel roads. For a description of the Rogue River Trail's next section, the 15 miles from Marial to Illahe, see Hike #85.

Other Options

The Rogue River Trail traverses sunny south-facing slopes that can be dizzyingly hot in August. For a cooler summer jaunt, park on the shoulder at the south end of the Grave Creek bridge and take the shady South Shore River Trail. It ends in 1.9 miles at a better viewpoint of Rainie Falls than the north shore offers.

If you'd really rather float the Rogue—usually a 3-day whitewater trip from Grave Creek to Illahe—write for permit information to the Rand Visitor Center, 14335 Galice Highway, Merlin, OR 97532, or call (541) 479-3735.

87   Mount Bolivar

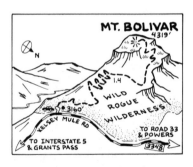

Moderate
2.8 miles round-trip
1160 feet elevation gain
Open May to mid-November
Map: Mount Bolivar (USGS)

Subalpine rock gardens and groves of old-growth trees line the path to Mt. Bolivar's lofty summit, where a 360-degree view encompasses the Rogue River's watershed from the Cascades to the California Siskiyous. Venezuela donated a bronze plaque for the summit because the peak honors Simon Bolivar (1783-1830), the Venezuelan-born liberator of Colombia and Peru.

To find the trailhead from Interstate 5, drive 22 miles north of Grants Pass (or 44 miles south of Roseburg) to Glendale exit 80, and head west 2.9 miles into Glendale. Opposite a small gas station, turn right on Brown Street (which becomes Reuben Road). After 12.3 miles turn left at a large brown signboard on the left. Follow a series of "Oregon Coast" pointers another 13 paved miles to a 6-way junction at Anuktuvuk Saddle. Then continue straight on Kelsay-Mule Road 32-8-31 for 3.3 miles to the trailhead spur on the left.

The view west from Mt. Bolivar.

If you're coming from Coos Bay, turn off Highway 101 south of town, take Highway 42 past Myrtle Point 3 miles, turn south through Powers 34 miles toward Agness, and turn left onto one-lane Road 3348, following Glendale signs 18.7 miles to the trailhead on the right, 0.9 mile after entering BLM land. (A washout closed this route late in 1996; call 541-439-3011 to see if it's repaired.)

The trail switchbacks a mile up a hot brushy slope with views and June rhododendron blooms. Then the path ducks into a cool forest of big Douglas fir, with lots of 6-petaled fawn lilies in May. Contorted yew trees form an understory. Then the trail climbs through a gorgeous rock garden of red Indian paintbrush, purple larkspur, and yellow stonecrop to the summit's former fire lookout site, now marked by foundation piers and a plaque.

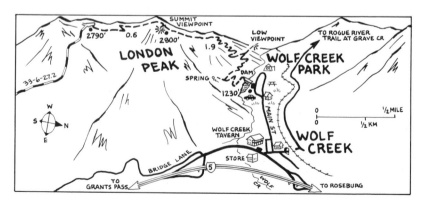

88　Wolf Creek Park

Moderate (to summit viewpoint)
3.8 miles round-trip
1570 feet elevation gain
Open all year
Map: Glendale (USGS)
Refer to map on previous page.
Right: London Peak from Wolf Creek Tavern.

If you've ever wished you could stretch your legs while driving Interstate 5 between Grants Pass and Roseburg, here's the perfect quick escape—a steep, little-known trail from a Wolf Creek swimming hole to a birds-eye viewpoint atop Jack London Peak. If the exercise makes you hungry, plan to stop for lunch at the trailhead's shady picnic area or at the Wolf Creek Tavern, a historic stagecoach inn nearby.

To start, take Interstate 5 north of Grants Pass 18 miles (or south of Roseburg 48 miles) to Wolf Creek exit 76, and drive half a mile to the Wolf Creek Tavern. Take a minute to tour this white clapboard landmark. Built between 1868 and 1875, it's typical of the hostelries that once fed weary travelers on the old Portland-Sacramento stagecoach line. The Oregon State Parks acquired the building in 1975, restored it, and reopened it to the public. There's no charge to look around and see the upstairs room where author Jack London penned a short story. London Peak behind town also honors the writer's famous stage-coach stopover. A private lessee operates the ancient inn's reasonably priced restaurant and 8 guest rooms.

To find the trailhead from the tavern, drive 100 feet into town to a "Wolf Creek Park" pointer, turn left on Main Street for 0.4 mile to the park, and keep left for 200 yards to a large paved parking lot and creekside picnic area on the left. Walk across a footbridge over Wolf Creek, a lazy, gravelly stream full of fingerling fish. In summer, a small dam backs up a swimming area.

On the far shore, the trail heads left 100 feet along a rocky bank festooned with triple-leafletted poison oak. Then turn up to the right on a switchbacking path through Douglas fir and madrone woods with sword fern, incense cedar, vine maple, Oregon grape, and vanilla leaf. After 0.5 mile ignore a side trail to the right to a disappointing lower viewpoint. The main trail zooms up the ridge steeply another 1.4 miles to a more satisfying clifftop viewpoint overlooking the town of Wolf Creek, the long arcs of Interstate 5, and the surrounding hills.

Other Hiking Options

If you prefer gentler trails, consider taking a new wheelchair-accessible shortcut to London Peak's summit viewpoint. To find the trailhead for this nearly level, 0.6-mile path, drive from the Wolf Creek Tavern 0.5 mile toward Grants Pass. Just before the I-5 on-ramp, turn right onto paved Bridge Lane for 2.1 miles. Beyond a small hill's crest, turn right on gravel Road 33-6-26 for 0.8 mile to a road cut. Then turn right on Road 33-6-27.2 for 1.7 miles, keeping uphill.

Northern
California

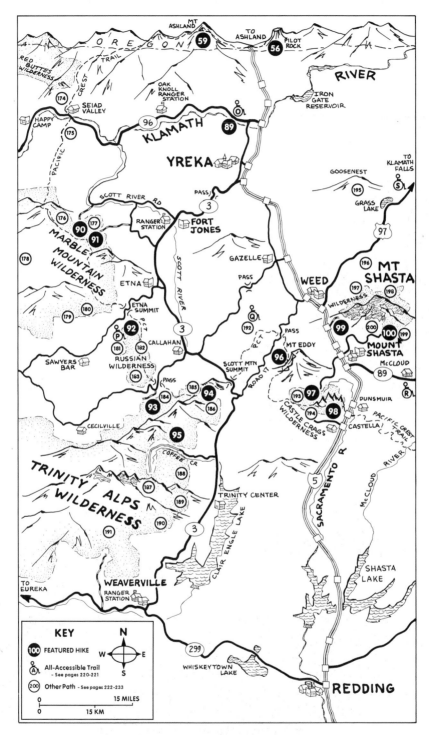

Opposite: Mt. Shasta from Castle Dome (Hike #98).

89

Klamath River

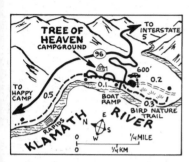

Easy
1.7 miles round-trip
50 feet elevation gain
Open all year
Use: hikers, bicycles
Map: Badger Mountain (USGS)

Twisting through a deep, remote rocky canyon, the Klamath River is an oasis for migratory birds—and for other north-south travelers as well. If you happen to be driving Interstate 5 between California and Oregon, consider slipping away from the freeway stress for a short side trip to Tree of Heaven Campground, where the glassy green river slides silently past ponderosa pines. Because the 300-mile-long Klamath cuts through a checkerboard of private land, the 2 short riverbank hiking trails at this campground are virtually the only public paths along the river.

To find the campground, drive Interstate 5 south of the Oregon border 11 miles (or north of Yreka 10 miles), take the Klamath River Highway 96 exit, and follow this road west 2.5 miles. Just before a river bridge, turn right to stay on Highway 96 for another 4.4 miles. Then turn left into the Tree of Heaven Campground entrance for 0.2 mile and park at the free day-use lot on the left. A small boat

Black oak leaf.

The Klamath River at Tree of Heaven Campground.

ramp here is a popular take-out point for whitewater rafters floating the 20-mile stretch of untamed river below Iron Gate Reservoir's dam.

Miners first visited Tree of Heaven's oxbow riverbend in the 1850s, when a gold rush sprinkled the Klamath River country with boomtowns. After the easy gold had been panned out of the riverbed gravels, ranchers began growing hay on the fertile riverbank fields. During the Depression, however, the fields were sold to a company that churned them up with an enormous floating dredge to extract the last few flakes of gold. The resulting barren rockpiles of cobbles are visible on both sides of the river.

The campground is named for the fast-growing, drought-tolerant ailanthus trees that were brought to California by Chinese miners in the 1800s for nostalgia and for shade. The tree's name comes from the Chinese *ailanto,* meaning "tree of heaven." An ancient ailanthus survives on the campgound's far loop.

The shorter of the 2 hikes begins as a gravel path beside the boat ramp and heads left along the riverbank past willow brush and wild grape vines. This 0.3-mile, wheelchair-accessible nature path features signs describing the many migratory birds that stop here on their seasonal journey between South and North America. To see the birds well, bring binoculars. When you reach trail's end, you can return on a loop by going straight 30 feet and turning left on an abandoned ranch road.

For the longer hike, walk 150 yards through the campground to a small parking spot at the end of the far loop. This prettier but rougher trail hugs the river for 0.4 mile to a foaming rapids, and then peters out 200 yards later at a sandy river bar of blackberries (ripe in August), thistles, and cobbles. On this hike it's useful to notice that the harmless black oak seedlings along the trail have leaves with pointy lobes, while poison oak's leaves have rounded lobes.

90

Sky High Lakes

Difficult
13.6-mile loop
2350 feet elevation gain
Open mid-June to mid-November
Use: hikers, horses
Map: Marble Mountain Wilderness (USFS)

A mountain of white marble looms above the lakes and wildflower meadows of the 2 alpine basins on this spectacular loop. The flower show peaks in July. By mid-September, cattle are typically herded here to graze. Backpackers planning to use a campfire in the Marble Mountain Wilderness need to pick up a free permit from the Scott River ranger station in Fort Jones.

To find the trailhead, turn off Interstate 5 at the Fort Jones exit just south of Yreka and follow Highway 3 for 16 miles to Fort Jones. At the far end of town turn right on Scott River Road for 14.1 miles to a pointer for Indian Scotty Campground and Lovers Camp. Turn left on one-lane, gravel Road 44N45 for 5.6 miles, and then turn left on Road 43N45 for 1.9 miles to its end at Lovers Camp's large parking area. Don't expect honeymoon suites in this romantically-named campground—just a few primitive walk-in sites without water.

The wide trail sets off from the left side of the parking lot, heads through the campsites, crosses a dirt road, and veers to the right into a cool old-growth forest. Some Douglas firs along the way are 7 feet in diameter. The woods are full of active chipmunks (with white eye stripes) and Douglas squirrels (without stripes). In early summer, white woodland flower include 7- to 9-petaled queens cup, the double bells of twinflower, and sprays of star-flowered smilacina.

If you keep right at all junctions for 4.7 miles you'll hike to the head of a broad, wooded canyon and climb through increasingly large meadows to Marble

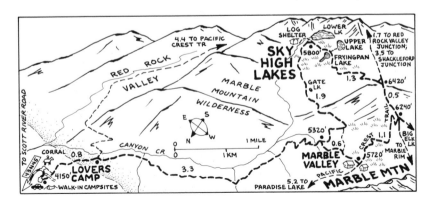

Lower Sky High Lake from the loop trail.   Opposite: Log shed at Marble Valley.

Valley. Beside the Pacific Crest Trail junction here you'll find a historic Forest Service guard station and a log-cabin-style shed. Both buildings are locked, but the area makes a nice rest stop anyway, with views across a meadow of hellebore (corn lily), goldenrod, and aster to the huge white wall of Marble Mountain.

The mountain's white marble has the same geologic age and origin as the marble of the Oregon Caves (see Hike #71). Not surprisingly, the rock here is riddled with caves too. Bigfoot Cave, the largest of the area's nearly 100 known caves, was discovered in 1976 and has proven more extensive than the Oregon Caves. Because of dangerous dropoffs, endangered bat habitat, and extremely fragile dripstone formations, however, casual scramblers are urged to stay away from cave openings. Serious spelunkers should check with the Scott River Ranger District (916-468-5351) for information.

To continue the loop hike, turn left on the Pacific Crest Trail through a natural rock garden of blue larkspur, red paintbrush, pink fireweed, and white marble. After climbing 1.1 mile to a pass with a 4-way trail junction, turn left along a panoramic ridgecrest for 0.5 mile. Then fork left at a "Sky High Lakes" pointer and descend 1.3 miles through more alpine meadows to the basin's lakes. Go straight past Fryingpan Lake (aptly named for its shape) and an unmarked side trail to Upper Lake. Near the large, lower lake, the trail becomes badly braided in the meadows. Keep right to find Lower Lake's grassy shore.

For a worthwhile detour, follow Lower Lake's outlet creek 200 yards downstream and hop across the creek to Sky High Shelter—a shake-roofed, 3-sided log shelter with a view of Marble Mountain. Then return to Lower Lake and turn right through the meadow to find the continuation of the loop trail. After 1.9 miles, turn right on the 4.1-mile trail back to Lovers Camp.

Other Hiking Options

For a less visited 13.2-mile loop, hike to Marble Valley, and follow the Pacific Crest Trail left 3.3 miles. Then turn left to descend back to Lovers Camp through the Red Rock Valley—a quiet canyon named for its red peridotite bedrock.

91   Campbell Lake

Moderate (to Campbell Lake)
9.3-mile loop
1360 feet elevation gain
Open mid-June to mid-November
Use: hikers, horses
Map: Marble Mountain Wilderness (USFS)

Difficult (to Cliff and Summit Lakes)
13.3-mile loop
2120 feet elevation gain

Outcroppings of glacier-polished marble form dramatic borders to the popular mountain lakes at the head of Shackleford Creek. For a moderate loop hike, tour the wooded shore of Campbell Lake. For a longer loop, continue onward to the huge-walled cirque of Cliff Lake and the subalpine meadows at swimmable Summit Lake. Backpackers planning to use a campfire need to pick up a permit, available free at the Scott River ranger station in Fort Jones.

To drive here from Interstate 5, take the Fort Jones exit (a mile south of Yreka) and follow Highway 3 for 20.5 miles. At a service station 4.5 miles beyond Fort Jones, turn right on Quartz Valley Road. Follow this paved road for 5.8 miles, making sure not to miss its left-hand zigzag after Mugginsville. Then turn left at a "Shackleford Trail" pointer onto gravel Road 43N21 for 7 miles to road's end. Park horse trailers in a lot to the left, while cars park on the right. Groups on the trail are limited to 25 and horse grazing is not allowed before July.

The Shackleford Trail follows a dusty, abandoned roadbed for its first half mile. Then the trail narrows and crosses a cattle gate at the 1-mile mark. From here on, the path passes small meadows full of huge-leaved hellebore (also known as corn lily), red-and-yellow columbine, fuzzy red spirea, red paintbrush, white yarrow, and blue aster. The meadows are also full of grazing cattle from mid-July through September. The cows wear tinny clanging bells to help cowboys find them. The calves don't need bells because each cow recognizes its offspring's bawl and stays close. Luckily, the cattle avoid the area's lakes.

After 2.8 miles, veer left at a fork and climb steeply through dense woods for 1.3 miles to Campbell Lake—a large lake with a many-bayed shore worth exploring. The main path parallels the shore for half a mile to a trail junction in the woods. If you're ready to take the shorter loop back, turn right past a "Shackleford Creek Trailhead" pointer, descend 0.7 mile to an X-shaped junction at a large meadow's edge, and go straight for 4 miles to your car.

If you'd like to take the longer loop, continue straight at the junction beside Campbell Lake—and continue straight through 4 other junctions in the next 400 yards. After 0.8 mile you'll climb to Cliff Lake, a deep pool rimmed on 3 sides by 1000-foot rock walls. Acres of bleached driftwood jam the outlet. The trail continues past a nice beach before ending at the lake's far end.

To continue the loop, head back from Cliff Lake 0.6 mile and turn left at a "Summit Lake" pointer. This path climbs over a hill to reach Summit Lake in

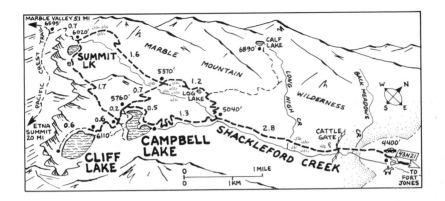

1.7 miles. Smaller and warmer, this lake is surrounded by pointy Shasta red firs, pink heather, colorful metamorphic rocks, and a cliffy mountain face. Beyond Summit Lake, follow the main loop trail downhill 1.6 miles to an X-shaped junction at a large meadow's edge. Turn left here and then go straight for 4 miles back to your car.

Cliff Lake.   Opposite: Cow along Shackleford Creek.

92 Paynes Lake

Moderate (to Upper Ruffey Lake)
4.2 miles round-trip
1200 feet elevation gain
Open late June to mid-November
Use: hikers, horses
Map: Marble Mountain Wilderness &
    Russian Wilderness (USFS)

Difficult (to Paynes Lake)
12 miles round-trip
2210 feet elevation gain

Hikers often drive past the Russian Wilderness on their way to its larger, more famous neighbors, the Trinity Alps and Marble Mountain Wilderness Areas. But this craggy chunk of the Salmon Mountains rivals those more crowded destinations in scenery. For a first-rate sample of the Russian Wilderness' charms, take the Pacific Crest Trail along a view-packed ridgecrest to Paynes Lake's dramatic granite basin. Car drivers for this trip will appreciate that the route to the trailhead is entirely paved. Backpackers planning to use a campfire need to pick up a free permit from the Scott River ranger station in Fort Jones.

From Interstate 5, take the Fort Jones exit (a mile south of Yreka) and follow Highway 3 for 27 miles. When the highway turns left toward Callahan, go straight for 0.5 mile into the quaint village of Etna. In downtown Etna turn right on Collier Way—which becomes the road to Sawyers Bar—and climb for 10.4 miles to Etna Summit. Just 100 yards beyond the pass, turn left into an unmarked parking lot beside a radio tower.

From the parking area, walk 100 feet up a road beside the radio tower and veer right onto the Pacific Crest Trail. This path climbs gently past sparse, storm-battered Shasta red firs along a slope of red-limbed manzanita brush, yellow sulphur flowers, and schist scree. After half a mile the trail enters denser woods with firs up to 4 feet in diameter.

At the 1.7-mile mark the PCT crosses an old mining road. If you're wearing

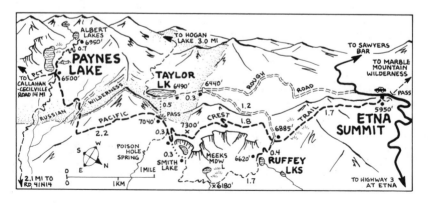

The Pacific Crest Trail south of Etna Summit. Opposite: Paynes Lake.

down, the best bet is to turn left on this road, which promptly becomes an 0.4-mile path down to woodsy Upper Ruffey Lake—an acceptable day-hike goal. If you're headed for the craggier granite scenery at Paynes Lake, however, stick to the PCT for another 4.3 miles. Along the way you'll pass a cliffy slope with views across Smith Lake to distant Mt. Shasta, a saddle with a view west to Taylor Lake, and a series of granite steps with bouquets of goldenrod, blue aster, and red paintbrush. When you reach a junction by Paynes Lake's outlet creek, turn right to a large wooded area with dozens of campsites overlooking the lakeshore.

Other Hiking Options

Much of the Russian Wilderness is accessed by rough trails or scramble routes. Here are 4 top goals for adventurers:

Albert Lakes. Hike to the far end of Paynes Lake and climb to the far, upper end of a steep meadow to find a faint, boggy trail that leads 0.7 mile up through alder brush and wildflowers to a rugged alpine lake basin.

Paynes Lake Trail. This shorter, but steeper and fainter route to Paynes Lake gains 2100 feet in 2.1 rocky miles, mostly through old clearcuts. To find its trailhead, drive Highway 3 south past Etna 4.5 miles, turn right on French Creek Road, and follow signs for 9 increasingly rough miles.

Taylor Lake. Nearly as pretty as Paynes, this lake is a bit closer. To get there, drive past Etna Summit 0.4 mile, turn left on a very rough dirt road for 2.4 miles, and walk a very easy 0.3-mile path to the lake. Adventurers can also scramble down to the lake from the PCT, but the slope is very steep and rocky.

Smith Lake. A faint trail continues 1.7 mile past Upper Ruffey Lake to this rock-rimmed pool. A very steep scramble trail continues 0.3 mile up a rocky ridge to a switchback of the PCT, making possible a rugged loop.

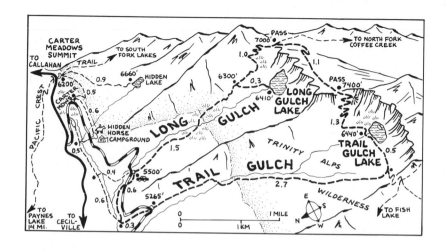

93   Long Gulch Lake

Moderate (to Long Gulch Lake)
3.6 miles round-trip
910 feet elevation gain
Open late June to mid-November
Use: hikers, horses
Map: Trinity Alps Wilderness (USFS)

Difficult (to Trail Gulch Lake)
9.6-mile loop
2280 feet elevation gain

Cars often pack the trailhead parking lots on the southern side of the popular Trinity Alps Wilderness, but here on the northern side, just an hour and a half's drive from the Oregon border, you can hike all day without meeting another group. Two of the Trinity Alps' prettiest lakes are hidden in a pair of subalpine canyons here. For a trip the whole family can manage, head for Long Gulch Lake. For a longer loop, continue over a panoramic divide to cliff-backed Trail Gulch Lake. If you plan to camp in the Wilderness, be sure to pick up a free permit at the Fort Jones or Weaverville ranger stations.

To drive here from Oregon, take Interstate 5 just past Yreka to the Fort Jones exit and follow Highway 3 west for 40 miles to the village of Callahan. (If you're coming from Redding, take I-5 north past Mount Shasta 22 miles to the Gazelle exit and follow signs 26 miles west to Callahan.) At a major junction just outside Callahan, turn off Highway 3 toward Cecilville. Follow this paved road 12 steep miles up to Carter Meadows Summit, continue 0.8 mile down the far side of the pass to a "Carter Meadows Trailheads" pointer, and turn left for 1.8 miles on a gravel road. Just beyond a creek culvert, park at a pullout and message board on the left for the Long Gulch Lake trail.

The trail up Long Gulch sets off through a forest of incense cedars and Shasta red firs with grassy openings of bracken, white yarrow, and granite rocks. The woods seem full of juncos, flashing their white tail-feather Vs as they swoop past. Midnight-blue Stellar's jays scold and tip their pointy topknots.

After 0.7 mile the path hops Long Gulch Creek in a meadow. Then the trail climbs more steeply 0.8 mile to a fork. Veer right for 0.3 mile to Long Gulch Lake, backed by a headwall of cliffs. The swimming's fine. If you're camping, pick a spot in the woods away from the shore.

If you're continuing on the loop, backtrack 0.3 mile from Long Gulch Lake, turn right at the junction, and climb 1 mile to a pass. Just beyond the saddle, fork to the right on a new trail that traverses 1.1 mile to another picturesque pass. For a quick view of Mt. Shasta and the high Trinity Alps peaks, scramble 400 yards to the right up an open ridgecrest to a rocky summit. Then continue on the main trail across the pass, switchbacking 1.3 miles down a dramatic, cliffy amphitheater to Trail Gulch Lake. A small bouldery island is evidence that a massive avalanche once skittered rocks onto the lake's winter ice.

The trail briefly becomes faint after crossing Trail Gulch Lake's outlet creek in a meadow; head left through a campsite into the lakeshore woods. Then the trail is obvious for 3.2 miles down Trail Gulch to a trailhead on the gravel road. Your car is 0.8 mile to the right, but rather than trudge back on the road, walk across it and return on a pleasant network of horse trails, following "Long Gulch" pointers 0.9 mile to your car.

Trail Gulch Lake. Opposite: Bigelow's sneezeweed.

Tangle Blue Lake.   Opposite: Incense cedar tree.

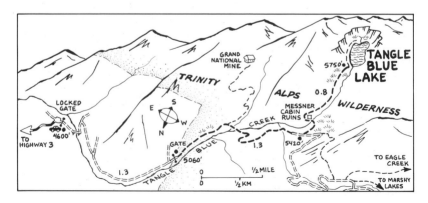

94   Tangle Blue Lake

Moderate
6.8 miles round-trip
1170 feet elevation gain
Open late June to mid-November
Use: hikers, horses
Map: Trinity Alps Wilderness (USFS)

Massive incense cedars and sugarpines stand guard along the trail to this lovely blue lake, set in a high granite half-bowl in a less-visited corner of the popular Trinity Alps Wilderness. Backpackers headed here should be sure to pick up a free overnight permit from the ranger station in Fort Jones or Weaverville.

If you're driving here from the north, take Interstate 5 a mile past Yreka to the Fort Jones exit and follow Highway 3 through Fort Jones and Callahan for a total of 49 miles. Beyond the Scott Mountain summit 4.3 miles (between mileposts 80 and 81), turn right at a "Tangle Blue Trail" pointer and follow a rocky road for 3.7 miles to a message board at a T-shaped road junction. (If you're driving here from Redding, take Highway 299 west toward Eureka 49 miles to a "Trinity Center" pointer in downtown Weaverville, and turn right on Highway 3 for 50 miles. At a "Tangle Blue Trail" sign between mileposts 80 and 81, turn left for 3.7 rough miles to the T-junction.)

Park by the message board at the T-shaped road junction and hike the road to the right past a locked gate. Follow this ancient mining road 1.3 miles to another gate at the Wilderness boundary, keeping right at all junctions. Along the way, notice the huge, straight-trunked sugarpines that scatter foot-long pine cones in the road.

Then continue 1.3 miles on a narrower track that passes through a grove of incense cedars, some of them 4 feet in diameter. The grove is particularly remarkable because foresters often claim this droopy-limbed, water-loving tree species cannot grow in pure stands. Soft and straight-grained, incense cedar is the wood used in most pencils. Its aromatic incense is instantly familiar as the smell of a freshly sharpened pencil.

Next the trail crosses boulder-strewn Tangle Blue Creek and climbs to a well-signed fork at the 2.6-mile mark. Turn left on a footpath that enters a meadow and recrosses the creek. Here the trail skirts the flattened walls and rusty wood stove of the former Messner cabin before launching the final climb to Tangle Blue Lake.

A meadow just before the lake is full of color: green bracken fern, white yarrow, blue aster, yellow buttercup, and pink mallow. The lake itself is bordered by fir woods with campsites, patches of alder brush, and granite rock outcroppings suitable for use as swimming or sunbathing platforms.

Hodges Cabin

Moderate
7.2 miles round-trip
1200 feet elevation gain
Open June through November
Use: hikers, horses
Map: Trinity Alps Wilderness (USFS)

The hike to this little-known hideaway in the heart of the Trinity Alps Wilderness traces Coffee Creek's north fork through a rugged canyon with a chilly swimming hole. The hike's goal, a historic 2-story, 6-bedroom lodge from the early 1920s, is usually open for tours from about June 20 to mid-September, when volunteer caretakers are in residence. If you plan to camp in the Wilderness you'll need to pick up a permit, available free at ranger stations in Fort Jones or Weaverville.

The spacious cabin began as the dream of Walter and Agnes Hodges, a Los Angeles couple who made their fortune in the sand and gravel business when LA began paving its streets. The Hodges already had vacation homes in San Diego, Hawaii, and old Trinity Center (now inundated by Clair Engle Reservoir), but they wanted an even more remote retreat. For three summers they employed a crew of up to 50 men to build this 2400-square-foot cabin at a creekside meadow high in the Trinity Alps.

The project proved enormously difficult. All of the lumber and furnishings had to be packed in on horseback over the North Fork Coffee Creek Trail. Snows buried the worksite up to 10 feet deep each winter.

After the house was finally complete, the Hodges entertained guests here for many summers. At one time there were gardens, a small swimming pool, and a generator for electric lights. The Hodges finally sold the cabin to a famous racehorse jockey. But then the Southern Pacific railroad company resurveyed their checkerboard holdings in the area and discovered that they had owned this land all along. In 1986 the company traded the property to the Forest Service, which set about preserving the historic building for the public.

To drive here from Oregon, take Interstate 5 just past Yreka to the Fort Jones exit and follow Highway 3 through Fort Jones and Callahan for a total of 62 miles. Between mileposts 67 and 68, turn right onto Coffee Creek Road for 6 miles of pavement and an additional 2.7 miles of gravel. Just before the road crosses Coffee Creek on a bridge, look for a sign on the right identifying the North Fork Coffee Creek Trail.

If you're driving here via Redding, take Highway 299 west toward Eureka 49 miles to a "Trinity Center" pointer in downtown Weaverville, turn right on Highway 3 for 37 miles, and turn left on Coffee Creek Road for 8.7 miles.

The trail begins by climbing a dry canyon slope high above the creek through a sparse forest of orange-barked Jeffrey pines, gnarled canyon live oak, lush

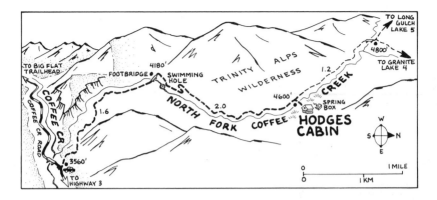

incense cedar, Douglas fir, and manzanita brush. Western fence lizards scamper across the rocks. On rare occasions, the rattlesnakes that hunt the lizards have been sighted here too. After 1.6 miles the path crosses the creek on a 100-foot steel footbridge. Just 250 yards later you'll reach a small creekbank campsite beside an 8-foot-deep swimming hole. Small waterfalls tumble over boulders nearby. Indian rhubarb grows on the bank.

After hiking up the creekside trail 2 more miles you'll see Hodges Cabin to the right. Turn across a gravel bar and a plank footbridge to the welcome shade of the cabin's porch. Then walk behind the cabin to the left to find a trap door over a spring box with a big ladle and plenty of deliciously ice cold water.

Other Hiking Options

If you continue up the North Fork Coffee Creek Trail 1.2 miles, you'll cross another footbridge and come to a fork. Keep left for 0.5 mile to reach Saloon Creek and the site of Saloon City, an 1850s gold rush boomtown built mostly of tents. All that remains is the stucco ruin of Frenchies Cabin. If you keep left at another junction and continue 4.5 miles, you'll end up at Long Gulch Lake, described in Hike #93.

Hodges Cabin.   Opposite: Manzanita.

96 Deadfall Lakes

Easy (to Middle Lake)
3.4 miles round-trip
800 feet elevation loss
Open July through October
Use: hikers, horses
Maps: South China Mtn, Mt Eddy (USGS)

Moderate (to Upper Lake)
5.4 miles round-trip
1400 feet elevation gain

Difficult (to Mount Eddy)
9 miles round-trip
2635 feet elevation gain

Perhaps nowhere in Northern California can you see so many different kinds of wildflowers on a single trail as when hiking through Deadfall Meadow to this string of alpine lakes below Mount Eddy. And if you're a fan of viewpoints, just keep following the trail up to the abandoned lookout on Mount Eddy's summit. At 9025 feet it's the highest point in the entire Klamath Mountains, with a breathtaking front-row view of Mt. Shasta.

To find the trailhead, drive Interstate 5 south of Yreka 27 miles (or north of Weed 3 miles), take the Stewart Springs Road exit, head west on a highway for 0.4 mile, turn left onto Stewart Springs Road for 4 miles, and turn right on one-lane, paved Road 17 for 9.3 miles to a pass. The Pacific Crest Trail crosses the road here, offering a longer, less interesting hiking route to the Deadfall Lakes. But to find the recommended trail, continue driving on Road 17 beyond the pass 1.3 miles to a hairpin curve. Park on the right, inside the hairpin curve. Then walk across the road to a "Deadfall Meadow" sign, where the trail strikes off through the fields. This path has a few boggy spots, so boots are a good idea.

Look in this first meadow for blue aster, purple clover, pink mallows, and white angelica. After 250 yards the path hops across Deadfall Creek on wobbly stepping stones and enters a forest of incense cedar, long-needled Jeffrey pine, prim Shasta red fir, and 5-needled white pine. Soon you'll cross a side creek with

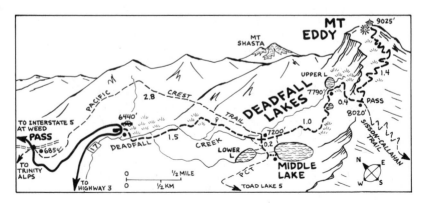

Mt. Eddy from Upper Deadfall Lake.   Opposite: Mt. Shasta from Mt. Eddy's summit.

wild roses, and then you'll recross Deadfall Creek—this time amidst pungent purple wild onions, bright blue gentians, and tiny yellow monkeyflowers.

Next the path climbs through a surprising field of *sagebrush*, brightened with yellow lupine, red paintbrush, and scarlet gilia. Keep your eyes peeled for an even stranger botanical oddity—a patch of insect-eating *Darlingtonia* pitcher plants, resembling a crop of green light bulbs in a boggy trailside spring.

At the 1.4-mile mark a side trail forks to the right to Lower Lake—a lovely pool, but no match for the other Deadfall Lakes. So continue straight 100 yards to an X-shaped junction with the Pacific Crest Trail, turn right for 0.2 mile to a "Deadfall Creek" sign, and bushwhack to the left 60 yards over a small rise to Middle Lake. This gem has an open, swimmer-friendly shore with gnarled mountain mahogany trees, rock outcroppings, and still more wildflowers.

If you're not yet ready to head back, return to the X-shaped PCT junction, turn right, and climb 1 mile to Upper Deadfall Lake, a small but gorgeous alpine pool reflecting the red metamorphic rock cliffs of Mt Eddy. Like the other lakes, this one also has swimming spots and campsites. If you're climbing Mt. Eddy, continue 0.4 mile past the upper lake to a pass. Then turn left along the ridgecrest on a well-graded trail that switchbacks steadily up the mountainside. The only trees at this elevation are stunted whitebark pines, with limbs so supple they can be tied in knots. In addition to dwarf blue lupine and yellow sulphur flower, look for bladderpod, a bizarre locoweed relative that produces inch-long, mottled purple balloons instead of ordinary flowers.

At the summit, the rickety ruin of a lookout stares eye to eye with Mt. Shasta. Notice the dark pyramid of Black Butte directly below Shastina's white cone. Also note Lake Shastina in the Shasta Valley to the left, with Oregon's Mt. McLoughlin on the horizon. To the south, look for snowy Mt. Lassen. Far to the west, the snowcapped crags of the Trinity Alps form a long, jagged silhouette.

97 Castle Lake

Easy (to Little Castle Lake)
2.4 miles round-trip
640 feet elevation gain
Open June to mid-November
Map: Mt. Shasta Wilderness & Castle
Crags Wilderness (USFS)

Moderate (to Heart Lake)
3.4 miles round-trip
880 feet elevation gain

Wintu Indians believed this large, cliff-rimmed mountain lake was the fortress of Ku-ku-pa-rick, an evil spirit who made ominous rumbling noises here in winter. An 1851 gold rush brought swarms of white miners to these headwaters of the Sacramento, muddying the river below and destroying the Indian's supply of salmon. The Wintu burned several of the intruder's cabins in response. Then they retreated to the bluffs above Castle Lake, where, with nothing but bows and arrows for defense, they were decimated by an impromptu army of heavily armed miners in the 1855 Battle of Castle Crags.

Today, easy paved access from Interstate 5 makes Castle Lake a popular summer picnic spot. For a short hike, take a 1.2-mile trail over a small, steep pass to a meadow at Little Castle Lake. For a better sample of the Castle Crags Wilderness—a landscape essentially unchanged since the days of the Wintu—track a faint trail to Heart Lake, a deep, swimmable pond in a high rock basin with a view across Castle Lake to Mt. Shasta and distant Mt. McLoughlin.

To start, drive Interstate 5 to the town of Mount Shasta, take the Central Mount Shasta exit, and follow "Siskiyou Lake" signs west for 3.5 miles through several forks and turns. Drive past the reservoir's dam 0.3 mile and turn left on Castle Lake Road for 7.3 miles to a large parking lot at road's end. Motorboats aren't allowed on the still, 47-acre lake, but canoeists often launch from a small boat ramp beside the parking lot. And although camping is banned near the shore, there's an official campground 0.3 mile back down the road.

For the hike, walk left around the Castle Lake's shore through a forest of Shasta red fir and white fir. Look for dragonflies and fuzzy red spirea blooms along the bank. The path soon climbs away from the lake and steepens to a pass in open, high country with whitebark pines, orange paintbrush, white yarrow, and red-limbed manzanita bushes. The colorful jumble of rocks here are metamorphic—old serpentinite and limestone that were cooked together and crystallized into veins when great bubbles of hot granite rose through the Earth's crust to form the Castle Crags.

Cross the pass, descend 0.5 mile to a meadow, and fork to the right to Little Castle Lake, a muddy-bottomed pond surrounded by spirea bushes and dramatic, July-blooming Cascade lilies. Scramble around the lake to a white granite cliff for the best views of Mt Shasta.

If you'd like a longer hike—and you have some pathfinding skills—consider a side trip to Heart Lake. From Little Castle Lake, walk back 0.5 mile to the pass.

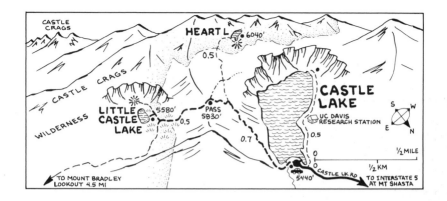

Just 5 steps beyond the summit, turn left on a faint path. After 150 yards you'll come to a confusion of faint trails on a barren rock tableland. Veer left, angling uphill toward a rocky ridgecrest for 0.3 mile. Then climb a short, steep trail to a little pass behind a small rock knoll. On the far side is Heart Lake, surrounded by bedrock, whitebark pines, Shasta red firs, and pink heather.

Little Castle Lake.   Opposite: Castle Lake.

Castle Crags

Moderate (to Indian Springs)
3.6 miles round-trip
1040 feet elevation gain
Open except in winter storms
Map: Mt. Shasta Wilderness & Castle
    Crags Wilderness (USFS)

Difficult (to Castle Dome)
5.4 miles round-trip
2120 feet elevation gain

Towering above Interstate 5 and the headwaters of the Sacramento River, the granite spires of the Castle Crags are one of the most popular hiking goals of Northern California. For a quick bit of exercise walk to Indian Springs, where cold water spurts from a cliff. For a tougher hike, continue up to Castle Dome, an enormous granite monolith with a panoramic view of the Mt. Shasta area.

The Castle Crags' granite domes look as though they rose straight up from the depths of the planet—and they did. For several hundred million years the North American continent has been crunching its way over the Pacific plate. In the process, the descending seafloor drags down a lot of sand and mud with it. When this relatively light sedimentary material gets deep enough it melts to form granite. Then it bubbles up through the continent toward the surface. Castle Dome, like Yosemite Valley's Half Dome, is the rounded top of a granite bubble that cooled underground and was later exposed by erosion.

In the late 1920s, photographs of these picturesque crags were used in the campaign to create California's state park system. Today the park includes a

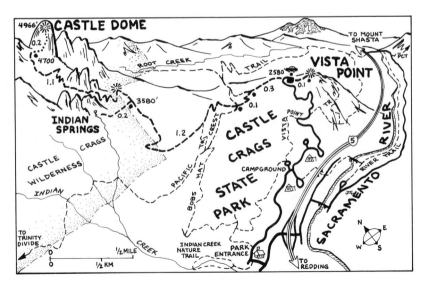

Castle Dome.   Opposite: Mt. Shasta from Castle Crags.

campground, several short nature trails, 7 miles of the Pacific Crest Trail, and a portion of the Castle Crags Wilderness. Dogs are not allowed on park trails.

Start by driving Interstate 5 south of Mount Shasta 14 miles (or north of Redding 48 miles). Then take the Castella exit and follow "Castle Crags State Park" pointers 0.4 mile to the park's entrance booth. Expect to pay a day-use parking fee of about $5 a car. Also expect to have rangers check your car to make sure food and cooler chests aren't visible. Black bears in this park have become so savvy that they sometimes smash windows if they spot an easy meal.

Beyond the entrance booth, turn right and follow "Vista Point" signs through the campground 2.1 miles on a winding, paved road that's so narrow it's closed to trailers and motorhomes. Park in a lot at road's end. For a quick warm-up walk, take a 150-yard path from the far end of the parking lot through oak woods to Vista Point, a hilltop with views of Mt.Shasta and the Castle Crags.

Then walk back across the parking lot and down the road 50 yards to a sign for the Crags Trail on the right. This wide path climbs gradually through second-growth Douglas fir woods with incense cedars, dogwoods (white blooms in April), and some triple-leafletted poison oak. After 0.3 mile, keep left at a fork. Then cross the PCT and continue straight, climbing steadily through viewless woods for 1.2 miles to the Indian Springs cutoff. Turn left for 0.2 mile to sample the delicious water that springs from a crack in a granite wall. Red-and-yellow columbines bloom here in a glen of 6-foot-thick Douglas fir.

If you go straight back to your car from Indian Springs you'll miss the best views. So when you return to the Crags Trail turn left and go up it at least another 150 yards to catch the trail's first viewpoint of Castle Dome. Then, of course, it'll be hard to turn back. Although the trail steepens beyond this point, the views only improve as the path winds up past fantastic spires, clefts, and tilted crags. Finally the trail crosses a bedrock granite upland of manzanita bushes and peters out at the base of Castle Dome itself.

The final 300-yard climb to the summit of Castle Dome doesn't require technical climbing gear, but is too dangerous for most hikers. Confident scramblers should attempt it only when wearing shoes with good-gripping soles and only when the steep, slippery granite is dry. From the trail's end, scramble up to the right to reach the dome's bare granite face. From there, climbers have to use their hands while following faint ledges up the rock slope and then chimneying up large cracks to the top.

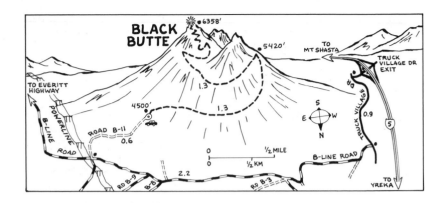

99   **Black Butte**

Difficult
5.2 miles round-trip
1858 feet elevation gain
Open late May to mid-November
Map: Mt. Shasta Wilderness (USFS)

Wedged beside Interstate 5, this strange, steep-sided volcano boasts a close-up view of Mt. Shasta and a wide-angle panorama that stretches from the Sacramento Valley to Oregon. The convenient, well-graded trail to Black Butte's summit is perfect for a few hours of earnest exercise. Just don't forget your hat and water bottle in hot weather, because the route lacks shade.

Black Butte looks like a cinder cone, but it was formed by a very different kind of eruption. When magma rose toward the surface here 10,000 years ago the rock didn't spray out as cinders. Instead it blasted a crater and then oozed up through the hole like dough from a cookie press, creating 4 adjacent lava domes. As the domes cooled the outer rock shattered into boulders, surrounding the central plug with a conical skirt of rockslides. About the same time, a similar lava dome erupted 7 miles away, much higher on Shasta's slopes. That dome is now Shastina.

To find the trailhead from Interstate 5, drive south of Weed 4 miles (or north of Mount Shasta 5 miles), take the Truck Village Drive exit, follow signs 200 yards to Truck Village Drive, turn left on this paved road for 0.9 mile, and then turn right on B-Line Road. This gravel road crosses a private timber plantation with a lot of poorly marked junctions and side roads with names like B-3, B-8, and B-9. But if you stick to the largest road for 2.2 miles—keeping to the right when in doubt—you'll come to a 4-way intersection underneath a big, triple-wired powerline. Turn right here onto Road B-11 and follow this rough gravel track 0.6 mile to its end at a cramped, steep turnaround.

The trail that starts at the end of the turnaround sets off through a sparse forest of firs and pines struggling to grow amidst a jumble of gray and red andesite boulders. Black Butte's lava is rich in hornblende. If you look closely you'll see this black mineral has formed crystals resembling fossilized fir needles in the rock. At times, yellow and black lichens seem to be the only life to have gained a foothold on this relatively fresh lava. Elsewhere the trail passes surprisingly lush patches of gooseberry bushes, orange paintbrush, red fireweed, lavender pennyroyal, and yellow rabbitbrush. Viewpoints are everywhere.

At the 1.3-mile mark the path makes its first switchback, high above the double ribbon of Interstate 5. Then 9 increasingly short switchbacks climb the final 1.3 miles to the cliff-edged summit and the mortared stone foundation of a long-gone fire lookout. The original cupola-style building blew off in a 1962 windstorm. Its replacement was removed by helicopter in 1975 because fire surveillance was being handled increasingly by aircraft.

From the summit, massive 14,162-foot Mt. Shasta rises above a patchwork of timber plantations—and the sharp triangular shadow of Black Butte itself. As you turn to the right, look for snowy Mt. Lassen, the flat Sacramento Valley, the jumbled Castle Crags, snow patches on Mt. Eddy to the west, the dimpled plain of Shasta Valley to the north (with Lake Shastina's reservoir below Pilot Rock's landmark knob), and Mt. McLoughlin's dark cone, 70 miles away in Oregon.

Mt. Shasta from Black Butte.   *Opposite: Black Butte from Interstate 5.*

100　Mount Shasta Meadows

Easy (to Panther Spring)
1.1-mile loop
280 feet elevation gain
Open mid-July through October
Map: Mt. Shasta Wilderness (USFS)

Moderate (to Squaw Meadow)
3.6-mile loop
850 feet elevation gain

Left: Mt. Shasta from Gray Butte.

"Lonely as God, and white as a winter moon, Mount Shasta starts up sudden and solitary from the heart of the great black forests of Northern California." So wrote 19th-century poet Joaquin Miller, the first of many white visitors to leave his heart amid the alpine wildflower meadows on this 14,162-foot peak. Naturalist John Muir later spread the mountain's fame with glowing reports of his many climbs, including one harrowing trip when he was trapped overnight on the summit in a subzero blizzard without a sleeping bag. Muir survived only by rolling all night in a sulphurous hot springs puddle.

Shasta has long inspired religious awe. The local Wintu tribe, to whom the peak was taboo above timberline, believed it to be the great white wigwam of a spirit who began creating the world from this point, and whose cooking fire sometimes wafts smoke from the summit. Those who smile at the old Indian myth should consider that the mountain is now held sacred by the Knights of the White Rose, the Rosicrucians, and Association Sananda and Sanat Kimara, the Radiant School of the Seekers and Servers, Understanding Inc., and the I AM Foundation. This latter group was founded by Guy W. Ballard, a Chicago paperhanger who claimed to have met a Lemurian on the mountain's slopes in 1930. Ballard reported that Lemurians have walnut-sized sense organs on their foreheads and live in tunnels inside Mount Shasta, but are actually refugees from the ancient kingdom of Mu, now submerged beneath the Pacific Ocean.

To hike through this mountain's strangely inspirational meadows for yourself, drive Interstate 5 south of Yreka 38 miles (or north of Redding 62 miles) and take the Central Mount Shasta exit—the *second* exit for this city in either direction. Drive east on Lake Street through downtown for 1 mile, curve left onto the Everitt Memorial Highway for 12.7 paved miles, and pull into the Panther Meadows parking lot on the right. From here, several little trails loop past 10 free walk-in campsites with picnic tables but no water. This is the only campground on the mountain itself, and no reservations are taken, so plan to come early if you want a site. Dogs are not allowed inside the Wilderness.

To start the hike, take the leftmost trail from the parking area and keep left for 0.3 mile, following a gurgling mountain brook through Lower Panther Meadow's pink heather, orange paintbrush, yellow monkeyflower, and blue aster. Stay on the trail to protect these fragile plants! After entering a grove of Shasta red fir you'll reach the start of a 0.3-mile loop. Follow a "Panther Spring" pointer to the right, and keep right until you've passed the gushing spring. At a junction 300 yards later you'll face a choice: either turn left to complete a short loop back down to your car, or turn right for a longer loop to Squaw Meadow. If you opt for Squaw Meadow, you'll climb 0.2 mile to another parking area. Turn right and keep right on a trail that ambles above timberline to a pass with views not only of massive Mt. Shasta, but also of the distant Castle Crags, snowy Mt. Eddy, and the jagged Trinity Alps on the horizon. Beyond the pass the trail descends past an ice-cold spring to Squaw Meadow's sandy bowl, slung between Mt. Shasta and Red Butte's ruddy cliffs. At first these meadows seem barren, but a closer look reveals thousands of western Pasque flowers. Also known as "old man of the mountain," this charming alpine anemone develops a tall, white-bearded seedhead by late summer.

Turn right at a junction in Squaw Meadows. This trail becomes faint when it hits a slope of glacier-polished bedrock. Continue straight and slightly downhill to find the true path. If you're still going strong when you reach a well-marked junction just beyond a saddle, consider turning left for a 1.8-mile detour to Gray Butte, a knoll with the world's best view of Mt. Shasta. Otherwise, keep right for 0.6 mile to Lower Panther Meadow and your car.

Other Hiking Options

Climbing Mt. Shasta is a serious undertaking that requires crampons, an ice ax, survival gear, mountaineering skills, and lots of stamina. Most climbers set out from the large Bunny Flat Trailhead on the Everitt Highway 1.7 miles before Panther Campground. If you're not intent on reaching the top, however, more scenic alpine rambles begin from the Upper Ski Bowl parking area at the end of the Everitt Highway. A ski resort that once marred this area was obliterated by a 1978 avalanche, leaving a network of hikable alpine roadbeds and trails. Climb 0.8 mile along these steep, braided paths to a piped spring in a patch of yellow monkeyflower. Or continue another 0.8 mile to a panorama at the avalanche-smashed ruin of a radio facility. New radio equipment has since been set up on Gray Butte, a safer distance from Mt. Shasta's sometimes vengeful spirits.

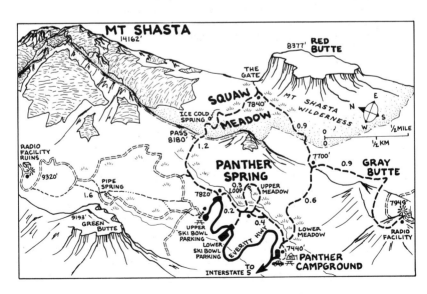

All-Accessible Trails in Southern Oregon

People with limited physical abilities need not miss the fun of exploring new trails. Here are 18 paths within a 2-hour drive of the Rogue Valley accessible to everyone. Nearly all are surfaced with asphalt or packed gravel. Unless otherwise noted, the paths are open year round. For more information, contact the trail's managing agency, listed at the end of each entry.

UPPER UMPQUA RIVER (map on page 13)

A. Deadline Falls. The first 0.2 mi of the North Umpqua River Trail has been widened and graveled for easy access from Tioga Trailhead to an overlook of fish jumping at this river chute. See Hike #2. (Roseburg BLM, 541-440-4930)

B. Susan Creek Campground. 2 graveled paths lead to N Umpqua River viewpoints—a 0.3-mi loop east from campsite #19, and a 0.3-mi path west from the campground's overflow parking lot. (Roseburg BLM, 541-440-4930)

DIAMOND AND CRATER LAKES (map on page 47)

C. Diamond Lake. Entire 11.5-mi paved lakeshore loop is accessible, as are 28 campsites at Broken Arrow Campground, 8 sites at Diamond Lake CG, the Diamond Lake Info Ctr, and a fishing jetty at the resort's marina. Open June-Oct. See Hike #20. (Diamond Lk Ranger Dist, 541-498-2531)

UPPER ROGUE RIVER (map on page 75)

D. Stewart State Park. Paved bike path traces Lost Creek Lake's shore 3.6 mi through woods, passing campground, picnic area, boat ramp, and marina. For a loop, return on paved 2.4-mi path through grassy fields near Hwy 62. See map on p 78. (Oregon Parks, 503-378-6829)

E. Mammoth Pines. Interpretive 0.3-mi nature loop trail (packed gravel) visits some large ponderosa pines, but the huge sugarpines that gave this trail its name have been cut down to protect visitors from windfall. Drive 6 mi N of Prospect on Hwy 62. (Prospect Ranger Dist, 541-560-3400)

F. Natural Bridge. Paved 0.2-mi path crosses Rogue River to fenced viewpoint of lava tube where river vanishes underground. Open Apr-Nov. See Hike #34. (Prospect Ranger Dist, 541-560-3400)

G. Rogue Gorge. Paved 0.2-mi loop along rim of chasm where the Rogue River churns through a 100-ft-deep slot. From Medford, drive Hwy 62 to Union Creek at milepost 56, continue east 0.2 mi, turn L at "Rogue Gorge" sign. Open Apr-Nov. See map on p 82. (Prospect Ranger Dist, 541-560-3400)

SOUTHERN CASCADES (map on page 99)

H. Whiskey Springs. 1-mi graveled loop through meadows and lodgepole pine woods circles a beaver pond and passes a gushing spring. From Medford, drive Hwy 62 east 14.5 mi, turn R on Butte Falls Hwy 15 mi to Butte Falls, continue straight 8.3 mi, turn L on Parker Mdws Rd 0.3 mi, turn L into Whiskey Spg CG entrance, keep R to picnic area. Open Apr-Nov. (Butte Falls Ranger Dist, 541-865-3581)

I. High Lakes Trail. Wide graveled 9.3-mi bike path links Fish Lake with Lake of the Woods (see Hike #52). For an easy trip, try the trail's nearly level eastern half from the Great Meadow trailhead past Lake of the Woods to the start of the Brown Mtn lava flow. Steepish grades make the western segment to Fish Lk suitable only for wheelchair athletes. Open June-Oct. (Klamath Ranger Dist, 541-885-3400)

Bridge on Big Pine Trail.

EASTERN SISKIYOUS (map on page 127)

J. Lithia Park. The first 1 mile of the path through Ashland's Lithia Park (Hike #57) is all-accessible. (Ashland Parks, 541-488-5340)

K. Bear Creek Greenway. Entire 15-mile paved path from Ashland to Central Point is open to all (see Hike #149). (Oregon Parks, 503-378-6829)

WESTERN SISKIYOUS (map on page 159)

L. Grayback Campground. Graveled path follows Grayback Creek 200 yards from barrier-free campsite near Oregon Caves Nat'l Mon. In Cave Junction, turn W toward Oregon Caves 11.6 mi. (Illinois Valley Ranger Dist, 541-592-2166)

M. Big Pine Trail. Choice of 3/4-mi Challenge Loop, 1/2-mi Sunshine Loop, 1/3-mi Big Pine Loop, or 1/6-mi Creek Loop. See Hike #83. (Galice Ranger Dist, 541-471-6500)

N. London Peak. New 0.6-mi packed gravel path to clifftop viewpoint above Wolf Creek and Interstate 5. See Hike #88. (Medford BLM, 541-770-2200)

NORTHERN CALIFORNIA (map on page 195)

O. Klamath River. Riverside packed gravel 0.3-mi nature path from Tree of Heaven Campground (see Hike #89) includes displays describing migratory birds. (Oak Knoll Ranger Dist, 916-465-2241)

P. Taylor Lake. Gravel 0.3-mi path to gorgeous lake in Russian Wilderness (see Hike #92) was built to be all-accessible, but is now too eroded for wheelchairs, and the access road is too rough for most vans. Open July-Oct. (Salmon River Ranger Dist, 916-467-5757)

Q. Lower McCloud Falls. Paved 0.2-mi trail along McCloud River connects Fowler Campground and waterfall with swimmable plunge pool. From I-5 south of Mt Shasta, take McCloud exit, drive E on Hwy 89 for 17 mi, and turn R at Fowlers Camp sign. (McCloud Ranger Dist, 916-964-2184)

R. Kangaroo Lake. Easy 0.2-mi path from CG to scenic mtn lake with fishing dock. Open July-Oct. See Hike #192. (Scott River Ranger Dist, 916-468-5351)

S. Juanita Lake. Start at campground with all-accessible fishing docks, circle lake on 1.7-mi loop trail. Drive Hwy 97 north of Weed 38 mi (or S of Klamath Falls 36 mi) to Goosenest Ranger Station, turn W on Ball Mtn Rd, and follow signs 7 mi to Juanita Lake. (Goosenest Ranger Dist, 916-398-4391)

100 More Hikes in Southern Oregon

Adventurous hikers can discover plenty of additional trails within a 2-hour drive of the Rogue Valley. The list below covers the most interesting--from park bike paths to rugged wilderness trails. Directions are brief, so be extra careful to bring appropriate maps. Estimated mileages are one-way. Most paths are open only in summer and fall, but symbols note which hikes are open all year and which are suitable for kids, horses, bicycles, or backpacking. For more information, check with the trail's administrative agency.

The appropriate ranger district or other offices are abbreviated: (AP)-Applegate, (AS)-Ashland, (B)-Butte Falls, (C)-Crater Lake National Park, (D)-Diamond Lake, (G)-Galice, (I)-Illinois Valley, (K)-Klamath, (M)-Mt. Shasta, (N)-North Umpqua, (O)-Oak Knoll, (P)-Prospect, (SA)-Salmon River, (SC)-Scott River, (T)-Tiller, (W)-Weaverville. Agency phone numbers are on page 11.

UPPER UMPQUA RIVER (map on page 13)

101. Wolf Creek Nature Trail. Cross the Little River on a dramatic suspension footbridge to a 0.6-mi loop through oak/ash woods with wildflowers in April and May. Start at picnic area of Wolf Cr Campground (map, p 29).(N)

102. Little River Overhang. Basalt cliff is 0.3 mile up river path through old-growth woods. From Hwy 138 at Glide, take Little River Rd 27 for 16.2 mi, turn R on Rd 2792 for 0.2 mi to White Creek CG. (N)

103. Shadow Falls. Rock grotto with 90-foot triple cascade is the goal of a 0.8-mi downhill path. From Hwy 138 at Glide, take Little River Rd 6.5 mi S, turn right on Cavitt Cr Rd 11.5 mi to pullout. (N)

104. Big Squaw Mountain. Hunt for blue-banded agates on 1.5-mi path that gains 900 ft to viewpt peak. From Hwy 138 at Glide, take Little River Rd 27 for 18.8 mi to end of pavement, fork R on Black Cr Rd 2719 for 10 mi, turn L on Rd 625 for 1.5 mi, turn R on Rd 626 for 0.1 mi. (N)

105. Riverview Trail. Paralleling Hwy 138, nearly level trail starts on Hwy 138 W of Steamboat Cr 0.2 mi, climbs 0.4 to N Umpqua River viewpoint above Steamboat Inn, continues on old roadbed 3.8 mi to Bogus Cr CG and another 1.4 mi to Rd 4710. (N)

106. Cougar Shelter. Visit a rustic 3-sided shelter by walking 0.6 mi on closed Road 630 or by climbing 2700 ft on steep 4-mile path from N Umpqua River Tr (see map, p 18). For upper access route, turn across Wright Cr Bridge between mileposts 33 and 34 of Hwy 138, follow Rd 4711 for 8 mi, and turn L on Rd 600 for 3 mi. (N)

107. Fuller Lake Shelter. Easy 0.7-mi tr drops 200 ft to rustic shelter by secluded, 600-ft-long lake. Drive as to Bullpup Lk (Hike #6), but follow Rd 3850 an extra 3.5 mi to Rd 3810 and keep L for 1 mi. (N)

108. Dog Creek Caves. Rare pink *Kalmiopsis* blooms, falcons, and caves make this area so sensitive that access roads are closed Jan-July 3.8 miles before the steep, downhill 0.9-mi trail. Drive Hwy 138 east of Steamboat Cr 1.5 mi, turn L on Rd 4713 for 4.5 mi, turn R on Rd 100 for 3 mi, turn R on Rd 120 for 3.2 mi, walk R on Rd 130 for 0.6 mi to tr. (N)

109. Mizell Viewpoint. Boulder Cr Wilderness vista on an unmarked 200-yd spur near the crest of the faint 3.8-mi Perry Butte Stub Trail (map, p 29). It's possible to hike east 2.2 mi from the Boulder Cr Tr (gaining 1700 ft), but easier to hike west 1.6 mi (and 800 ft up) from Rd 4775. For this option, drive Hwy 138 to a Slide Cr sign near milepost 55, turn N on Rd 4775 to pavement's end in 4 mi. (D)

110. Clearwater River. Popular with mtn bikers, a nearly level 1.5-mi riverside path from Toketee Lk passes small cascades (map, p 36). For loop, return on parallel path through woods. (D)

111. Cow Creek. Well-graded 6.1-mi Nat'l Rec Trail starts with awkward wade of 40-ft Cow Cr, gains 1700 ft through woodsy canyon to gravel rd and historic shake shelter at Railroad Gap. From Azalea exit 88 of I-5, take Upper Cow Cr Rd for 19 mi and turn R on gravel Rd 3232 for 1 mi to lower trailhead, or continue 10.3 mi to upper trailhead. (T)

112. Donegan Prairie. Faint but level 3.7-mi path ambles through scattered subalpine wildflower mdws (with cows July-Oct) atop Rogue-Umpqua Divide. Path starts and ends on Road 800. From Abbott Butte trailhead (Hike #36), drive 100 yds north and fork left for 0.2 mi to first trailhead, or continue 2.3 mi to second trailhead. (T)

113. Cougar Butte. Scattered wildflower mdws with big incense cedars (and cows July-Oct) highlight this faint 5.1-mi ridgetop spur of Rogue-Umpqua Divide Trail (map, p 86). Drive as to Hike #36, but then go N toward Tiller 8 mi on Rd 68. (T)

114. Anderson Mountain. Sandstone Trail climbs through viewless Wilderness forest 4 mi (and up 1950 ft) to Rogue-Umpqua Trail. Bushwhack up another 0.3 mi through wildflower mdw to views and burned lookout remnants atop broad Anderson Mtn. Take Canyonville exit 98 of I-5, drive 23.3 mi to Tiller, fork L on Rd 46 for 5.3 mi, turn R on Rd 29 for 17.5 mi, go R on Rd 300 for 3.2 mi. (T)

115. Castle Creek. Quiet path follows fork of S Umpqua 4.5 mi into the forested heart of Rogue-Umpqua Divide Wilderness (gaining just 800 ft), then climbs 1700 ft in 3.1 mi to Fish Cr Valley Rd 870 (map, p 94). For lower trailhead, drive as to Hike #10, but stick to Rd 2823 a total of 6.5 mi. (T)

116. Whitehorse Meadows. Hike a beautiful, relatively level trail into the Rogue-Umpqua Divide Wilderness 0.6 mi, detour left 0.3 mi to narrow Wolf Lake, then continue 2.4 mi to flowers at Wildhorse Mdws, in a pass overlooking Castle Cr valley. Path continues 2.9 mi to Windy Gap (see map on p 94). From Roseburg, drive Hwy 138 east past milepost 50 nearly a mile, turn R on Rd 28 for 14 mi to a 5-way jct, turn L on Rd 950 for 3.5 mi to trailhead at jct in a pass. (D)

117. Skookum Lake. Easy path descends 0.4 mi to small woodsy lake at 5500 ft elevation. From Roseburg, drive Hwy 138 past milepost 60, turn R on Fish Cr Rd 37 for 7 mi, fork L on Rd 3703 for 8 mi, and turn L on Rd 200 for 4 mi to its end. (D)

118. Calamut Lake. Easy 1.4-mi hike gains 350 ft to kid-friendly mtn lake with sandy beaches, warmish water, flat campsites. From Hwy 138 between mileposts 73 and 74, turn N on Windigo Pass Rd 60 for 7 mi, turn L on Rd 700 for 2.4 mi, turn R on Rd 740 for 0.3 mi. (D)

119. North Umpqua Headwaters. 8-mi segment of N Umpqua River Tr climbs valley into Mt. Thielsen Wilderness to river's source at Maidu Lk, gaining 1800 ft (see map on p 43). Between mileposts 73 and 74 of Hwy 138, turn N on Windigo Pass Rd 60 for 4.5 mi, then keep R for 1.2 mi to Kelsay Valley Trailhead. (D)

DIAMOND AND CRATER LAKES (map on page 47)

120. Rodley Butte. Motorcycles rule this trail from Diamond Lk's outlet (see map on p 52). Path climbs through dry woods 3.3 mi (and 1600 ft up) to within a 0.2-mi scramble of a viewpt atop this cone. Main path continues 3.7 mi down to gravel Rd 4786, but becomes faint. (D)

121. North Crater Trail. Viewless 8.7-mi horse trail through woods by Diamond Lake provides a return route for equestrians making longer loops through Mt. Thielsen Wilderness. Trail starts at Howlock Mtn Trailhead (see map on p 48), parallels Hwy 138 to N Crater Trailhead at the Cascade summit and Pacific Crest Tr jct. (D)

122. Red Cone. Cinder cone near Crater Lake's rim affords views to Mt. Thielsen and 3 Sisters. Trailless 1.3-mi route to top gains 800 ft. Park at a turnout on National Park's N entrance rd, 1 mi N of the Rim Drive jct. Walk X-ctry through pumice mdw toward obvious cone to NW. (C)

123. Sphagnum Bog. Floating moss landscape in Nat'l Park hosts 4 species of carnivorous plants. Park on Crater Lake's N entrance rd, 2.5 mi N of the Rim Drive jct. Hike Pacific Crest Tr W 4.8 mi (passing Red Cone Spr), turn R on Crater Spr Tr 3.6 mi to springs above bog area. Camping banned within 0.5 mi. Mosquitoes common. (C)

124. Stuart Falls via Pumice Flat. Gentler, longer route to Stuart Falls than Hike #42 crosses pumice plain in Crater Lk Nat'l Park. Drive Hwy 62 east of Mazama Village jct 2.8 mi to pullout. Hike 2.9 mi (up 400 ft) to Pacific Cr Tr, continue straight 2.5 mi (down 900 ft) to falls. (C)

UPPER ROGUE RIVER (map on page 75)

125. Denman Nature Trail. In wildlife area beside Rogue River, 1-mi interpretive nature loop passes frog ponds, oaks, grassland. From Medford, drive Crater Lk Hwy 62 for 6.3 mi to White City, turn L on Antelope Rd 0.3 mi, turn R on Agate Rd 1 mi, and turn L on Touvelle Rd 0.7 mi to tr on L. (Oregon Fish & Wildlife)

126. Viewpoint Mike. Path to columnar basalt overlook of Lost Cr Lake gains 1000 ft in 2.5 mi (map, p 78). From Medford, drive Hwy 62 east for 30 mi. Just after Rogue River bridge, turn R for 0.3 mi to Big Butte Park. Tr starts on L above rd. (US Army Corps of Engineers)

127. Sugarpine Creek. Faint trail follows gravelly creek 3.1 mi with

Barr Creek Falls, on the Mill Creek Falls Trail (Hike #129).

Easy
Moderate
Difficult

shady woods, bridgless creek crossings, and cows, to spring at jct with Coalmine Creek. Gains 400 ft. From Medford, drive Hwy 62 east for 26 mi, turn L on paved Elk Cr Rd for 11.1 mi, turn L on Sugarpine Rd 2 mi, fork R on Rd 6610 for 1 mi, and park on R near Rd 050. Walk down this rough rd for 0.2 mi and wade creek to trail. (P)

128. Bitterlick Creek. Faint path descends from Grub Box Gap through lodgepole/sugarpine woods, losing 700 ft in 0.5 mi, then follows shady creek (with many bridgeless crossings) down 1300 ft in 3.9 mi to private land, cows. From Medford, drive Crater Lk Hwy 62 east for 26 mi, turn L on Elk Cr Rd for 13.8 mi, turn L on Rd 66 for 3.8 mi to end of pavement, turn L on Rd 6640 for 4.3 mi to signed trailhead. (P)

129. Mill Creek Falls. Spectacular 174-foot fall spills into Rogue River canyon of columnar basalt cliffs. Wide 0.4-mi trail loses just 200 ft. Short spurs lead to narrower Barr Cr Falls, giant boulders by river. From Medford, drive Hwy 62 east almost to Prospect. After milepost 42, turn R on Mill Cr Rd 0.3 mi, then turn left 0.7 mi. (Boise Cascade)

130. Golden Stairs. Named for a failed gold prospect, path climbs rocky ridge 1600 ft in 4.3 mi to Rogue-Umpqua Divide Trail. From there, either turn L for 1.4 mi to Elephant Lk (see Hike #36) or turn R for 0.9 mi to an upper trailhead at Yellowjacket Camp. From Medford, drive Hwy 62 east to between mileposts 51 and 52, turn L on Rd 68 for 5 mi, turn R on Rd 550 for 2 mi to lower trailhead. (P)

131. Anderson Camp. Early 1900s sheepherder tr gains 750 ft in 1.4 mi to wildflower mdws, views on broad Anderson Mtn. Tread becomes faint in mdws, but go straight 0.1 mi to Rogue-Umpqua Divide Tr and turn R for 2 mi to better views. Drive E of Medford on Hwy 62 to between mileposts 51 and 52, turn L on Rd 68 for 2.7 mi, go straight on gravel Rd 6510 for 5.8 mi, and turn L on Rd 6515 for 5 mi. (P)

132. Garwood Butte Lookout. 1.4-mi path gains 1000 ft to views at abandoned lookout tower on 7017-ft butte near Mt. Bailey. From Diamond Lk, drive Hwy 230 toward Medford 3 mi to milepost 21, turn R on S Umpqua Rd 3703 for 6 mi to tr on R, opposite 3 Lakes Camp.(D)

133. Minnehaha Creek. Motorcycle-marred path follows cascading stream through old-growth woods 2.9 mi to boggy Soda Springs. From Medford, drive 69 mi E toward Diamond Lake. Just after milepost 12 of Hwy 230 turn R at a Hamaker CG pointer. Follow Rd 6530 for 0.9 mi, turn R on Rd 800 for 300 yds to tr on L. (P)

SOUTHERN CASCADES (map on page 99)

134. Varmint Camp. Steep 3.1-mi motorcycle trail along Crater Lake Nat'l Park border gains 1800 ft. Path crosses Varmint Cr, climbs wooded ridge, crosses wildflower mdw to campsite at dirt road. Take Hwy 62 east of Medford 45 miles, turn R into Prospect for 0.7 mi to hotel, turn L on Butte Falls Road 1 mi, turn L on Red Blanket Road 0.4 mi, and fork L on gravel Rd 6205 for 10.5 miles to tr sign on L. (P)

135. McKie Meadow. Loop through Sky Lakes Wilderness follows Tom & Jerry Tr 5.4 mi to McKie Mdw (1930s shelter, springs, rock outcrops) and returns on Mudjekeewis Tr past Kerby Hill's view of Middle Fk Rogue River canyon. Rocky at times, the 11.1-mi loop gains 2400 ft in all. Take Hwy 62 east of Medford 45 miles, turn R into Prospect for 0.7 mi to hotel, turn L on Butte Falls Road 2.8 mi, turn L on Rd 37 for 3 mi, fork L on Rd 3795 for 5.5 mi, turn L on Rd 650 for 0.8 mi to its end. The only horse trailer turnaround is 0.5 mi before trailhead. (P)

136. Middle Fork Rogue River. Snow-free by mid-May, river valley path in old-growth woods is the first Sky Lks Wilderness trail open each year. The first 3.2 mi gain a mere 400 ft, tracing the bottom of a colossal U-shaped valley carved by a vanished glacier. Drive Butte Falls Hwy 1 mi E of Butte Falls, turn L toward Prospect 9 mi, turn R on Rd 34 for 8.5 mi, keep L on Rd 37 for 5 mi, turn R on Rd 3790 for 3 mi. (B)

137. Alta Lake Trail. Long-cut to Alta Lk (compare Hike #43) follows dry Gopher Ridge, gains 2000 ft in 5.3 mi. Drive Butte Falls Hwy 1 mi E of Butte Falls, turn L toward Prospect 9 mi, turn R on Rd 34 for 8.5 mi, keep L on Rd 37 for 2.2 mi, turn R on Rd 3785 for 3.5 mi. (B)

138. Willow Prairie. 19 miles of horse-only trails explore forests, mdws from campground. Drive Hwy 140 E of Medford 35 mi. Just before Fish Lk, turn L on Rd 821 for 1.5 mi, turn L on Rd 3738 for 1.5 mi. (B)

139. Rye Spur and Billie Creek. An easy 1-mi creekside loop and a tough 3.3-mi viewpoint hike (gaining 1200 ft) both start at the same trailhead. From the Lake of the Woods exit on Hwy 140, drive west 200 yds on Hwy 140, take the first dirt rd to the R, and keep R for 100 yds to the trail signboard. (K)

140. Sky Lakes via Cherry Creek. Alternate route to Trapper Lk (compare Hike #51) gains 1300 ft in 5.2 mi. Drive Hwy 140 to between mileposts 43 and 44, turn N on Westside Rd for 10.9 mi, turn L on Rd 3450 for 1.8 mi to its end. (K)

141. Mountain Lakes via Lake of the Woods. Slightly longer than the Varney Cr route into the Mtn Lks Wilderness (Hike #54), this 4.8-mi path gains 2000 ft to the central loop, passing small Lk Waban along the way. From Hwy 140 near Lake of the Woods, turn S on Dead Indian Hwy for 200 yds and turn L on Rd 3660 for 1.5 mi to trailhead on L. (K)

142. Mountain Lakes via Clover Creek. Shortcut into Mtn Lks Wilderness passes creekside meadows (with cows) and small Clover Lake, gaining 1380 ft in 3.4 mi to the central loop (see map, p 126). From Ashland, drive Dead Indian Mem Hwy east past milepost 28, turn R on paved Clover Cr Rd for 5.7 mi, turn L on Rd 3852 for 3.2 mi to its end. From Klamath Falls, drive Hwy 66 west 8 mi to sharp curve, go straight on Clover Cr Rd for 15.7 mi, turn R on Rd 3852 for 3.2 mi. (K)

143. Brown Mountain Trail. Conveniently near Boy Scout Camp McLoughlin at Lake of the Woods, this viewless 7.8-mi forest trail goes around (not over) Brown Mtn, passing lava and crossing the Pacific Crest Trail. Drive Hwy 140 to between mileposts 35 and 36, turn S on Rd 3601 and promptly turn R on gravel Rd 3640 for 0.6 mi to poorly marked trailhead on R just before hill. (K)

144. Beaver Dam Creek. Beavers actually are active along this easy streamside loop. From Ashland, drive Dead Indian Mem Hwy east to between mileposts 21 and 22, turn L on Rd 37 for 2 mi. Park at Daley Cr Campground, hike tr downstream 0.6 mi to start of 0.9-mi loop. (A)

145. Dunlop Meadow. Stroll 0.4 mi to a mdw (the old ranch of a 1920s bootlegger), then descend 700 ft in 1.1 mi to S Fk Little Butte Creek. From Ashland, drive Dead Indian Mem Hwy east 18.6 mi. Just past Lily Glen Horse Camp turn L on Shell Pk Rd for 1.6 mi, keeping R at forks. Then continue on Rd 100 another 5 mi to Dunlop Trail on R. (A)

146. Soda Springs. Stroll 0.2 mi to mineral springs by Dead Indian Cr, then gain 1300 ft in 2.3 mi up steep ridge of oaks and pines to an upper road. From Ashland, drive Dead Indian Memorial Hwy east to between mileposts 13 and 14, turn L on Conde Cr Rd for 11.3 mi, turn R on Lake Cr Rd for 3.7 mi, turn R on Rd 800 for 0.6 mi. (A)

147. Little Hyatt Lake. Old-growth trees survive on level, 1.5-mi segment to Little Hyatt Reservoir. From Ashland, drive Hwy 66 east to Green Springs Inn (between mileposts 17 and 18), turn L toward Hyatt Lk 2.9 mi to a rd junction. The PCT crosses here. Follow it L. (A)

EASTERN SISKIYOUS (map on page 127)

148. Roxy Ann Peak. In Medford's Prescott Park, this wooded knoll is circled by a hikable 2.9-mi loop road that's closed to cars in winter. From the loop, an 0.8-mi spur path and a gated 0.5-mi service road gain 550 ft as they climb to a summit viewpoint. From Medford exit 27 of I-5, take Barnett Rd E 1 mi, turn L on Black Oak Dr 1 mi, turn R on Hillcrest

Rd 3.2 mi, and turn L on Roxy Ann Rd 0.4 mi to gate. If closed, walk up the road 2 mi to the start of the loop. (Medford Parks)

149. Bear Creek Greenway. Paved 15-mi bike path follows Bear Cr from Ashland through Talent, Phoenix, and Medford to county fairgrounds in Central Point. Path is often near I-5 freeway. For a stroll, walk 2 mi from Talent's Newbry Park (at I-5 exit 21) south past ponds to Hwy 99 at S Valley View Dr (near Ashland exit 19). (Oregon State Parks)

150. White Rabbit Trail. Mtn bike route drops 700 ft in 2.3 mi from Ashland Loop Rd 2060 to Park St at the green entrance gate to Ashland's Siskiyou Mountain Park. Start as for the 28.5-mi loop of Hike #57, but 2 mi past Granite St Reservoir look for trailhd on L.(AS)

151. Bull Gap. Old Mt Ashland Rd built by CCC in 1930s has been converted to 2.5-mi trail. Loses 980 ft. Drive as to Hike #59 but continue 1.5 mi to ski area parking. See map on p 132 to plan an 8-mi mtn bike loop via Bull Gap, gravel Rd 2080, and paved Rd 20. (AS)

152. Wrangle Gap. Follow the Pacific Crest Tr through high forest and mdws 3.8 mi around Red Mtn, gaining 850 ft. Easy 3-mi car shuttle between trailheads. Drive to Mt Ashland (see Hike #59) and continue straight on rough gravel Rd 20 another 8 mi to PCT crossing at milepost 17, just after Siskiyou Gap. For shuttle, drive 3 mi more. (AS)

153. Mule Mountain. Climb through grassy pine/oak woodlands with spring flowers to views of Applegate Valley. From Ruch, drive Upper Applegate Rd 11.5 mi S, past Jackson Picnic Area 2 mi. Park at trail sign on L. Path crosses private land with 2 gates, gains 1700 ft in 2 mi to ridgecrest viewpoint, continues 2 mi to Baldy Pk Trail. (AP)

154. Grouse Loop. Woodsy 2.8-mi loop with glimpses of Applegate Lk gains 600 ft. Begin at Hart-tish Park entrance (map, p 141). (AP)

155. Squaw Lakes. Easy 3.3-mi loop circles 2 mtn lakes popular with anglers, gains 240 ft. From Ruch, drive Upper Applegate Rd 14.4 mi south, turn L across Applegate Dam, go straight 8.5 mi on Rd 1075 to parking area. Walk gated road L around Big Squaw Lk 1.5 mi to Mulligan Bay campsites, turn L on 1.1-mi trail through woods past Little Squaw Lk, turn R for 0.7 mi on Rd 1075 to your car. (AP)

156. Cook and Green Loop. Challenging 15.5-mi loop near Red Buttes tours creek canyons, Echo Lake, Siskiyou crest. Gains 3500 ft. Drive as to Frog Pond (Hike #66), but only go 3.7 mi on Rd 1040 before turning L at Horse Camp Tr pointer. Hike this trail 3.9 mi steeply up to Pacific Crest Tr (map, p 147), turn L for 2.6 mi to pass, turn L on Cook and Green Tr for 8.2 mi, turn L on Rd 1040 for 0.8 mi to car. (AP)

157. Butte Fork Trail. In Red Buttes Wilderness, hike up canyon of old-growth 6.8 mi to Cedar Basin (gaining 2000 ft), then fork R for 0.9 mi to popular Azalea Lk or fork L for 1.4 mi to gorgeous little Lonesome Lk. For a grand 24.5-mi loop, keep L via PCT, Echo Lk, and Horse Camp Tr back to your car. Drive as to Frog Pond (Hike #66), but take Rd 1040 a total of 7.6 mi to Shoofly Trailhead on L (map, p 148). (AP)

158. Whisky Peak Lookout. Abandoned lookout building affords sweeping Siskiyou views. Steep 0.5-mi trail to top gains 580 ft. Drive to

Middle Fork Trailhead (see Hike #66), then continue driving up Rd 1035 for 9 mi and turn L on Rd 350 for 2.4 mi to Rd 356 on R. (AP)

WESTERN SISKIYOUS (map on page 159)

159. Sucker Creek Loop. Follow mining area creek 2.7 mi to mdws, huge cedars, and rustic Sucker Cr Shelter (see also Hike #68), then keep right on Boundary Tr (with views) and Fehley Gulch Tr (with old-growth firs) to complete 7.9-mi loop through Red Buttes Wilderness. Drive as to Oregon Caves (Hike #71), but only go 13.4 mi on Hwy 46. Beyond Grayback CG 1.5 mi, turn R on Rd 4612 for 10 mi. Then fork L on Rd 098 for 4 mi. (I) 🐾🏕️

160. East Fork Illinois River. Rugged 9.7-mi path into Siskiyou Wilderness fords knee-deep river 4 times, passes good swimming holes en route to Youngs Valley (map, p 168). Drive as to Hike #75 (Polar Bear Gap), but when pavement ends on the Bridgeview-Takilma Rd, fork R on Rd 011 for 0.8 mi. (I) 🏊🏕️🐾

161. Sanger Peak Lookout. Views extend from the Pacific Ocean to Mt Shasta atop this summit, accessed by a 0.6-mi path that gains 460 ft. Rock climbing site is nearby. Drive as to Hike #76 (Raspberry Lake), but instead of turning R on Rd 4803, turn L for 1.5 mi. (I)

162. Island Lake. Rugged trail to Siskiyou Wilderness hideaway drops 700 ft in 0.9 mi to easy ford of S Fk Smith River, then gains 2100 ft in 3.2 mi to a cirque pool backed by Jedediah Mtn. Permits (available at Gasquet ranger station) are required only for campfires. Drive as to Hike #77 (Devils Punchbowl), but after 10 mi on Little Jones Cr Rd turn R on paved Rd 16N02 for 2.5 mi and turn L on rough Rd 16N28 (closed in rainy season) for 1.8 mi to its end. (SR) 🏕️

163. South Kelsey Trail. This 27-mi path across the Siskiyou Wilderness is a remnant of a 200-mi Army mule train route built from Crescent City to Fort Jones in the 1850s. Drive Hwy 199 E of Crescent City 10 mi, turn R on paved S Fork Rd for 14 mi to a fork, go R on paved Rd 15 for 3.5 mi, turn L on Rd 15N39 for 2 mi to road's end. The path follows the S Fk Smith River 7 mi, climbs 4400 ft in 6 mi to Baldy Pk's views, and follows a ridge 3.1 mi to small Harrington Lk, a good goal. (SR) 🏕️

164. Baldface Creek. Walk a rocky roadbed 2.8 mi (and down 500 ft) to views on Biscuit Hill, then continue on a steep trail down 1500 ft in 1.7 mi to ford of remote, bouldery creek. Drive Hwy 199 south of Cave Jct 7 mi to O'Brien, turn R on County Rd 5550 (which becomes FS Rd 4402) for 13 mi, and turn R on Rd 112 for 3 mi to roadbed/trail on L. (I) 🏕️

165. Doe Gap. Starting point for backpack explorations of southern Kalmiopsis Wilderness trail network. Drive as to Hike #166, but continue on Rd 112 for 1.5 mi to barricade. Walk old ridgecrest road 7 mi to pass with views. Trails branch left to Chetco Pk and Vulcan Lk or right to Cold Springs Camp and Babyfoot Lk (Hike #78). (I) 🏕️

166. Whetstone Butte. Red rock ridgecrest route offers views of Kalmiopsis Wilderness and beyond. Path gains just 300 ft in 1.6 mi. For a longer hike, continue 1.6 mi (gaining 1000 ft) to Eagle Mtn or 3.1 mi to Chetco Pass. Drive as to Babyfoot Lk (Hike #78), but at the pass of

Rd 4201 follow signs 0.8 mi R to Onion Camp. (I)

167. Chetco River. Ugly mining road accessing remote center of beautiful Kalmiopsis Wilderness is drivable only in summer with diehard 4WD vehicle, and subject to restrictions even then. Drive as to Fall Cr (Hike #79), continue across low-water river bridge to McCaleb Ranch, take center fork through pvt land for 5.1 awful miles to Chetco Pass, continue 0.6 mi to gate, and park. Hike closed road 3.6 mi to knee-deep Chetco River ford and junction with several Wilderness trails. (I)

168. Pearsoll Peak Lookout. Open for free overnight use, this restored 1954 lookout on Kalmiopsis Wilderness rim has panoramic views, but lacks heat and water. Drive to Chetco Pass via awful road (see Hike #167) or hike there via nice 4.7-mi trail (Hike #166). Then walk N for 5.9-mi loop to lookout, gaining 1500 ft. (I)

169. Limpy Creek. Easy 1-mi nature loop through botanical area identifies many wildflowers, trees. Take Hwy 199 west of Grants Pass 7 mi to Applegate River, turn R on Riverbanks Rd 4.5 mi to sign, go L 2.5 mi to parking lot. (G)

170. Shan Creek. Handy 0.3-mi path to a swimming hole continues 1.8 mi up canyon slope, gaining 1100 ft to logging rd. Open to motorbikes. From Grants Pass, take Hwy 199 west 7 mi to Applegate River, turn R on Riverbanks Rd 5 mi, go L on Shan Cr Rd 1.2 mi. (G)

171. Dutchy Creek Trail. 1.8 mi of mining roads interrupt the middle of this 7.9-mi route from Sam Brown Campground (see Hike #82) over a wooded ridge to Rd 050 near Silver Falls (see below). (G)

172. Silver Falls. Confusing, muddy, poorly signed roads make this 1-mi hike a trip for explorers only. From Galice, drive 0.3 mi toward Merlin, turn west on paved Galice Access Rd 9.5 mi to 5-way jct, turn L on Rd 35-9-1for 4.2 mi, and fork L on rough Rd 050 for 6 mi to its end at possibly unmarked trailhead. Path goes over rise, then loses 500 ft, switchbacking into wooded canyon with 60-ft falls. (G)

173. Silver Peak. Wild, tough trail traces dry ridgecrest 12.5 mi to peak, then dives 4.5 mi down to Illinois River Trail. Crosses forest thinned by 1987 wildfire. From Galice, drive paved Galice Access Rd west 11 mi, turn L toward Hobson Horn on Rd 2411 for 4 mi to trail on R. (G)

NORTHERN CALIFORNIA (map on page 197)

174. Devils Peaks. Challenging 4.9-mi climb on Pacific Crest Tr gains 3700 ft from Klamath River to blockbuster viewpoint atop Lower Devils Peak. Or climb another 2 mi (gaining 960 ft) to Upper Devils Pk. Drive I-5 south of Oregon 11 mi, go W on Klamath River Hwy 96 for 44 mi to Seiad Valley, continue 0.7 mi to trail sign on R. (O)

175. Grider Creek. Easy loop, open all year, follows PCT up bouldery stream 1.6 mi, turns R across creek on 1.5-mi Grider Cr Tr past campsites, swimming holes. Drive I-5 south of Oregon 11 mi, go W on Klamath River Hwy 96 for 42 mi. Before Seiad Valley 2 mi, turn L for 100 ft, turn R for 2.5 mi, turn L for 2.3 mi to Grider Cr CG. (O)

176. Paradise Lake. Idyllic Marble Mtn Wilderness pool rimmed by wildflower meadows and the cliffs of Kings Castle is the goal of the 2.8-mi Rye Patch Tr (gains 1400 ft). Drive as to Hike #90 (Sky High Lks) but stick to Rd 44N45 for a total of 11.2 mi. (SC)

177. Wright Lakes. Demanding 5.5-mi climb gains 3140 ft to spectacular wildflower mdws at Lower Wright Lk, below Boulder Pk, highest pt in the Marble Mtn Wilderness. Continue 0.6 mi (and 500 ft up) to smaller upper lk. Drive as to Hike #90 (Sky High Lks), but only take Rd 44N45 for 1.6 mi and turn L for 2 mi to Boulder Cr Trailhead. (O)

178. Haypress Meadows. Marble Mtn Wilderness meadows in old-growth woods are an easy 1.7-mi walk. Backpackers can continue along Sandy Ridge 5.8 mi, then either turn R for 0.6 mi to 3 charming Cuddihy Lks, or turn L for 2.8 mi to 56-acre Ukonom Lk, the area's largest. Drive I-5 south of Oregon 11 mi, turn W on Hwy 96 (through Happy Camp) for 106 mi to Somes Bar, turn L on Rd 88 for 13.6 mi, turn R for 1.3 mi to trailhead at road's end. (Ukonom Ranger Dist)

179. Chimney Rock. Rugged Garden Gulch Trail into Marble Mtn Wilderness gains 2300 ft in 2 mi, dips 900 ft in the next 3.3 mi to jct on shoulder of Chimney Rock. Turn R for 2.6 mi to remote Clear Lk (or for 5.8 mi to huge Hancock Lk). Drive as to Hike #92 (Paynes Lk), but continue 15 mi to Sawyers Bar, go straight on hwy another 4 mi, and turn R on a gravel road 5 mi to its end. (SA)

180. North Fork Salmon River. Trek up a long, forested valley in Marble Mtn Wilderness 12.5 mi to headwaters at English Lk, gaining 3100 ft. Then hike over high pass 1.5 mi to huge Hancock Lk. Drive as to Hike #92 (Paynes Lk), but continue 9 mi past Etna Summit to Idlewild CG, turn R on Rd 41N37 for 2 mi. (SA)

181. Taylor and Hogan Lakes. Broad, easy 0.3-mi path in Russian Wilderness to gorgeous Taylor Lk (see p 203) continues faintly 3 mi to equally scenic Hogan Lk, but gains 400 ft and loses 800. (SA)

182. Duck Lakes. Large, popular Russian Wilderness lakes require 2000 ft climb. Hike 2.9 mi, partly on old roads, then fork left 0.4 mi to Big Duck Lk, or fork right 0.8 mi to Little Duck Lk. To start, drive 4.5 mi S of Etna on Hwy 3, turn R on French Cr Rd, follow signs 8 mi. (SC)

183. Russian and Waterdog Lakes. View-packed, shadeless Deacon Lee Trail contours 3.7 mi to granite pass high in Russian Wilderness. Turn L for 0.2 mi to Waterdog Lk and 0.2-mi bushwhack route up through mdws to spectacular, swimmable Russian Lk. Drive Hwy 3 to Callahan and turn W toward Cecilville 19 mi. Past Trail Cr CG 3 mi, turn R on Rd 39 for 7 steep mi, and then turn R on a dirt road 2 mi. (SA)

184. Hidden Lake and South Fork Lakes. Cute lakes on N edge of Trinity Alps Wilderness are accessed from Carter Mdws Summit (see p 204). Easy path to Hidden Lk gains 460 ft in 0.9 mi. Tougher route to S Fork Lks follows PCT 1.2 mi (losing 400 ft), then climbs steeply 950 ft in 1.2 mi. (SC)

185. East Boulder Lake. Alpine mdws, sagebrush, and grazing cattle surround this high, large lake on N edge of Trinity Alps Wilderness. A

1.7-mi trail gains 930 ft to the lake; continue 0.8 mi to 3 small upper pools. Drive Hwy 3 to downtown Callahan, turn W on South Fk Rd, follows signs 7 mi to E Boulder Tr. (SC)

186. Big Bear Lake. Steep 4-mi trail into Trinity Alps Wilderness gains 2800 ft to scenic granite basin with peaks, large lake. Drive Hwy 3 south of Callahan 15 mi (or N of Weaverville 48 mi); near milepost 78, take Bear Cr Loop 1 mi to trailhead. (W)

187. Caribou Lake. Spectacular 9-mi trail climbs 2500 ft to huge, granite-rimmed lake in heart of Trinity Alps Wilderness. Horrendously steep path continues 6 mi over Sawtooth Ridge to Sapphire Lk (Hike#192). Drive as to Hike #95 (Hodges Cabin), but continue 10 mi farther to end of Coffee Cr Rd at Big Flat CG. (W)

188. Boulder and Little Boulder Lakes. Easy hike in eastern Trinity Alps Wilderness gains 600 ft in 1.4 mi to a fork. Either go R for 0.5 mi to picturesque Boulder Lk, or go L 0.6 mi to a smaller pool that's tops for swimming. Drive Hwy 3 south of Callahan 26 mi (or N of Weaverville 36 mi). Near milepost 67, turn W at a Boulder Lakes pointer on a gravel road for 10.5 mi. (W)

189. Granite Lake. Hike into Trinity Alps Wilderness along Swift Creek 1 mi to a footbridge, turn L on steeper 4-mi trail up Granite Cr (with waterfall) to wildflowers of Gibson Mdw and large, lovely lake in cliffy granite cirque. Route gains 1900 ft. To start, drive Hwy 3 north of Trinity Center 0.2 mi, turn L at Swift Cr pointer for 6 mi. (W)

190. Stuart Fork to Sapphire Lake. Popular backpack route into the craggy granite heart of the Trinity Alps Wilderness follows Stuart Fork of Trinity River 13 mi to shallow green Emerald Lk and deep blue Sapphire Lk, beneath jagged Sawtooth Ridge. Gains 3200 ft. Drive 8 mi N of Weaverville on Hwy 3 to milepost 39, turn L for 4 mi. (W)

191. Canyon Creek. Most heavily used Trinity Alps Wilderness trail climbs along wooded slope 4 mi to 20-foot waterfall with swimmable pool, then continues 1.9 mi to jct ; either go L 1.6 mi to Boulder Lks, or go R 1.5 mi to Canyon Cr Lks. Both goals are stupendous granite cirques with flowers and views. Drive Hwy 299 W of Redding 57 mi to Junction City, veer R on Canyon Cr Rd 13.4 mi. (Big Bar Ranger Dist)

192. Kangaroo Lake. Paved road leads to campground and easy 0.2-mi trail to pretty lake. Turn R to climb 600 ft in 0.8 mi to PCT and ridgetop views of Mt. Shasta area. From I-5 between Weed and Yreka, take one of the Gazelle exits, follow signs to this hamlet, turn W toward Callahan 15 steep mi, turn L on Rd 41N08 for 7 mi to its end. (SC)

193. Gray Rock Lakes. Little-known cirque lake cluster in Castle Crags Wilderness affords views of Mt. Shasta. Take Central Mt Shasta exit of I-5, follow Siskiyou Lake signs 3.5 mi, go straight on Rd 26 for 9 mi, park at wood bridge on L. Cross bridge, turn R, hike 2.6 mi up steep, rocky road to old trailhead, and climb 0.7 mi on nice trail to Gray Rock Lk. Then continue 0.5 mi to either Timber Lk or Upper Gray Rock Lk. Entire 3.8-mi route gains 1470 ft. (M)

194. Burstase Falls. Stroll the nearly level PCT beneath the granite spires

Boulder Lake (Hike #188).

Easy
Moderate
Difficult

of the Castle Crags Wilderness to a shady grotto with a 40-ft waterfall. Drive I-5 south of Mt Shasta 14 mi (or N of Redding 48 mi), take Castella exit, head W on Castle Cr Rd 3.3 mi, park at Dog Trailhead on R. Hike 0.7 mi up to PCT, then either go right 0.6 mi to Sulphur Cr (and Castle Crags views), or go left 1.7 mi to Burstase Falls. (M)

195. Deer Mountain. Climb cross-country, gaining 800 ft in 2 mi to summit of a 7006-ft butte with a magnificent view of nearby Mt Shasta. From I-5 at Weed, drive Hwy 97 N 15 mi, turn R on Deer Mtn Rd 4 mi to snowmobile park, turn R on Rd 44N23 for 2 mi. Park anywhere and walk uphill. (Goosenest Ranger Dist)

196. Goosenest. Climb 1000 ft in 2 mi to the panoramic summit of an arid 8280-ft butte 20 mi N of Mt Shasta. From I-5 at Weed, drive Hwy 97 N 20 mi. Just before Grass Lk, turn L on Rd45N22 for 7 mi, then turn L on Rd 45N72Y for 2.5 mi. (Goosenest Ranger Dist)

197. Clear Creek Trail. Hike an ancient road to Wilderness vistas of the Watkins Glacier on Mt Shasta's rarely visited SE flank, gaining 1800 ft in 2.3 mi before the route peters out above timberline. No dogs. From the McCloud exit of I-5 just S of Mt Shasta, drive Hwy 89 E for 10 mi to McCloud, continue 3 mi farther, turn L on Rd 13 for 5 mi, turn L on Rd 41N15 for 5 mi to an X-jct, go straight on Rd 41N61 for 1.1 mi, and fork L for 2 mi. (McCloud Ranger Dist)

198. North Gate. Uncrowded Wilderness path to timberline on Mt Shasta follows brook 1 mi before fading. Then continue upstream 1 more mi to a spring with flowers and views, gaining 1700 ft in all. No dogs. From I-5 at Weed, drive Hwy 97 N for 15 mi, turn R on Military Pass Rd 7 mi, and turn R on Rd 42N76, following signs 4 mi to trailhead. (M)

199. Whitney Falls. Hike to a dramatic chasm with a 200-ft falls (sometimes dry) high on Mt Shasta's north flank. In the Wilderness, but partly on old logging roads, the route gains 1000 ft in 2 mi. No dogs. Climbers can continue above timberline 3 mi to Bolam Glacier. From Weed exit of I-5, drive Hwy 97 N 11.7 mi, turn R on dirt Rd 43N21 for 4 mi. (M)

200. Mount Shasta. Not a hike, the adventure of climbing this glaciated peak requires crampons, an ice axe, survival gear, good weather, the stamina to gain 7270 ft in 6 mi, and a very early morning start (at least 3:30am). No dogs. Take the Central Mt Shasta exit of I-5, drive E for 12 mi on what becomes Everitt Mem Hwy , park at Bunny Flat Trailhead. From there it's 1.6 mi to the Sierra Club Hut at timberline. (M)

Index

William L. Sullivan (photo by Paul Neevel)

About the Author

William L. Sullivan is the author of 6 books and numerous articles about Oregon, including a regular outdoor column for *Eugene Weekly*. A fifth-generation Oregonian, Sullivan began hiking in Southern Oregon at the age of 6 and has been exploring new trails ever since. After receiving an English degree from Cornell University and studying at Germany's Heidelberg University, he earned an M.A. from the University of Oregon.

In 1985 Sullivan set out to investigate Oregon's wilderness on a 1,361-mile solo backpacking trek from the state's westernmost shore at Cape Blanco to Oregon's easternmost point in Hells Canyon. His journal of that 2-month adventure, published as *Listening for Coyote*, was a finalist for the Oregon Book Award in creative nonfiction. Since then he has authored *Exploring Oregon's Wild Areas* and a series of *100 Hikes* guidebooks to the regions of Oregon.

He and his wife Janell live in Eugene, but spend summers in a log cabin they built by hand on a roadless stretch of Oregon's Siletz River.